COMBAT HANDGUNS

The photograph on the jacket is a Heckler & Koch 9mm Parabellum Polizei Selbstlade-Pistole (Police Self-loading Pistol). This was one of the successful competitors in the 1978 West German police pistol trials. It qualified for issuance to German State Police and is designated the P7 (Pistole 7). This is one of the more interesting combat-handgun designs introduced in the past twenty-five years, and it is described in more detail in chapter 2. (Courtesy Heckler & Koch)

George Nonte's

COMBAT HANDGUNS

edited by Edward C. Ezell

Stackpole Books

COMBAT HANDGUNS
Copyright © 1980 by
Stackpole Books

Published by
STACKPOLE BOOKS
Cameron and Kelker Streets
P.O. Box 1831
Harrisburg, Pa. 17105

First printing, March 1980
Second printing, August 1981

Published simultaneously in Don Mills, Ontario, Canada
by Thomas Nelson & Sons, Ltd.

Printed in the U.S.A.

Library of Congress Cataloging in Publication Data

Nonte, George C
  Combat handguns.

  Includes index.
  1. Pistols.   2. Pistol shooting.   3. Police—
Equipment and supplies. I. Ezell, Edward Clinton.
II. Title.
HV7936.E7N65 1980   683'.43   79-21398
ISBN 0-8117-0409-2

Contents

Foreword

GEORGE C. NONTE, Jr., was a handgun enthusiast and an automatic-pistol specialist. For more than a dozen years, he had been thinking and talking about writing a book on automatic handguns for combat. It was his opinion that combat handguns had not been given enough serious attention by the people who carried them and whose lives depended upon their reliability and lethality. Nonte also believed that the self-loading pistol was better suited for combat use than the more commonly used revolver. He began to put his thoughts down on paper in the mid-1970s.

Unfortunately, Nonte did not have the opportunity to complete his book. He was just beginning to convert his rough notes into draft chapters when he suffered a fatal heart attack in late June 1978. Three people—Dick Eades, Lee Jurras, and I—discussed the unfinished manuscript with Nonte's eldest son, David, and with Clyde Peters and Neil McAleer at Stackpole Books, Nonte's publisher. All agreed that the book should be completed. Jurras, with David Nonte's help, gathered all of the author's notes and draft chapters and took them home to New Mexico, where he arranged them, revised chapter 8 on ammunition—a topic to which he had personally contributed so much—and put out a call to the handgun community for additional data. Once Jurras had all the materials in hand, he sent them to me in Virginia.

Upon receipt of the manuscript, I began to assemble the materials into book form. Since the years 1977–1979 had seen many new handgun developments, I gathered new and supplemental information, especially for chapters 2, 5, and 6. As is always the case, a book of this kind is made possible only through the cooperation of many people and organizations. I cannot possibly list everyone who assisted me, but I would especially wish to thank the following: Colt Firearms, Hartford, Connecticut; Detonics .45 Associates, Seattle, Washington; Dick Eades, Hurst, Texas; H. Dietsheim and the Eidgenossische Waffenfabrik, Bern, Switzerland; Fabbrica d'Armi Pietro Beretta S. p. A., Gardone Val Trompia, Italy; R. Chavee, C. Davila, C. Gaier, V. Vanderperren and the Fabrique Nationale-Herstal, Herstal-Liege, Belgium; Dr. Otto Sailer and the Federal Republic of Germany Embassy, Washington, D.C.; Klaus Minberg and the Federal Republic of Germany Ministry of Defense; W. Fritze, J. Huber, H. Schober, H. Zink and the Heckler & Koch GmbH, Oberndorf am Neckar, Federal Republic of Germany; Illinois State Police Ordnance Unit, Springfield, Illinois; Interarms, Alexandria, Virginia; Jack Krcma, Willowdale, Ontario, Canada; Valmore Forgette, Jr. and the Navy Arms Co., Ridgefield, New Jersey; New York State Division of Criminal Justice Services, Albany, New York; J. P. Sauer & Sohn GmbH, Eckernforde, Federal Republic of Germany; Schweizerische Industrie-Gesellschaft (SIG), Neuhausen am Rheinfall, Switzerland; Sile Distributing, New York, New York; Richard S. Smith, Belleville, Michigan; Roy G. Jinks and Smith & Wesson, Springfield, Massachusetts; Sterling Arms Corporation, Gasport, New York; Masami Tokoi, Tokyo, Japan; Jim Swenson and the U.S. Air Force, Eglin Air Force Base, Florida; Richard Dorbeck, and the U.S. Army Armament Materiel Readiness Command, Rock Island, Illinois; U.S. Navy; Tom Wagster, Fraser, Michigan; Carl Walther Sportwaffenfabrik, Ulm/Donau, Federal Republic of Germany; Wildey J. Moore and the Wildey Firearms Company, Inc.

Linda, my wife, deserves special thanks for her editorial assistance and for typing the manuscript. She now knows more about handguns than she cares to admit.

Although *Combat Handguns* is not exactly the same book George Nonte would have written had he lived to complete the project, we think that we have been faithful to his goal of presenting a balanced discussion of combat handguns. While we have attempted to present a reasonably comprehensive book, it is not exhaustive. Some handguns are not discussed here because they did not meet Nonte's criteria for combat handguns and some very new guns were not included because the manufacturers were not ready to have them publicized. Still, we believe that *Combat Handguns* presents new and useful information about combat automatic handguns that will be of interest to handgunners. And we hope that we have done it in a manner that George Nonte would have found acceptable.

EDWARD C. EZELL

Preface

I HAVE PLAYED and worked with handguns of all sorts—modern and obsolete, revolvers and autoloaders alike—since my age could be set down with a single numeral. In the beginning, and for a good many years thereafter, I shared a commonly held view that "a handgun is a handgun," and that any given one would serve as well as any other one.

Generally speaking, there were only two types of handguns—revolvers and automatics. Within each of these types, the only meaningful differences were in their size and their power. For many years, police officers thought it was enough to be armed with any handgun. A 200-pound New York City policeman armed with a diminutive .32 caliber Colt Police Positive Revolver or a Smith & Wesson Regulation Police Model Revolver felt quite confident to handle any situation that might come his way. During the first three decades of this century, the New York State Police officer carried the .45 caliber Colt New Service six-gun. But seldom did either of these officers fire his handgun, be it in training or in actual combat situations. Most officers of the law were fortunate enough to retire after twenty or thirty years of service without ever once having to draw their service revolvers. Only a small percentage ever had to take aim and fire at another human being.

Contrary to fictional accounts—of either the literary or motion picture variety—shootouts were few. Often as not, those that did occur involved rifles and shotguns. Handguns were usually considered weapons of personal protection to be used in close-quarter combat of the last resort. Thus, since they were carried for their deterrent effect, the basic criteria for a defensive firearm was simply that it be small, light, and unobtrusive. Law enforcement officers counted upon its menacing appearance and the noise produced when it was fired to deter unpleasant individuals from painful and unlawful acts. For the most part, this system seemed to work during the first four decades of this century. Before 1945, there were only a few genuine handgun enthusiasts in the United States, and those handgunners who also happened to be police officers were generally concerned with target accuracy rather than with combat performance.

Note that all references to police handguns thus far have been to revolvers. Until very recently, not one law-enforcement officer in ten thousand—excluding, of course, military policemen and the hard-boiled Texas Rangers—would be caught dead carrying an autoloader. Self-loading pistols were viewed with suspicion; they were categorized as being complex and unreliable pieces of machinery. Autoloaders might be suitable for army personnel, who carried them primarily for show, or for an individual whose other duties would not permit him to tote a rifle, but they were not acceptable for police work. Most of the men in blue preferred their tiny .32 caliber revolvers to the heavyweight .45 caliber automatics. The revolver reigned supreme and, in fact, is still the basic armament for most policemen.

In a 1972 police-equipment survey conducted by the Law Enforcement Standards Laboratory of the National Bureau of Standards on behalf of the Law Enforcement Assistance Administration, it was estimated that 99 percent of the handguns used on duty and off duty by police officers were revolvers. Of the more than 484,752 police officers in the United States, 71 percent (334,679) used .38 Special caliber handguns; 25 percent (119,266) used .357 Magnum handguns; 1 percent (7,578) used .45 caliber handguns; 2 percent (9,537) used 9mm Parabellum handguns; and a fraction of 1 percent (3,692) used handguns of other calibers. Few of the larger, city-police forces used anything other than the .38 Special revolver. Of the 445 police agencies that responded to the survey, 97 percent used handguns of either Colt or Smith & Wesson manufacture.

While I intend to make the case for the automatic pistol as the primary armament of police officers, it should be made clear from the outset that the police departments of the United States are going to have to be convinced that this change is a reasonable one to make. The .38 or .357 revolver is so firmly entrenched that only the strongest of arguments is likely to change minds that appear to be so firmly made up.

Using either a revolver or an automatic, police officers are being called upon to use their handguns more frequently as the number of encounters with armed criminals increases. Ironically, the increased use of handguns by the police comes at a time in our history when the utilization of "deadly force" by law enforcement personnel is being more rigorously controlled. Therefore, police today must be trained to use firearms effectively in a combat situation, but they must also be prepared by that same training to know when deadly force should not be employed. A 1979 statement on "The Use of Firearms by Special Agents" by the Federal Bureau of Investigation summarizes the problem.

> The FBI realizes that arrest situations often call for split-second decisions. These decisions are reached more through reaction based upon training and experience than they are through any conscious train of thought. Bureau training is and has been geared to arrest plans in which the subject is outmanned, outgunned, and outmaneuvered so that it is immediately apparent to him that he has no alternative but to surrender. It is because of this training and implementation of these arrest techniques that the FBI

has been able successfully to arrest dangerous individuals without harm either to Agents or to the subjects. Our training will continue to stress these techniques.

A question which has been presented with increasing frequency is under what circumstances an Agent may use a firearm. No definitive policy can be set forth, therefore we must continue to rely on good training and experience in arrest situations to produce the proper response in situations in which the use of deadly force may be necessary.

There are many situations in which Agents may draw their weapons when making an apprehension without being confronted with existing deadly force. This is a question of judgment which must be evaluated in terms of the individual or individuals to be apprehended, and the circumstances under which the apprehension is being made.

It is the policy of the Bureau that an Agent is not to shoot any person except, when necessary, in self-defense, that is, when he reasonably believes that he or another is in danger of death or grievous bodily harm.

Self-defense was defined by Mr. Justice Holmes, in language with which the courts still agree, as follows: "Many respectable writers agree that if a man reasonably believes that he is in immediate danger of death or grievous bodily harm from his assailant, he may stand his ground, and that if he kills him, he has not exceeded the bounds of lawful self-defense. That has been the decision of this court." (*Brown* v. *U.S.*, 256 U.S. 5 [1921].)

The term "self-defense" also includes the right to defend another person against what is reasonably perceived as an immediate danger of death or grievous bodily harm to that person from his assailant. 40 *American Jurisprudence* 2d, 170–17.

Emphasis must be placed on planning arrests so that maximum pressure is placed on the individual being sought, and he has no opportunity either to resist or flee. Any situation of this type can deteriorate in an instant, and continuing alertness, extreme care, and good judgement are necessary to enable Agents to control the situation. If a subject initiates action which may cause physical harm, there should be no hesitancy in using such force as is necessary to bring the subject under control effectively and expeditiously.

The increased probability of a law-enforcement officer having to use his handgun has led to improvements in such sidearms. The sole purpose of the weapons described in this book is to incapacitate an adversary who is threatening the life of the officer or the lives of others. The handguns described here are not toys. They are lethal instruments that should be taken seriously, and the discussion that follows is directed to the professional whose life might depend on a handgun.

As you read this book, you will understand that the ideal combat handgun has yet to be developed. Most police officers carry revolvers, and it is my hope that this book will help convince the law-enforcement community of the utility of switching to self-loading handguns. I also hope that by being better armed, police officers will be able to deter those who would use firearms in the pursuit of criminal activities. It would please me to learn that an officer carried the perfect combat handgun for an entire career without once having to use it, but should he need to draw and fire his weapon I hope that it will do its job and thereby protect his life.

GEORGE C. NONTE, JR.

George C. Nonte, Jr.:
A Biographical Sketch

MAJOR GEORGE CHARLES NONTE, JR. was one of the most prolific writers on the subject of firearms in this or any other century. He got his start in the field with an article in a military journal in 1957. That same year he published his first piece in a gun magazine. It was the beginning of a brilliant career.

Numerous books and countless magazine articles bear his by-line (which includes pen names C. George Charles and David Wesley) and his brand of thorough, investigative reporting. When Nonte retired from the Army in 1964 as an ordnance major after a twenty-year career, he was well-established in the gunwriting field and ready to freelance for a living. His output was tremendous; it was not uncommon for him to publish 175 articles a year.

In a field crowded with experts, Nonte was one of the most skilled and knowledgeable. His magnificent tome on the subject of *Pistolsmithing*, published in November 1974, has already become a classic in its field and has been reprinted four times. Not only was this his most popular work, it was also his personal favorite.

George C. Nonte, Jr. (Courtesy Lee Jurras)

As befits a man in his profession, Nonte was a man of action. An ardent hunter—and a very successful one at that—Nonte went to Africa several times, and he hunted extensively in Europe and some parts of Asia, as well as in Canada, Alaska, and Mexico. He also owned and operated a professional firearms testing, evaluation, and consultation service. Although modest about his achievements, Nonte was also a competitive shooter with the military. He alternated between a Shockey .45 and a Smith Model 52 Master .38; but he always favored Smith & Wesson's Model 41 in .22.

George C. Nonte, Jr. died in June 1978. At that time, he was in the middle of his rough draft of *Combat Handguns*, the first comprehensive book on the topic. Nonte was concerned that combat handguns had not been given the serious attention that was crucial for guns which are carried by people whose lives depend on them. *Combat Handguns* is Nonte's last achievement in a field where he will long be remembered for his contribution of vast learning and personal experience with firearms.

1

Autoloader Versus Revolver

IN THIS BOOK, the position is taken that the best handgun for most combat situations is the self-loading, or automatic, pistol; but the most popular American handgun has been the revolvers. Americans traditionally have been six-gun fans—nurtured on novels, films, and television programs in which the venerable single-action revolver always wins the fight. Likewise in the popular media, only a small number of uniformed or plainclothes policemen are seen carrying automatic pistols. Most American police forces still rely on revolvers. In the United States, large-caliber automatic pistols have been reserved for military use, while the .22 rimfire has been used for plinking, small game, and target shooting. Millions of shooters during the past seventy-five years have purchased tiny automatics for home and personal defense; and they have usually chosen guns with an attractive price or size rather than determining their effectiveness or reliability. Most of these individuals would probably rather have a revolver, but the automatic handgun was usually cheaper and smaller. Still, 99 percent of these small automatics would not qualify by today's standards as combat firearms.

Generally speaking, autoloading pistols have a reputation for unreliability. This is generally not justified, but the tales have been told and retold so often that virtually everyone without the personal experience of using a good automatic handgun paired with good ammunition still believes that "automatics always jam." The reputation autoloaders have for jamming goes back to the turn of the century when designers of both guns and ammunition were just beginning to solve the problems connected with automatic firing. Many of those early designs did malfunction, and this was an especially acute problem when the ammunition used was not loaded to the precise specifications required by a particular automatic pistol. By the second decade of this century, a number of the new autoloaders had demonstrated remarkable reliability.

Prominent among the more dependable handguns was the Colt/Browning .45 caliber automatic pistol, adopted in 1911 by the U.S. Army. Some problem areas remained; but they were primarily the result of misunderstandings between the manufacturers of the handguns and the makers of the cartridges, rather than problems inherent in the guns. For example, the Parabellum Luger performed beautifully with German ammunition manufactured to match it, but it would not always perform as well with American-made cartridges that were loaded to slightly different specifications. In recent years a high degree of international standardization for handgun cartridges has been achieved, and cartridge-loading variability has been eliminated as a major source of concern, as has the problem of unreliable cartridges with bad primers.

Following World War II, there was another rash of sentiments against automatic pistols, based again on demonstrable unreliability. The troubles almost invariably occurred with souvenir handguns brought back by soldiers. Many of these guns were battlefield pickups in deplorable condition, and many others were of late-war production when the quality of the workmanship and the materials had deteriorated very severely in Europe. Furthermore, most of the malfunctions were aggravated by the use of poor-quality, military-surplus ammunition.

In spite of all the bad press—some justified, some not—that autoloaders have received over the past seventy-five years, it can be clearly demonstrated today that a modern automatic with ammunition intended for it will generally survive a 5000-round, functional firing test without difficulty, sometimes without any malfunctions at all. The handguns most successfully tested to date are several variants of the Colt Government Model (M1911), the Smith & Wesson Model 39, the Browning Hi-Power (M1935), and the Walther P–38. Numerous government agencies have tested these automatics, and the evaluators are satisfied that modern autoloading pistols are as reliable for service use as the best revolvers.

Users of handguns for combat situations need to know how reliable revolvers are and how their reliability compares with automatics. Still-confidential, computerized reliability and endurance studies of automatic and revolver-type handguns by a major manufacturer of both have indicated that the automatic pistol is significantly more reliable than the revolver. Generally, the reason for this result is that currently manufactured autoloading pistols are designed to be rugged so that they will overcome the bad reputation this class of handguns has had in the past. If one examines the component parts of a typical, good-quality, double-action, large-caliber revolver and those of a comparable quality and caliber automatic, it becomes immediately evident that many of the essential operating parts of the revolver are smaller and more fragile than those of the automatic. Accordingly, the above-mentioned study indicates that over a long period of use, automatic handguns demonstrated greater functional reliability than revolvers.

Some further contrasts can be made between automatics and revolvers. Bulk and concealability is one category of comparison. While a revolver of comparable power may appear more graceful and less bulky than an automatic, it is actually more difficult to carry and conceal. It requires a large-diameter cylinder to house the cartridges and an otherwise superfluous mass of wood and metal as a handle. In addition, for a given barrel length, caliber, and cartridge capacity, a revolver is larger than an automatic. Autoloaders usually take up less space than a revolver, but the uniformed officer does not have to worry about concealability. For plainclothes officers or for users required to carry their handguns during off-duty hours, the automatic pistol can be a major improvement. For instance, the 9mm Parabellum Smith & Wesson Model 39 automatic pistol is 7.44 inches (189 millimeters) overall, with a 4-inch (102-millimeter) barrel. The Smith & Wesson .357 Magnum Model 19 is 7.5 inches (191 millimeters) overall, but has only a 2.5-inch (64-millimeter) barrel. A Model 19 with a 4-inch (102-millimeter) barrel is 9.5 inches (241 millimeters) overall. While the Model 39 is not potentially as powerful as the Model 19, a plainclothes officer can have less bulk and a longer barrel (hence greater accuracy) with the Model 39 than he can with the comparably barreled model of the Model 19 revolver.

When it comes to cartridge capacity, even the heaviest and best revolvers can hold only six cartridges without becoming overly bulky. On the other hand, an automatic of comparable power may contain as many as two and a half times that number—fifteen or sixteen cartridges in the case of the Smith & Wesson Model 59. The trained and experienced officer can also recharge an empty autoloader with a filled magazine in about one-fourth the time required to place new cartridges in a revolver. This gives the autoloader many times the firepower of the revolver and seems to allow new officers to be trained to an acceptable level of marksmanship proficiency in less time.

These characteristics of the autoloader indicate that it can be viewed as an acceptable combat sidearm. While revolvers are still favored by law-enforcement agencies throughout the United States, some departments and agencies are replacing them with modern combat autoloaders after extensive laboratory evaluations and field tests. The Illinois State Police was among the first police organizations to completely switch over to the self-loading pistol. Having made such a pioneering change, their ordnance personnel were constantly asked about the results of their decision. The following is a

Size comparison of the Smith & Wesson Model 19 Revolver and the Model 39 Automatic Pistol. (Courtesy Smith & Wesson)

verbatim reproduction of the report they used to answer questions asked by others contemplating the use of the new automatics. It is an excellent statement of the case favoring the self-loading pistol.

Report of Justification for Adopting
The 9mm Semi-automatic Pistol as Service Weapon
By The Illinois State Police

Prepared By
Ordnance Unit
Illinois State Police
Revised February 10, 1972

In 1966, several problems were identified in connection with the use of the standard revolver by the Illinois State Police. At that time, all personnel were required to furnish, from personal funds, a service revolver which had to meet the following criteria:

1. fire either .38 special or .357 magnum ammunition, and

2. be equipped with 4, 5 or 6 inch [102-, 127-, or 152-millimeter] barrel, and

3. be one of several different models of Colt or Smith and Wesson manufacture.

Since it was the policy of this agency (and continues to be) that all personnel carry star [badge], I.D. Card and weapon at all times while off-duty, it was found that many of our officers were also purchasing smaller weapons to carry while in off-duty or plain clothes situations. The only requirement of the department was that the off-duty weapon be of .32 caliber as a minimum. A survey of all personnel was conducted within the department and it was learned that because of the need for concealment and comfort, the vast majority of our men had purchased and were carrying (off-duty) a rather surprising assortment of guns.

It was determined that there was a wide range of types and styles of guns and ammunition. More importantly, it was learned that there were serious discrepancies in the condition of many of these off-duty weapons.

Since legal decisions were making it increasingly obvious that the courts were going to hold the department responsible for the training of its police personnel in the use of firearms and, more importantly, for their competency in using those weapons, the Illinois State Police found itself in a situation of concern. In an effort to over-come this problem, all personnel were required to fire their off-duty weapon as well as their service gun for qualifica-tion. Our Marksmanship Qualification Course (50 rounds) was fired 10 times on an annual basis, 7 times as Practice Shoots and 3 times as Qualification Shoots. The results of firing the off-duty weapon for qualification were somewhat startling.

Weapon	Ammunition	Score (Possible 500)	
Service Revolver	.38 Special Target Wadcutter	393	(Statewide Field Average)
Off-Duty Weapon	.38 Special Target Wadcutter	217	(Statewide Field Average)

For purposes of comparison

Smith & Wesson Model 39	Our Own Special Police Service Load	387	(Statewide Field Average)

Our weakness was very obvious—the "off-duty" weapon! We were faced with two alternatives:

1. Greatly increase the level of training and practice with the off-duty firearm and continue the program of training and practice with the "on-duty" weapon, or

2. issue a state-owned firearm which by design and weight and overall competency would serve as both "on-duty" and "off-duty" weapon and maintain a training and practice program for that *one* gun.

Because at that time the State did not own any of the guns used by State Police personnel, it was felt, that it would be very difficult to raise the level of competency and condition of the "off-duty" weapons carried and owned by members of the Illinois State Police. Additionally, it was recognized that a training program sufficient to raise the level of "shooter" competency with the "off-duty" weapon would be very expensive from the standpoint of both ammunition and man-hours. All recruits had received 50 hours of training with their service revolvers during their assignment at recruit school. There had been *no* training with the "off-duty" weapon. Also, because of the very wide range of types and condition of "off-duty" guns, it was recognized that the design and implementation of a training program directed toward "off-duty" guns would be very questionable as to its effectiveness. It was decided to survey available police weapons then in use with a view toward trying to find *one* firearm that would satisfy both the "on-duty" and "off-duty" police needs of our department. Thus, the time and cost of training in the "off-duty" weapon would be removed and the department would control the condition and competency of firearms carried by its members in "off-duty" situations.

Many tests were conducted, but they will not be repeated here because we were also experimenting with many different loads. Our tests did show that the 9 mm is no panacea with respect to being the *only* police service weapon. The 9 mm is no different than any other caliber from .32 through .45. The final determination is dependent upon the component parts of the weapon being used and the capability of the person handling the weapon. A good cartridge can be made in all these calibers if the manufacturer is desirous of doing so. At the present time one of the leading manufacturers [Winchester-Western] in this country is taking an interest in this project and has been working very closely with our department in ballistically testing various combinations of load and bullet weight.

One important reason for eliminating the small revolver was that they lacked either sufficient stopping power or practical accuracy. In eliminating these weapons, it was not necessarily because they were not capable of being fired accurately. It was because the average trooper could not master these weapons in the training time that was available. We further decided that any weapon not capable of delivering a bullet with foot-pounds of energy approximately 400 F.P.E. [Foot-Pound Energy] to the "right address" would not be a satisfactory service weapon.

This foot-pound energy, we felt was a "must," so an attempt was made to utilize a medium size 4-inch [102-millimeter] revolver by lightening the projectile and lessening the recoil. To do this, it was necessary to increase the velocity for compensation. This proved successful to a point; however, current revolver sights would not handle the variation in hits caused by the small variation in bullet weights. Knowing that semi-automatics were less prone to these variations, we next turned to the following:

The .45 caliber [M1911 Colt] fell from our list quickly as it has always been a weapon hard to master with a limited amount of training and, in reducing the weights of the bullets, functional difficulties developed. Also, the noise level was high and speed with safety was a problem so we decided to experiment with modern semi-automatics.

The .38 Caliber Super [Colt] Commander was one of the last weapons we eliminated and only because the Smith & Wesson Model 39 has additional features which make it more like our faithful friend, the revolver—safe and fast for the first shot.

The Model 39 had many features we felt were advantageous to a policeman:

A. Weight—less than two-thirds the weight of our lightest permissible service revolver (26½ ounces [751 grams]).

B. Width—three-fourths the width of our .38 caliber special revolver (1⅛" to 1½" [28.6-38 millimeters]) with no sudden or uneven bulges like the cylinder on the revolver.

C. Length—two inches [50.8 millimeters] shorter than the four-inch [102-millimeter] revolver (7⁹⁄₁₆ inches [192 millimeters] long), yet, the barrel lengths are the same. Also, the cartridge is completely encased by the barrel with no side splash of lead that all revolvers display to some degree.

D. Height—(5½" [139.7 millimeters]) which is ¼" [6.35 millimeters] lower than the revolver. It has a grip for larger hands due to the trigger being almost one inch [25.4 millimeters] higher on the semi-automatic, permitting the wrist to be straight and not cramping the fingers.

E. The balance or grip is such that there are no two or more ways to grip this pistol as on the revolver. In fact, the hand falls into one position on the grips, making this pistol an excellent pointer with a minimum of training or effort.

F. Safety—By removing the magazine, the pistol becomes inoperative even with a live round in the chamber. If this magazine is then placed in the uniform trouser pocket with the car keys, etc., one will not forget to reload the pistol on dressing for duty. When storing the gun with magazine out, the manual safety should be in the "on" position since we found that with the inertia-type firing pin, if the gun is dropped from a height of four (4) feet [1.2 meters] or more and lands directly on the end of the barrel, the firing pin will go forward with enough momentum to fire the round in the chamber. If the manual safety is "on" this locks the firing pin in place and the round cannot fire through mishandling.

1. *Magazine Safety*—Even with the magazine inserted and a round in the chamber, this pistol is as safe as a loaded revolver because the hammer is down and either has to be cocked or fired double action.

2. *Thumb Safety*—This safety is applied first when loading a round in the chamber. This always leaves the hammer in a safe position (down), with the manual movement of the slide.

G. Also, once in action, a trooper has more ammunition at his command (50%) with the option of reloading much faster, even in the dark without removing his eyes from the target. Additionally the more accurate single action type of shooting after the first shot results in quicker hits.

Ammunition

We found the caliber of this weapon (9 mm) to offer some advantages when compared to any .38 caliber revolver of comparable size for several reasons:

1. The same diameter as the .38 caliber and .357 magnum.

2. It can be loaded to pressures of 33,000 psi. Revolvers of comparable weight can stand but half this amount.

3. Regardless of the bullet weight or propellant, the point of impact does not vary as radically as it does with a revolver.

4. Lighter bullet weight (100 gr.) permits more velocity (1380 feet per second [420.6 meters per second]) within *working* ranges (100 yards [91.4 meters] or less), then loses speed and range rapidly, and further

reduces extreme ranges (¾ mile [1.2 kilometer]) and dangerous richochets. Thus, it is safer than the 158 or 200 grain .38 Special service loads (900 F.P.S.) with one and one-half mile [2.4-kilometer] range.

5. Due to the light jacketed bullet at high speed, penetration through auto bodies, seats, and rubber tires is comparable to the .357 Magnum. Yet, the 9 mm with 385 foot pounds of energy will only penetrate eight inches [203.2 millimeters] of flesh.

6. Accuracy—4" [102-millimeter] group at 25 yards [22.9 meters] and adequate at 100 yards [91.4 meters].

7. By substitution of a .30 caliber barrel and nothing else, this becomes a .30 caliber Luger with much more velocity. This could become an advantage in future years when smaller calibers at even greater speeds might come into use. The continuous trend seems to be toward lighter and faster bullets.

Malfunctions

We have had some malfunctions due mainly to three (3) causes:

1. Quality control in production of the gun at the factory.
2. Quality control in production of ammunition used.
3. Improper maintenance.

Cause #1: Smith and Wesson has worked very closely with our Department, and the production quality control problems that were in the gun itself have been corrected.

Cause #2: Probably more malfunctions have been caused by ammunition than any other single cause. Without some refinements on the loading ramp, this gun has trouble feeding exposed lead nose bullets, therefore, we do not recommend that this type of bullet be used for anything except practice. It is hard to control the quality of reloaded ammunition to the requirements of this gun. This again has been one of our problems. Because of this, we insist that only factory manufactured rounds be used for service work.

We re-load our own practice ammunition but it is used in range practice only.

Cause #3: (Dry Slide) After the gun has been fired a considerable number of times and burned powder residues begins to accumulate in the gun action, unless the slide has been oiled, the action starts to drag. Here again reloads may fail to eject. We have not found this to be a problem with factory ammunition.

We could go on and on as to the advantages which we believe are numerous over other weapons we tested for our needs. We realize that the noise level of the Model 39 is high, so we have issued ear guards with each pistol to be used on the practice range. We further feel that if absolute *dependability* were the *only* consideration, we might favor one of the new service revolvers with a perpetual inspection to insure against malfunction. However, from a practical standpoint, we found that the 9 mm Model 39 will maintain reliability for a longer period and it can be restored more quickly and easily without technical knowledge.

We maintain our own repair section for all state-owned weapons. Any Department furnishing weapons to their personnel should consider having a well-trained gunsmith regardless of whether they have revolvers or semi-automatics. For our Department (1700 men), the added advantage of interchangeable parts and barrels is also desirable.

In conclusion, it should not be implied that the Illinois State Police feel we have found the *one* and *only* firearm solution to the needs of police service today. Each police department must examine their own needs and base their decision upon the *needs* of *that* agency. There are many very competent guns and ammunitions available and all should be very carefully considered by any Department contemplating a change of firearms. After carefully weighing the practical factors and needs of our Department, we believe the 9 mm Smith & Wesson Model 39 best meets the needs of the Illinois State Police.

2

A Historical View

WHILE THE WHOLE story of handgun development cannot be recounted in this book, a few historical notes are in order. The modern handgun dates from the mid-1800s when many creative individuals began experimenting with multiple-shot firearms. Two key inventions made the modern revolver possible—the percussion cap for igniting gunpowder and the self-contained metallic cartridge. Toward the end of the nineteenth century, the manufacture of smokeless powder helped create the environment in which the self-loading (or automatic) pistol could emerge.

REVOLVER-TYPE HANDGUNS

The idea behind the revolver is an old one. Revolving-cylinder or revolving-barrel firearms date back to the sixteenth century and include weapons that were ignited by matchlock, wheel lock, and flintlock. Prior to the introduction of the percussion cap, all these ignition forms required the placement of a small amount of gunpowder next to a vent, or touch hole, which led to the powder chamber. The problems associated with containing this loose powder while the cylinder or barrel was rotated and with protecting the powder from the flash of the ignition of an adjacent chamber were major stumbling blocks for early designers.

Samuel Colt was the first person to successfully solve the revolver problem. While fragile and relatively low-powered by modern standards, Colt's early revolvers made at Patterson, New Jersey, established the basic pattern for the handguns that were to follow. Three elements set Colt's Patterson revolvers apart from those that preceded his. First, building on improvements in manufacturing technology and metallurgy, Colt could make a reasonably reliable handgun at a reasonable price. Second, the basic design concept of his early revolvers was a sound one. Third, he exploited the benefits of a practical system—the percussion cap ignited the gunpowder in a group of chambers in a single cylinder.

Although the Patterson revolver was a good idea, it required further perfection. While better than earlier designs, it was still too fragile for the treatment American frontiersmen gave it. Also, the cost of manufacturing handguns on a large scale was still too costly, and Colt needed a better manufacturing and financial system to underwrite such an enterprise.

By 1847, Colt had improved the design of his revolvers considerably. The result was the massive .44 caliber (11mm) handgun, popular with soldiers mounted on horseback. This "Walker" model Colt, made at the Whitneyville, Connecticut, armory of Eli Whitney, Jr., was adopted by the U.S. Army as the Model 1847. This revolver was an improvement, but it was still far from perfect. Problems with it during the Mexican-American War (1846–1848) led to the improved Colt Dragoon series. In a parallel development, Colt introduced his smaller-caliber, and hence smaller-frame, revolvers in the late 1840s. This work led to the 1851 Navy model, the 1860 Army model, and ultimately the Colt Model P, which is more widely known as the Colt Single-Action Army Model 1873, or the Colt Frontier Six-Shooter. Thus, by the early 1850s, the single-action revolver had become the standard American

Three variants of the Colt Patterson-type revolver. The top gun is shown with its folding trigger extended in the firing position. (Courtesy Colt)

sidearm. The centerfire Colt Single-Action Army was manufactured continuously from 1873 until World War II. After a brief hiatus, it was reintroduced by Colt, and a host of other companies have also produced variations since the 1950s.

This .44 caliber M1847 Colt Whitneyville Walker military revolver was quite a handful. It weighed about 4.85 pounds (2.2 kilograms), or about twice the weight of the .45 caliber M1911A1 Colt Automatic Revolver. (Courtesy Colt)

Single-action Revolvers

The basic compliments that can be paid the Colt single-action mechanism are that it is mechanically simple, it is easily repaired, and it is not especially difficult to manufacture. The popularity of this type of revolver led to many copies being made during the late percussion period and the early cartridge era. There were numerous attempts to circumvent Colt's patents, to copy the design outright without payment of royalties, and to develop improved or superior mechanisms.

The major improvement on Colt's design in the United States came with the Remington 1858 revolver. Functionally it was quite similar to the Colt, but instead of having separate barrel and grip assemblies the Remington had a solid frame. Although it was a more durable and reliable gun, the Remington name never quite caught on with the American gun-buying public as did Colt. The popularity of the single-action revolver led many American buyers to shun even more advanced double-action revolvers of both American and European origin.

In 1857, the Smith & Wesson Company introduced the first revolver designed to fire a self-contained metallic cartridge. This was the diminutive "Number 1" revolver, chambered to shoot the cartridge we call today the .22 short. Metallic cartridges signaled the end of the percussion era.

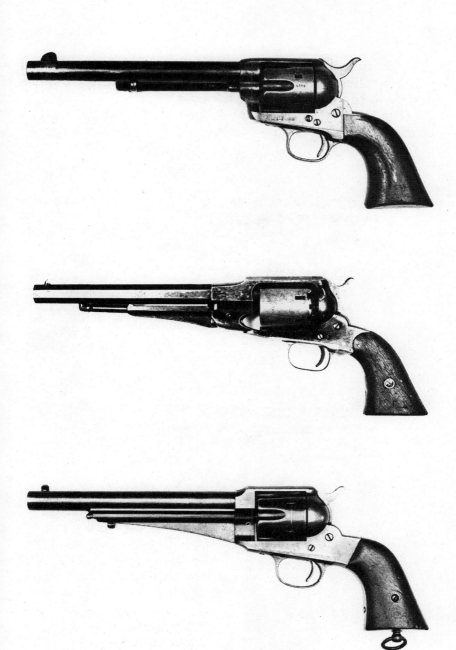

Three single-action revolvers. Top, a military-issue .45 caliber M1873 Colt Single-Action Revolver. Middle, a Civil War period .44 caliber percussion model. Bottom, a .44 caliber M1875 centerfire model. (Courtesy Masami Tokoi)

The American Civil War and certain patent rights prevented a larger-caliber rimfire revolver from being developed immediately in the United States, however.

The entire Civil War was fought with single-action percussion revolvers. Of the two American double-action hand-

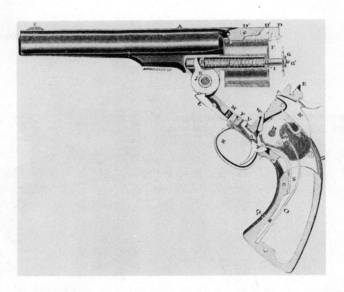

Schofield Smith & Wesson Army Revolver. This .45 caliber revolver was much easier to reload than the Colt M1873 Single-Action Army because of its top-breaking, simultaneous-ejection mechanism. (U.S. Army drawings)

guns, only the Starr was actually practical. However, neither the Starr nor the Savage revolvers survived to be manufactured in the postwar period. To satisfy the demands of the two contending military establishments, all manner of Colt copies and adaptations were manufactured in the North and South. Although the .44 Henry rimfire cartridge used in the Henry rifles and carbines would have been ideally suited for a military revolver, the Smith & Wesson Company held the license to Rollin White's patent for the bored cylinder that could be loaded from the rear (U.S. Patent No. 12649, 3 April 1855). This patent clearly prevented any other American company from selling a large-bore, metallic-cartridge pistol until 1873 when the White patent expired.

Smith & Wesson did introduce their .44 caliber rimfire "Model Number 3" in 1870. Although it was a single-action handgun, it offered a significant advantage over other revolvers because its top-break design permitted simultaneous extraction and ejection from all chambers. Rapid extraction could be followed by much easier reloading. While Smith & Wesson did not fully exploit the commercial potential of the Number 3 revolver on the domestic market (they were kept very busy filling orders for the Imperial Russian Army), they did sell the Schofield version of this gun to the U.S. Army in 1873. Meanwhile, Colt was ready with the Single-Action Army in 1872, as the White patent held by Smith & Wesson was about to expire.

In Europe, designers were producing high-quality, single-action and double-action revolvers, but these were never marketed successfully in the United States. Part of the problem facing the European manufacturers was the shipment of their arms to the U.S., but equally significant was the widespread consumer prejudice in America against foreign-made guns.

Double-action Revolvers

Late in the 1870s, Colt began to experiment with double-action revolvers. Colt's first double-actions were not terribly reliable; its parts were subject to wear and breakage. The

The Colt New Double-Action Self-Cocking Central-Fire Six-Shot Revolver with a 6.5-inch (165mm) barrel. This revolver was also called the Colt Lightning. (Courtesy Colt)

first Colt double-action was introduced in January 1877 as the New Double-Action Self-Cocking Central Fire Six Shot Revolver. Later Colt just called it the Lightning, and it was sold in .38 and .41 calibers. That same year, the .45 caliber Double-Action Army, also called the Double-Action Frontier, was introduced by Colt. Production of these double-action Colts continued for thirty years (1877–1907), and a total of approximately 212,000 handguns of this type were made.

Colt .45 caliber Double-Action Army Revolver. (Courtesy Colt)

Smith & Wesson began experimenting with double-action handguns in the early 1870s. By 1872, they were trying to sell such a revolver to the Russians. In 1881, they produced a double-action model of their top-break, hinged-frame revolver in .32, .38, and .44 calibers; but the men at Smith & Wesson soon saw the limitations and weaknesses of their design. The hinge was a failure point, and the double-action mechanism was fragile and overly complex. In 1894, Smith & Wesson began to work on a solid-frame handgun with a swing-out cylinder. The first model of this new type was introduced as the .32 Ejector Model of 1896. By the early 1900s, this design had been refined and became the mechanical basis for virtually all of Smith & Wesson's double-action revolvers. Only the frame size was varied to match the caliber of the handgun.

It was not long before Colt also recognized the design weaknesses of their double-action model of 1877. To replace that pistol, they introduced a .38 caliber, swing-out cylinder,

Two variations of the basic Model 1889 Colt military revolver mechanism. Top, a commercial version of the Model 1894–1896. Below, the Model 1905, manufactured for the U.S. Marine Corps. (Courtesy Colt)

double-action revolver in 1889. The first version of this gun was adopted by the U.S. Navy as the Model 1889. The U.S. Army followed in 1892. Field experience indicated that the hammer and firing pin of the M1889 and M1892 could be damaged if operated while the cylinder was open, so a modified lockwork was incorporated into the revolver design. The new gun was called the M1894. Several minor alterations were made during the next decade, culminating in the Army Special Model of 1908. This definitive pattern became the basis for Colt's entire line of double-action revolvers until the Mark III series was introduced in the late 1960s. Like the "definitive" Smith & Wesson design, the Colt revolver was produced in four basic frame sizes.

Colt Frames

Frame	Caliber	Model
Model D	.38 Special	Detective Special*
		Cobra
		Agent
		Diamond Back
		Police Positive
Model I	.357 Magnum	Official Police*
		Python*
		Official Police Mark III
New Service	.44	New Serice
	.45	Model 1917
		New Service Target
		Shooting Master
		Officers' Model Target
Model J	.357 Magnum	Lawman Mark III*
		Trooper Mark III*
		Metropolitan Mark III*

*Readily available in 1979.

Smith & Wesson continues to manufacture its basic military and police revolvers in three frame sizes—J frame (originally in .32 and later in .38 Special), K frame (originally in .38 Special and from the mid-1950s in .357 Magnum), and N frame (originally in .44 Special and later in .455/.45 and .44 Magnum). Following is a contemporary list of Smith & Wesson revolvers by model number with frame size and caliber indicated.

Two views of the "D" frame Detective Special Revolver manufactured by Colt. At the top is the revolver as manufactured before 1972; below, as manufactured in 1972 and after. (Courtesy Colt)

Smith & Wesson Revolvers

Model	Caliber	Name	Frame
10	.38 Special	Military & Police	K
12	.38 Special	Military & Police	K (Alloy)
13	.357 Magnum	Military & Police	K
14	.38 Special	K-38 Masterpiece	K
15	.38 Special	Combat Masterpiece	K
17	.22 Long Rifle	K-22 Masterpiece	K
18	.22 Long Rifle	.22 Combat Masterpiece	K
19	.357 Magnum	.357 Combat Magnum	K
25	.45 ACP	1955 .45 Target	N
27	.357 Magnum	Model 27 .357 Magnum	N
28	.357 Magnum	.357 High Patrolman	N
29	.44 Magnum	Model 29 .44 Magnum	N
31	.32 S&W Long	.32 Regular Police	J
34	.22 Long Rifle	1953 .22/.32 Kit Gun	J

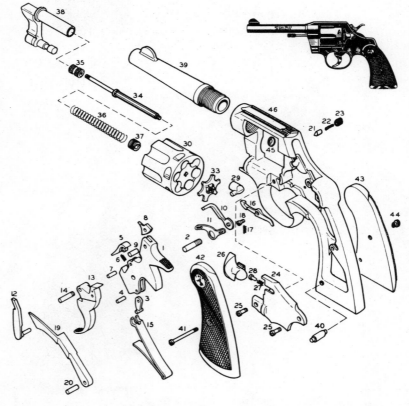

Exploded view of a typical Colt Model "I" revolver. (Courtesy Colt)

Model	Caliber	Name	Frame
36	.38 Special	.38 Chiefs Special	J
38	.38 Special	.38 Bodyguard Airweight	J (Alloy)
48	.22 Magnum Rimfire	K22 Masterpiece, M.R.F.	K
57	.41 Magnum	.41 Magnum	N
60	.38 Special	.38 Chiefs Special	J (Stainless)
63	.22 Long Rifle	1977 .22/.32 Kit Gun	J (Stainless)
64	.38 Special	.38 Military & Police	K (Stainless)
65	.357 Magnum	.357 Military & Police	K (Stainless)
66	.357 Magnum	.357 Combat Magnum	K (Stainless)
67	.38 Special	.38 Combat Masterpiece	K (Stainless)

Colt and Smith & Wesson were certainly not the only producers of revolvers in the United States after the Civil War. Before 1900, a number of other companies entered the American gun market with revolvers. Of those, only two are still in operation—Harrington & Richardson, established in 1873, and Iver Johnson, established in 1871. From the start, these two companies produced simple, low-cost revolvers of both solid-frame, fixed-cylinder, and hinged-frame types. While these were often purchased for personal protection and for recreational use, few police or military organizations looked with favor on these pistols for combat.

Colt .357 Magnum Python Revolver built on the "I" frame. (Courtesy Colt)

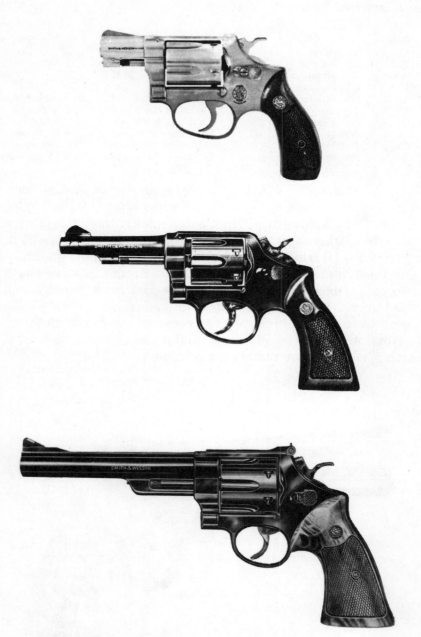

Contemporary Smith & Wesson revolvers. Top to bottom: Model 60, .38 Chiefs Special on the "J" frame; Model 10, .38 Special Military & Police on the "K" frame; and Model 29, .44 Magnum on the "N" frame. (Courtesy Smith & Wesson)

The Iver Johnson was the first *Safe* revolver made, and is the only revolver in which the *hammer never touches the firing pin*. Because of this patented unfailing safety device, it has gained for itself the slogan and design known all over the world as "HAMMER THE HAMMER," which convincingly portrays in every language its own story of positive, never failing safety. And yet, it is as safe as a toy until needed, and then it will never fail.

Because of the security against discharge by dropping or jolting, or accidental hitting of the hammer, the Iver Johnson Safety Automatic Revolvers are standard equipment in leading Banks, Express Companies and large institutions in this and other countries.

The Iver Johnson "Hammer the Hammer" revolver. (Iver Johnson Company catalog)

Iver Johnson did make a very important contribution to revolver design when they introduced the safety lifter, or transfer-bar safety, for revolvers. This type of safety interposes a bar or lever between the hammer face and the firing pin, which is housed in the revolver frame. The hammer cannot deliver its blow to the firing pin unless the transfer-bar is raised by its trigger linkage into position between the two. Raising of the transfer-bar does not occur unless the trigger is deliberately held to the rear. Old Iver Johnson advertisements feature a line drawing of a revolver with the hammer being struck by a carpenter's hammer, and in the ad the transfer-bar system is called the "hammer the hammer safety

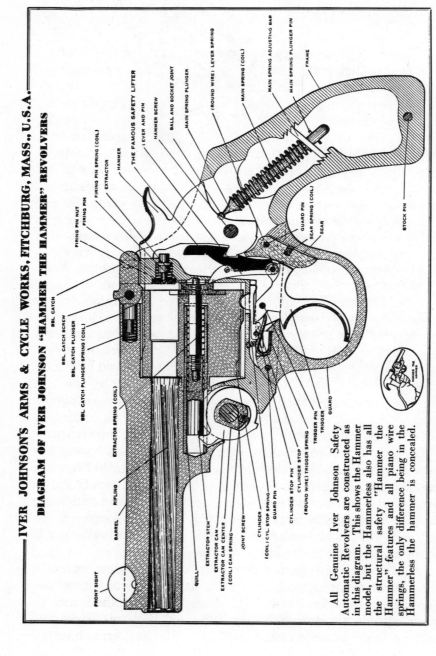

IVER JOHNSON'S ARMS & CYCLE WORKS, FITCHBURG, MASS., U.S.A.

DIAGRAM OF IVER JOHNSON "HAMMER THE HAMMER" REVOLVERS

FRONT SIGHT

BARREL

RIFLING

EXTRACTOR SPRING (COIL)

BBL CATCH

BBL CATCH SCREW

BBL CATCH PLUNGER

BBL CATCH PLUNGER SPRING (COIL)

FIRING PIN NUT

FIRING PIN

FIRING PIN SPRING (COIL)

EXTRACTOR

HAMMER

THE FAMOUS SAFETY LIFTER

LEVER AND PIN

HAMMER SCREW

BALL AND SOCKET JOINT

MAIN SPRING PLUNGER

(ROUND WIRE) LEVER SPRING

MAIN SPRING (COIL)

MAIN SPRING ADJUSTING BAR

MAIN SPRING PLUNGER PIN

FRAME

GUARD PIN

SEAR SPRING (COIL)

SEAR

STOCK PIN

QUILL

EXTRACTOR STEM

EXTRACTOR CAM

EXTRACTOR CAM CENTER

(COIL) CAM SPRING

JOINT SCREW

CYLINDER

(COIL) CYL. STOP SPRING

GUARD PIN

CYLINDER STOP PIN

CYLINDER STOP

(ROUND WIRE) TRIGGER SPRING

TRIGGER PIN

TRIGGER

GUARD

All Genuine Iver Johnson Safety Automatic Revolvers are constructed as in this diagram. This shows the Hammer model, but the Hammerless also has all the structural safety "Hammer the Hammer" features and all piano wire springs, the only difference being in the Hammerless the hammer is concealed.

The Iver Johnson "Hammer the Hammer" revolver. (Iver Johnson Company catalog)

system." It makes the point that even an extraordinary impact on the revolver's hammer will not cause the revolver to fire.

Although Iver Johnson no longer manufactures revolvers with the transfer-bar safety, this system has become very common since the mid-1960s on most high-quality revolvers. In 1964, Charter Arms reintroduced the transfer-bar safety in their Undercover revolver, which was designed by Douglas Meclannahn. Colt followed, including this element in their Mark III family of medium-frame, double-action revolvers. Dan Wesson (a great-grandson of D. B. Wesson, one of the founders of Smith & Wesson) also used the transfer-bar assembly in his recent line of Dan Wesson Arms. Sturm, Ruger and Company included this idea in their line of Security Six double-action revolvers. After some careless people shot themselves while "playing" with Ruger's copy of the Colt single-action revolver, that company incorporated the transfer-bar mechanism into that line of handguns also.

The transfer-bar safety was the greatest single advance in revolver safety since the introduction of the rebounding hammer at the beginning of this century in both Smith & Wesson and Colt designs. The only other important safety feature was the safety bar, or interrupter, employed by Smith & Wesson and Colt. These interrupters, operated by the trigger mechanism, blocked the hammer so that the firing pin could not reach the cartridge primer until the hammer was fully to the rear. While, practically speaking, interrupters were very effective, they were not so robust and were not totally fail-safe. At the end of the 1970s, Smith & Wesson was the only major American manufacturer of revolvers that had not taken steps to convert some of their designs to incorporate the transfer-bar safety. Still, the Smith & Wesson interrupter is just as effective in preventing most inadvertent discharges as the transfer-bar.

Between 1900 and the mid-1960s, few new revolver designs were introduced in the United States or elsewhere. Most new models were variations on established mechanisms. Since the mid-1960s, Charter Arms, Colt Firearms, Sturm, Ruger and Company, and Dan Wesson Arms have in-

The 7.65mm Schwarzlose self-loading pistol. (Schwarzlose manual)

troduced new designs. While many are interesting for their aesthetic appeal, none represent a fundamentally new idea for a revolver mechanism. All are combinations of early Colt and Smith & Wesson features and the transfer-bar safety. The real technological advances in handgun design since the beginning of this century have been in autoloading pistols.

AUTOMATIC HANDGUNS

The first successful autoloading handgun to use smokeless-powder ammunition was created in 1892 by the Austrian designer Joseph Laumann. Called the Schonberger, this pistol was a step forward from the mechanically operated black-powder, lever-action repeaters. The Schonberger was actuated by the rearward motion of the cartridge's primer. As was so often the case with early automatic pistols, the Schonberger was made in only small numbers.

Next came the self-loader designed by Andreas Wilhelm Schwarzlose. Although this Austrian designer is better known for his work with machine guns, he also designed several handguns. Schwarzlose's first design (1893) was more closely akin to the older mechanical repeaters. The cartridges were housed below the barrel with the point of the bullet pointing to the ground. Although this design was not successful, his second gun in 1898 was quite modern in appear-

PARTS of the self-cocking pistol.

Pistol.

1. Case with guide piece and fitting piece.
2. Barrel with sight and aim.
3. Breech cylinder.
4. Barrel holder.
5. Safety lever.
6. Setting lever.
7. Trigger with pin.
8. Magazine stop.
9. Ejector.
10. Magazine holder with spring and pin.
11. Guide bar.
12. Barrel spring.
13. Firing bolt.
14. Firing bolt spring.
15. Extractor.

Magazine.

16. Magazine case with bottom.
17. Magazine spring with button.
18. Transmitter with bar.
19. Grip pieces.
20. Grip bowls with screws.

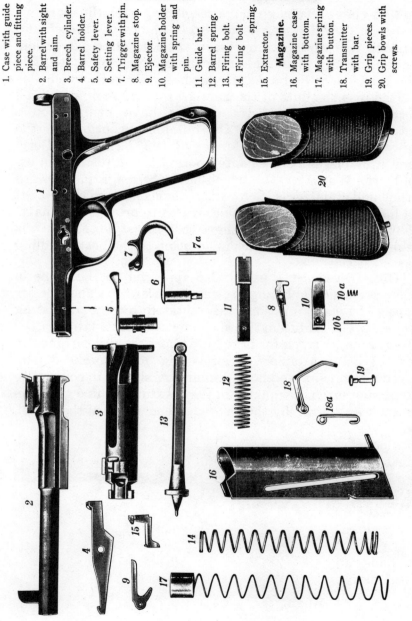

The 7.65mm Schwarzlose self-loading pistol. (Schwarzlose manual)

ance and much more typical of the automatic pistol as we
know it. The 1898 design had a recoiling barrel, the rearward
movement of which was harnessed to unlock the breech and
to relock it (through compressed springs) after extraction,
ejection, cocking, feeding, and chambering took place. The
Schwarzlose also had a detachable box magazine, which was
inserted into the butt of the handgrip. Since then, nearly all
successful automatic-pistol designs have utilized butt-
contained magazines, with the notable exceptions of the
highly successful Mauser Model of 1896, Theodore Berg-
mann's pistols, and a few contemporary target pistols (for example, the Walther OSP), which have the magazine forward
of the hand and trigger. Schwarzlose concentrated the weight
and bulk of his pistols in such a way as to provide a manageable weapon. Many people believe that this style of pistol has
the most pleasing aesthetics in addition to the best handling
characteristics.

Hugo Borchardt's pistol also appeared on the scene in
1893. Borchardt's handgun was awkward because of its
shape. The configuration was dictated by the operating
mechanism. In addition, the weapon was intended to be fitted
with a shoulder stock for firing as a short cavalry carbine. Instead of using a simple reciprocating bolt, Borchardt employed a toggle-jointed-bolt mechanism, similar in concept to
the locking mechanism used in the Maxim machine gun. Unlocking was started by the short-distance recoil of the barrel,

The 1893 Borchardt self-loading pistol. (Courtesy Jack Krcma)

The 1898 Borchardt-Luger in 7.65mm. (Courtesy Swiss Waffenfabrik, Bern)

and the bolt continued to the rear when the barrel assembly came to a stop. Like the Schwarzlose, the Borchardt was recoil-operated. The principle was the same, but the mechanical approach differed.

In its original form, the Borchardt was only a limited success. This pistol was significant because George Luger redesigned it to produce his world-famous handgun, called the Luger in America and the Parabellum in Europe. By 1900, the Borchardt/Luger pistol was being produced in significant numbers at the Deutsche Waffen und Munitionsfabriken. The Parabellum used a 7.65 x 22mm bottle-neck cartridge. In 1904, it was modified to take the 9 x 19mm Parabellum cartridge. By 1908, the operating mechanism reached the definitive form it would have until 1942, when the production of the gun ceased. While barrel lengths, sights, and safeties varied, over two million Parabellums were produced for several armed forces in Europe. In 1969, the Mauser factory in Oberndorf, West Germany, began to manufacture the Parabellum again. Still in production, this handgun is a variation of the Swiss pattern of the Luger design. Thus, the Borchardt/Luger/ Parabellum design has one of the longest production histories of all self-loading pistols.

Prototype Model 1896 Mauser self-loading pistol. (Courtesy Jack Krcma)

In 1896, the brothers Paul and Peter Mauser began manufacturing their commercially successful pistol. More than 1.5 million Mauser pistols were made before production came to a halt in the 1930s. The Spanish firm Esperanza y Unceta (ASTRA) produced thousands of their copy of the Mauser "broom handle" pistol as well. The Model 1896 and the Spanish copy were widely used by armed forces in Europe and Asia; and though it was never the official handgun of the German army, it was utilized in the hundreds of thousands by German troops in the 1914–18 and 1938–45 wars. When used with a shoulder stock, the Mauser served as a short repeating carbine for infantry and cavalry.

Mauser's 1896 pistol was also a recoil-operated design. The recoiling-barrel assembly unlocked the breech-bolt assembly. Unlike the Schwarzlose and the Borchardt, the Mauser magazine was placed in front of the trigger assembly. Whereas the Schwarzlose and Borchardt employed striker mechanisms (hammerless) to detonate the cartridge primer, the Mauser had an external, pivoted hammer at the rear of the frame that struck a firing pin in the bolt assembly.

At the close of the nineteenth century, the Parabellum

and the Mauser were the principal, high-power, autoloading pistols in use. They were not the only ones to be marketed in quantities, as dozens of designers and companies were rushing to produce self-loading handguns. Two designers, the Austrian Ritter Ferdinand von Mannlicher and the American John M. Browning, would challenge Luger and Mauser in the new century, but in the fading days of the 1800s the autoloading-pistol field was dominated by German designs.

Browning-type Handguns

John Browning was—and is—the most important designer of automatic handguns. His designs are still among the most popular and have been the most copied of any designer to date. John Browning was a mechanical wizard without equal. After unsatisfactory experiments with a gas-operated pistol, Browning concentrated on recoil-operated designs. The Colt Firearms Company put one of his self-loaders into production in 1900. This .38 caliber handgun was also recoil-operated, but it differed from earlier guns of this type by having a recoiling slide that enclosed the full length of the barrel. It

John M. Browning's Model 1900 .38 caliber Colt Automatic Pistol. (Courtesy Masami Tokoi)

did not have an exposed breech mechanism. It also differed from the Parabellum and Mauser in that the recoil spring used to feed and close the gun was housed in the slide beneath the barrel, instead of being in the frame. Browning's 1900 Colt design continued in production until 1929. While only 55,000 of this pattern were manufactured, this basic Browning design led ultimately to the American Model 1911 and the Fabrique Nationale Model 1935 Hi-Power pistols.

The early double-link locking system was extensively modified by Browning and the men at Colt. This work led to the elimination of the forward link and a number of less significant changes. Out of this activity emerged the U.S. Model M1911, or, as it is also frequently called, the Colt Government Model. The M1911 first saw combat use during the American 1916 punitive expedition into Mexico. It was later used in the Philippines campaign and in World War I. A series of minor changes were made to this handgun in 1926, and the modified product was called the M1911A1. This handgun is still the official handgun of the U.S. Army and is produced by Colt today. The following companies currently make either complete M1911A1-type pistols or major components for it:

Producers of the M1911A1

Manufacturer	Product(s) Made
A. R. Sales Company	frames
Arcadia Machine & Tool	A.M.T. frames
	slides
	barrels
	complete guns (A.M.T.)
Colt	complete guns (Colt Government Model)
Crown City Arms	complete guns (Crown City .45 Automatic)
Essex Arms Corporation	frames
Pacific International	complete guns (Vega)

Many of the early handgun designers were interested in capturing a portion of the military market for high-power pistols. Most of these guns were built around cartridges that produced chamber pressures that required the designers to use locked-breech-type handguns. John Browning probably saw more clearly than any of his fellow designers the market

U.S. Pistol, .45 caliber, Model of 1911. (Courtesy Richard Smith)

U.S. Pistol, .45 caliber, Model 1911A1. (Courtesy U.S. Army)

potential of a small, low-powered autoloader for the civilian market. Toward this goal, he developed several unlocked-breech patterns chambered for a short, semirimmed, .32 caliber (7.65 x 17mm SR) cartridge. (The cartridge is often referred to as the .32 Browning or the .32 ACP.) Browning and Fabrique Nationale, a Belgian firm, agreed to the production of the Model 1900 Browning. This pistol, first manufactured by Fabrique Nationale in 1899, became very popular with the forces of good and bad alike. Unwanted fame came to this little gun when one of them was used to kill the Archduke Francis Ferdinand of Austria—the spark that began the First World War. By the opening of hostilities, more than one million FN Model 1900 Brownings had been made. After World War I, many European police forces adopted the Model 1900 or similar handguns in .32 ACP (7.65mm Browning). For many years, the 7.65mm cartridge remained the standard police cartridge in Europe.

John M. Browning's Model 1900 Fabrique Nationale pistol. (Courtesy Fabrique Nationale)

Browning's work did not cease with this design. The fantastic success of the 1900 handgun caused the men at Colt to reconsider their initial rejection of a blowback pistol that Browning had designed in 1901. That gun became the Model 1903 Colt Pocket Pistol, and it was produced until 1946 in .32 ACP and .380 ACP (9 x 17mm Browning). A larger version chambered for the 9mm Browning Long (9 x 20mm SR) was made by Fabrique Nationale beginning in 1903, and it was adopted and used by armies in Europe and South America.

The initial success of these Fabrique Nationale and Colt Browning handguns spawned literally dozens of competitors. Some were pure copies. Many others borrowed heavily on Browning's ideas. Some of these handguns were good; some were bad; still others were terrible. Few made any original contributions to the field of automatic-pistol design. Whereas the Browning designs helped to popularize the compact, pocket automatic pistol, many of the copies and adaptations raised the specter of poor workmanship and unreliability.

There were some very interesting pre–World War I pistol designs of the non-Browning type also. These included the odd-looking family of Webley-Scott automatics; the eye-pleasing M1917 Savage; the boxy, but very reliable, M1910/14 Mauser Pocket Models; the rotating, barrel-locked Steyr-Hahn; and the basic Beretta of 1915. Only the Beretta, in a much refined and improved form, survived into the 1970s. Following the 1914–1918 war, only one new North American autoloader saw sizeable production—the Pedersen-designed Remington Model 51. In Europe, hundreds of small handguns were introduced in the next few decades.

European Autoloaders: 1918–1975

One of the most important new handgun developments of the post-World War I years came from the designers at Carl Walther Waffenfabrik. Carl Walther's eldest son, Fritz, introduced the Polizei Pistole (the PP) in 1929 and the Polizei Pistole Kriminal (the PPK) in 1931. The former (in 7.65 x 17mm and 9 x 17mm) was designed for use by uniformed police, while the PPK (in 7.65 x 17mm) was created for plainclothes

The Walther PPK in 7.65 x 17mm. (Courtesy Jack Krcma)

police. In addition to the fact that they were very handsome
pistols, both in outward shape and quality of workmanship,
the PP and PPK were significant because they were double-
action. These moderate-power, blowback handguns could be
fired from the hammer-down (uncocked) position by a single,
direct pull on the trigger in the same fashion as a double-
action revolver is fired. As a result, these guns could be safely
carried in an uncocked position, but still be ready for a quick
first shot. Although there has always been some controversy
surrounding the accuracy of the first shot from a double-
action handgun, revolver or automatic, many users seem to
prefer the quickness of the double-action first shot to the
slowness of the more accurate single-action first shot. For
combat shooting, double-action must be viewed as a preferable feature.

Toward the end of the 1930s, the Walther company introduced the 9mm Parabellum military pistol, called the P38
after its year of adoption. This handgun was significant be-

cause it was a positively locked autoloader with a double-action mechanism. Widely praised when it was introduced, the P38 was very rugged and reliable as a military combat handgun. More than 1.2 million P38s were produced during the war years, and in the postwar period Carl Walther Sportwaffenfabrik renewed and has continued production of the P38 for both military and police use (as the P1) and commercial sales. Although other designers did not follow suit immediately, the P38 ushered in the era of the big-bore, double-action pistol.

When John Browning died in November 1926, he was working on yet another automatic-pistol design. The completion of this gun, designed around the 9mm Parabellum cartridge, was carried out by Dieudonne J. Saive at Fabrique Nationale. That Belgian firm introduced the Model 1935 Grand Puissance, or, as it is known in English, the Browning Hi-Power, in 1935. Saive's contributions to the development of this pistol generally have been overlooked because Fabrique Nationale used the Browning name to help sell the gun. But Saive was responsible for taking a rough design and

Post-1945 manufactured Walther P–38 pistol. (Courtesy Interarms)

turning it into a finished piece of hardware. Most significant
was his development of the double-row magazine with the
large capacity of thirteen cartridges. Browning had believed
that such a magazine was an impossibility. Saive thought it
was possible and developed one, setting another precedent
for combat handguns—a large-capacity magazine. Basically a
refinement of the M1911 design, the M1935 Hi-Power has
been widely accepted for military use. Since its introduction,
more than two million have been manufactured.

In 1935, the French Army adopted the MAS–35 automatic pistol. This gun was designed by Charles Petter, who at
the time was working for the Société Alsacienne des Con-
structions Méchanique (SACM). Basically a Browning of the
M1911 type, the Petter pistol was unique because the hammer, sear, and mainspring assembly could be separated as a
unit from the gun. Fedor Vasilivich Tokarev, a Soviet
designer, evolved a similar system in the late 1920s.

The Schweizerische Industrie Gesellschaft (SIG) pur-

Preproduction FN Model 1935 Hi-Power pistol made in November 1934. (Courtesy
Fabrique Nationale)

The Swiss Army model of the 9mm Parabellum SIG P210 pistol. (Courtesy Masami Tokoi)

chased the patents of Charles Petter in 1937 and began development of an autoloader for the Swiss Army. Originally called the SP47/8 pistol, the SIG design is better known as the P210. Although an evolution of the basic Browning M1911 pattern, the P210 has some unique features. In most Browning-type pistols, the slide moves on grooves, or rails, machined on the outside of the main frame. The SIG design reversed this pattern; the rails were milled into the interior surface of the frame and into the exterior surface of the slide. In addition, the frame was somewhat longer, which supported the slide during a greater portion of the recoil and counter-recoil cycles. Although it is one of the most expensively produced handguns, the P210 is a high-quality and very accurate pistol.

Yet another variation of the Browning is the Tula-Tokarev 1930 pistol. Modified in 1933, this handgun was a standard military pistol for the Soviet Union and Warsaw Pact countries until the mid-1960s. Still further evidence of the excellence and popularity of the Browning locked-breech mechanism was the Spanish copies made by Gabilondo y cia and Bonifacio Echeverria. The former company marketed its handguns under the name Llama, while the latter sold its guns under the tradename Star. The full-size Llama series was introduced in the 1930s. Following World War II, Gabilondo y cia introduced scaled-down versions of their Browning-type pistols in .22, .32, and .380 calibers. Bonifacio Echeverria introduced their Llama Brownings in the 1920s, and the company continues to produce these pistols a half century later.

It is interesting to note that the original Borchardt/ Luger/Parabellum and Mauser locked-breech pistols were successful, but they were not copied or produced in large numbers by manufacturers outside their country of origin. The M1911 Browning-type pistol has been modified, copied, or improved in such diverse parts of the world as the Soviet Union, the United States, Switzerland, France, Poland, Spain, Brazil, and Mexico, to name a few. Whereas production of the Mauser was ended in the late 1930s and Parabellum military manufacture was terminated in 1942, Brownings of several types remain in production today.

In the years immediately before World War II, a number of small-caliber, blowback automatic pistols were brought onto the world market. Mauser and J. P. Sauer und Sohn, following the lead of Walther, introduced pocket automatics for police and military use. The Mauser HSc (Hahn Selbstpann variant c, or self-cocking hammer) was introduced in 1938 to compete with the Walther PP and PPK. Production of the HSc was interrupted by the close of World War II but resumed in September 1968. In 1967, the firm Heckler & Koch introduced the HK4 pistol, which bears a very strong resemblance internally to the HSc. The HK4 is set off from the HSc by an aluminum frame and the use of modernized production techniques, which make the Heckler & Koch pistol easier and less expensive to manufacture. The HK4 also is notable because it is available in four calibers—.22 Long Rifle, .25 ACP, .32 ACP, and .380 ACP. Hence its name—HK4.

Sauer und Sohn's Model 38H pistol was another competitor with the Walther guns. Like the HSc, the Model 38 was double-action. In addition, it had one specific feature that is

The Mauser HSc of post-1945 manufacture. (Courtesy Interarms)

Phantom view of the HK4 pistol. (Courtesy Heckler & Koch)

The J. P. Sauer und Sohn Model 1938(H). Note the cocking lever below the caliber 7.65mm designation on the slide. (Courtesy Masami Tokoi)

now found on many modern self-loading handguns. While both the Walther PP/PPK and the Mauser HSc have external hammers, the M38 has an enclosed hammer. The Sauer M38 can be fired double-action for the first shot by pulling the trigger all the way to the rear, or it can be cocked by using a cocking lever located just above the magazine-release button and to the rear of the trigger. Alternatively, the weapon can be uncocked (the hammer lowered) by pressing the cocking lever until the sear is released. Controlled release of pressure on that lever permits the hammer to be released safely. Another advanced feature incorporated into the design of the M38 is the magazine-disconnect safety. The pistol cannot be discharged if the magazine has been removed. At the end of the Second World War, J. P. Sauer und Sohn moved from Suhl in East Germany to Eckernforde in West Germany, where their production of fine sporting rifles and pistols was resumed.

Design layouts for the Heckler & Koch P9 series began in

1966, with continuous production beginning in 1970. The P9
pistol series was first chambered for the 9mm Parabellum
cartridge. The P9 is single-action only, and the P9S is double-
action. Both the frame and slide of the P9S are formed by
stamping and folding sheet metal with spacers and adding inserts. The machining often required in handgun manufacture
has been eliminated through the use of precision castings.
Surrounding the built-up frame are a trigger-guard assembly
and grips made of molded plastic. The most unusual feature
of the P9 series is the locking system, which is derived from
the roller-lock-breech mechanism of the G3 rifle. The only
other automatic pistol that uses a roller-locking system is the
Czechoslovakian Vz 52. After talking about a .45 ACP version of the P9S for several years, Heckler & Koch began
series production of a .45 caliber pistol in 1976. Demand for
this version of the P9S will probably exceed the supply for
many years.

There are several unique aspects of the P9 pistols. All P9
models have the side-mounted cocking lever after the pattern
of the Sauer Model 1938(H). In the single-action P9, this lever
is used to cock and unlock the pistol as necessary. In the
double-action P9S, the first round can be fired double-action
for a quick shot, or the cocking lever can be used to ready the
hammer for a more accurate single-action release. Instead of
conventional rifling, the engineers at Heckler & Koch chose
polygonal rifling. In addition to being easier to manufacture
—HK barrels are hammer-forged—these barrels supposedly
provide greater velocity and greater accuracy than conven-
tionally rifled barrels. Shooters who are accustomed to relat-
ing the accuracy of slide-type automatics to the close fit of
the muzzle end of the slide on the exterior surface of the barrel will be puzzled by the apparent looseness of the P9 barrel
and slide. Unlike Browning designs, the HK P9 series does
not rely upon forward-barrel bushing fit for accuracy. The
barrel-locking system is different, and the P9 behaves more
like a fixed-barrel handgun than a moveable one, as in the
Browning link-operated barrels. In any case, the P9 pistols
give good accuracy.

In the mid-1970s, SIG and J. P. Sauer und Sohn worked

Top, *the 9mm Parabellum P9S pistol.* Bottom, *the .45 ACP P9S pistol. Note the special target sights on the 9mm P9S.* (Courtesy Heckler & Koch)

together to produce the P220 and P230 pistol designs. All of the design work was carried out by SIG engineers, while the production was concentrated at the Sauer factory. The P220 has been produced in 9mm Parabellum, .38 Colt Super, and .45 ACP, but due to increased production costs it is currently produced only in 9mm. The P220, which became available in 1975, features a stamped and welded slide with a separate breech block (#34 in accompanying drawing), which is held in by the firing-pin retaining pin (#40, #41). Locking is a much modified Browning-type.

Unlike the conventional Browning/Colt, in the P220 there are no top lugs on the barrel and no recesses in the slide; instead the breech end of the barrel locks up into the ejection port. The movement of the barrel is controlled by the breech block (#34) and by the lever-barrel-lug-cam surfaces in a hardened steel "locking insert" (#24) inside the aluminum frame (#1). As a result, all of the firing and locking loads imposed on

The SIG-Sauer P220 9mm Parabellum automatic pistol. This weapon is the result of an extensive investigation into the attributes most desirable in a combat automatic. SIG-Sauer has incorporated the most advanced pressing, welding, and investment-casting techniques into the manufacture of this gun. (Courtesy SIG)

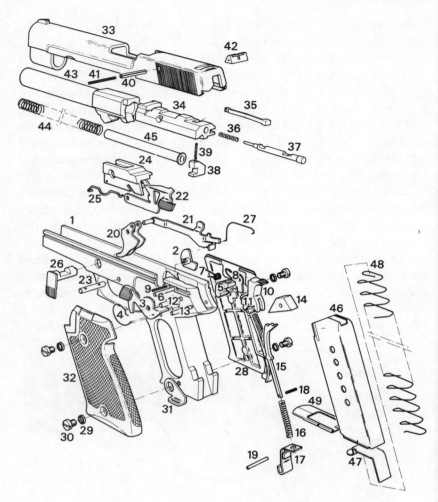

P220 disassembled.

the frame are taken by steel parts, and the peening, or bat-
tering, encountered in some aluminum-frame handguns is
avoided. As in the case of several of the newer automatic
handguns, the P220 has been equipped with a decocking
lever. The P220 does not have a manual safety because it has
an automatic, firing-pin safety mechanism. The firing pin is
locked until the trigger is pulled. If the P220 is carried with
the hammer down, it is impossible for the handgun to be inad-

vertently discharged. All things considered, the SIG-Sauer P220 is an excellent design, one upon which a person could rely in a combat situation. The Swiss Army has adopted this handgun as the Model 75 pistol.

SIG-Sauer had also introduced a new blowback pistol for police use in the P230. Chambered for the 9 x 18mm Police cartridge (midway in size between the 9 x 17mm, or .380 ACP, and the 9 x 19mm Parabellum), the P230 was created to compete with guns firing the .380 ACP (9 x 17mm) cartridge. While many European law-enforcement officers still carry .32 ACP (7.65 x 17mm) and .380 ACP automatic pistols, neither these sidearms nor the P230 are adequate for American police activities in the opinion of most experts. This topic is discussed more fully in chapter 8.

Carl Walther also introduced a 9 x 18mm Police caliber pistol in the mid-1970s called the PP-Super. Although slightly larger than the PP, the Super model is basically the same mechanically. The PP-Super has a reshaped pistol grip and a repositioned magazine-release button. A slide-hold-open latch

The SIG-Sauer P230 9 x 18mm Police pistol. (Courtesy SIG)

The Walther PP-Super caliber 9mm Ultra (9 x 18mm) and the Walther PP caliber .380 ACP (9 x 17mm). (Courtesy Masami Tokoi and Walther)

has also been added to the design. The accompanying drawing compares the PP-Super with other currently produced Walther pistols. With the introduction of the Walther P5 (see below), the future of the PP-Super is uncertain.

During the mid-1970s, the Walther firm introduced two variations of their P38 that have shortened barrels. Specifications for these new variants are as follows:

Walther Specifications

Model	Barrel Length	Length Overall	Weight
P38/P1	4.94 in (125mm)	8.5 in (216mm)	Steel, 33.6 oz (.95kg) Aluminum, 28. oz (.79 kg)
P4	4.5 in (114mm)	8.0 in (203mm)	29 oz (.82 kg)
P38K (kurz)	2.75 in (70mm)	6.38 in (162mm)	26 oz (.74 kg)

Germany and Switzerland are not the only European countries whose designers have introduced new 9mm Parabellum double-action pistols. In Italy, Beretta has produced the Model 92, which was evolved from the single-action military M951 Brigadier pistol. The locking system of the M951 and Model 92 is similar to that of the Walther P38. The Model 92 has a fifteen-cartridge magazine, compared with the eight-shot magazine of the M951. In 1975, the Czechoslovakian state export agency, Merkuria, announced the availability of a new 9mm Parabellum double-action combat handgun manufactured by the Ceska Zbrojovka factory at Strakonice. Ceska Zbrojovka borrowed the Browning locking system for their Model 1975 Parabellum Pistol. Looking like a cross between the FN Browning Hi-Power and the Smith & Wesson Model 39, this fifteen-shot handgun copies the SIG P210 pattern of having the slide ride on guides cut into the interior surface of the frame. Most other Browning-type slides ride on guide rails cut into the exterior surface of the frame. Several newer combat handguns have appeared in Europe since 1975, and they will be discussed later.

THP

PPK

PP

PP-SUPER

P 38 K

P 4

P 38

The current line of Walther automatic pistols drawn to the same scale.

Top, *Beretta M951 Brigadier 9mm Parabellum single-action pistol.* (Courtesy Beretta) Bottom, *Egyptian version of the M951.* (Courtesy Jack Krcma)

Top, *M92 with manual safety mounted on the frame.* Bottom, *M92S with manual safety mounted on slide.* (Courtesy Beretta)

The Ceska Zbrojovka Model 1975 Parabellum Pistol. (Courtesy Jack Krcma)

HANDGUNS IN THE UNITED STATES:
1945 TO THE PRESENT

For nearly seven decades, the M1911-type .45 caliber Browning/Colt has been the standard service pistol of the U.S. Army. There has been little support for changing to a smaller caliber or newer design because the M1911 has been a very reliable combat handgun and because so many were produced—about 2.4 million for the U.S. Government alone. Still, there have been recurring attempts to introduce a lighter, smaller-caliber pistol into the Army's inventory.

The Army Ground Forces staff looked into the desirability of a new handgun during the years 1946–1955. Official specifications established by the Ordnance Technical Committee in 1947 called for a handgun weighing no more than 25 ounces (.71 kilograms) and measuring no longer than 7 inches (178mm). The M1911A1 pistol weighs 40 ounces (1.13 kilograms) and is 8.62 inches (219mm) overall. A new requirement—influenced by the Walther P38—was the desire for double-action to eliminate the time-consuming, single-action

cocking of the M1911A1. Furthermore, the new guns were to
have a reduced caliber of .35 inch, or 9mm, with the Parabellum cartridge being the most logical ammunition candidate
because many European countries—which were to become
the nucleus of the North Atlantic Treaty Organization—were
standardizing the 9mm Parabellum.

Upon receipt of the Ordnance Technical Committee's
specifications, Springfield Armory approached three commercial manufacturers—Colt, High Standard, and Smith &
Wesson. Of these firms, Colt and High Standard immediately
agreed to submit prototypes. Smith & Wesson declined at

*A comparison of the .45 ACP SIG-Sauer P220, the 9mm Parabellum CZ Model 75,
and the Beretta Model 92. All three pistols are double-action. The 9mm pistols have
large-capacity magazines (fifteen cartridges), while the .45 caliber P220 holds only
seven cartridges in its magazine. Note also that the P220 has special target sights
unsuited for combat. (Courtesy Jack Krcma)*

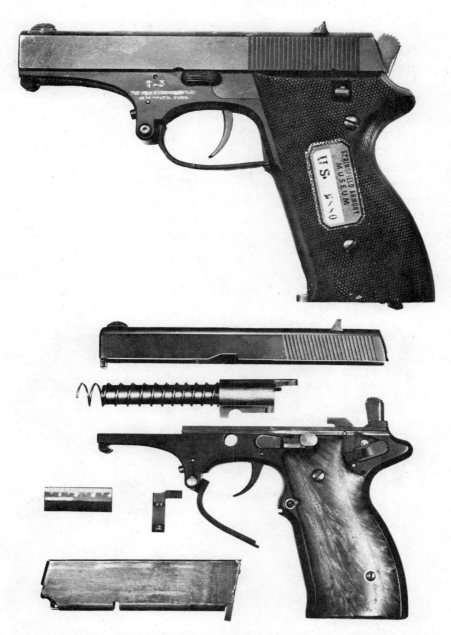

Top, *High Standard 9mm Parabellum T3 pistol.* Bottom, *High Standard T3 pistol (note winter trigger guard partially lowered and changes from model above).* (Courtesy Jack Krcma)

Two views of the Colt T4 9mm Parabellum pistol. (Courtesy Springfield Armory)

first because they considered themselves to be primarily revolver people. Initially, the following prototype models were
submitted: shortened M1911A1 in .45 ACP and 9mm Parabellum, Colt T4 in 9mm Parabellum, and High Standard T3
in 9mm Parabellum. A few lightweight, Inglis-made (Cana-
dian), Browning Hi-Powers were also tested during these
trials. From this experimentation came the Colt Commander
series and the Smith & Wesson Model 39 automatic pistol.

Work toward the Commander aluminum-frame handguns
began in 1947 when the people at Colt began discussions with
the Forgings & Castings Laboratory of the Sales Development
Division of the Aluminum Company of America. ALCOA engineers delivered sample frame-forgings in 1948. The Commander-type frames were also shorter, and a number of other
changes were made to lighten the gun. Early in 1950, the
short, lightweight pistol in 9mm Parabellum, .38 Colt Super,
and .45 ACP was introduced to the commercial public as the
Commander Model.

Smith & Wesson personnel began work on their automatic handgun after C. R. Hellstrom was elected president of
that firm in 1946. Joe Norman, who led the team of design
engineers, delivered the first prototype double-action 9mm
Parabellum Model 39-type pistol on 28 October 1948. This
gun was referred to as the X–46 at the factory. The first
model with an aluminum frame was manufactured in March
1949. These X–46 models had a grip with a twenty-five-
degree angle, instead of the fifteen-degree angle incorporated
into the production Model 39s. Between 28 October 1948 and
10 August 1954, 31 X–numbered guns were built by Smith &
Wesson to test various alloy and steel frames and different
modifications to the operating mechanism. Some of the
X–numbered guns were single-action. Production of the
Smith & Wesson automatic pistols began in November 1954.
When number designations were given to these handguns in
1957, the double-action version was called the Model 39. Only
ten of the single-actions were ever produced. Of all the 9mm
Parabellum double-action pistols, the Model 39 has probably

The 9mm Parabellum Colt Commander. (Courtesy Jack Krcma)

An experimental Smith & Wesson Double-Action Automatic Pistol of the Model 39 type. (Courtesy Masami Tokoi)

the best overall design shape and sizing. Aesthetically as well as mechanically, it is a very pleasing weapon to handle.*

The U.S. Army tested the Colt Commander and the Smith & Wesson Double-Action Automatic (M39) in 1955. On 7 July 1955, further experimentation with 9mm Parabellum pistols was terminated after the Deputy Chief of Staff of the Army for Logistics decided that there were ample stocks of M1911A1 pistols in the Army's inventory. Since handguns are seldom used in combat, a new handgun was not a necessity—so went the reasoning. Policemen and private citizens benefited from the Army's encouragement of 9mm pistol development, but the U.S. armed forces still had the old, but reliable, M1911A1 pistol.

---

*In 1971, Smith & Wesson introduced an improved extractor for the Model 39. Originally, the extractor was a wide spring-bar that extended from the manual-safety hole to the bolt face. Occasionally these extractors broke. The new extractor is shorter, narrower, and has a coil spring to apply the necessary pressure. Model 39s with the original extractor are marked 39-1; those with the improved extractor are marked 39-2.

U.S. ARMY EXPERIMENTAL HANDGUNS: 1946–1955

	1949 Specifications	Final Specifications	T3 High Standard	T4 Colt	9mm Colt Commander	9mm Smith & Wesson	.45 M1911A1-Type w/Aluminum Frame	Standard M1911A1
Weight:	Not to exceed 25 oz (.71 kg)	Not to exceed 29 oz (.82 kg) with magazine	1st 28 oz (.79 kg) 2d 32 oz (.91 kg)	30.05 oz (.85 kg)	27.8 oz (.79 kg)	26.5 oz (.75 kg)	26 oz (.74 kg)	39.2 oz (1.1 kg)
Length:	Not to exceed 7 in (178mm)	Not to exceed 7.5 in (191mm)	7.525 in (191mm)	6.867 in (174mm)	7.8 in (198mm)	7.44 in (188.9mm)	7.8 in (198mm)	8.6 in (218.4mm)
Caliber:	9mm Parabellum	9mm Parabellum	9mm Parabellum	9mm Parabellum	9mm Parabellum	9mm Parabellum	.45 ACP	.45 ACP
Magazine capacity:	7–10	13	7 for initial models	13	7	8	7	7
Trigger operation:	Double-action	Double-action	Double-action	Double-action	Single-action	Double-action	Single-action	Single-action
Operation: Winter trigger to permit use with mittens	Winter trigger to permit use with mittens	Winter trigger to permit use with mittens	Yes	Yes	No	No	No	No
Slide lock: Hold open after last cartridge	Hold open after last cartridge	Hold open after last cartridge	Yes	Yes	Yes	Yes	Yes	Yes
Breech operation: Blowback	Blowback	Blowback	Yes	Modified Browning	Browning	Modified Browning	Browning	Browning
Magazine release: Similar to M1911A1	Similar to M1911A1	Similar to M1911A1	Yes	Yes	Yes	Yes	Yes	Yes

In the mid-1970s, the M1911A1 pistol was joined by a new .45 caliber handgun, the M15 General Officers Pistol. The M15 was basically a modified version of the National Match model of the old standard .45. For decades, Army officers upon reaching the rank of Brigadier General (one star) were issued a .32 or .380 ACP Colt Pocket Model Pistol (sometimes called the Pocket Model M). Between April 1941 and February 1945, the U.S. Government purchased 17,330 .32 caliber and 1,113 .380 caliber Pocket Models from Colt. Until December 1964, the generals had the option of purchasing their pistols upon retirement; after that date these officers could keep the guns without charge.

Between 1965 and 1967, studies and tests of replacement sidearms for generals were carried out by the Army. The Walther P38, FN Browning Hi-Power, Colt Commander, and Smith & Wesson Model 39 were among the candidates ex-

Pistols for generals. Top, the .45 ACP M15 General Officer Model ready for engraving a general's name on the plate in the grip. Bottom, the .32 ACP Colt Pocket Model M, the type of handgun issued previously. (Courtesy U.S. Army)

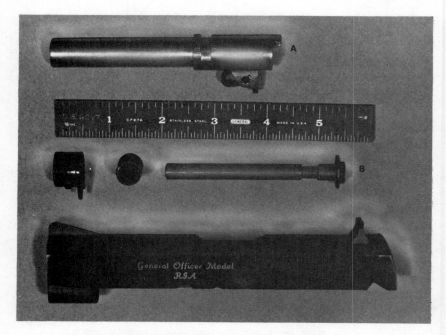

The slide and internal parts of the M15 General Officer Pistol. Note the modified and shortened barrel (A) and the new recoil spring and plunger assembly (B) required by the shortened barrel and slide. (Courtesy U.S. Army)

amined. Despite the ready availability of these 9mm Parabellum automatic pistols, the men at Rock Island Arsenal responsible for the selection of a new pistol decided that general officers should have something special. Colt submitted a 9mm General Officers Pistol M1969, but the Army elected to keep the .45 caliber cartridge. Therefore, Army design engineers made a series of prototypes in 1971 that culminated in the XM15. On 12 October 1972, the M15 General Officer Model RIA was standardized.

Production of the M15 began in the summer of 1972. The men who make the M15 belong to the same specialized team of armorers who produce National Match pistols and rifles. They begin by cutting down a standard M1911A1 frame, rather than use the shortened Commander frame. They also utilize a shortened M1911A1 slide, rather than the Commander slide. The M15 has a redesigned recoil-spring mecha-

nism consisting of two tubes and a spring to compensate for
the shortened barrel and slide. As modified, the M15 weighs
about 2.25 ounces (.064 kilogram) less than the standard
M1911A1. Each general officer pistol is a work of craftsman-
ship, and the individuals who carry them have excellent, but
exclusive, pieces of armament.

The Smith & Wesson Model 59 is yet another commercial
handgun influenced by military needs. During the Vietnam
war, the U.S. Navy Seal (Sea, Air and Land) Teams established the requirement for a silenced automatic pistol. Smith
& Wesson first modified steel-frame Model 39s to meet this
need. After experimentation with these prototypes, the Navy
in 1968 asked Smith & Wesson to build a small quantity of
fourteen-shot pistols. Smith & Wesson engineers had made
two fourteen-shot prototypes in 1964, but this project had
been shelved due to more pressing work. In 1968, those prototypes were used to design the Mark 2, Mod. O Silenced Pistol.
Also called the Hush-Puppy, this weapon had a locked slide
to prevent the loss of gas and the movement of the slide upon

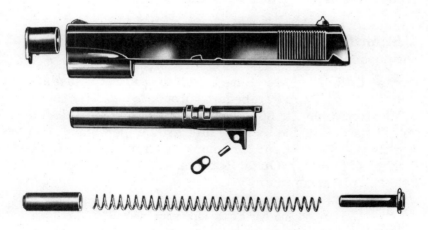

*Standard Colt Commander slide, barrel, and recoil spring and plunger assembly.
Compare with M15 barrel and note modified locking lugs. Note also the different
recoil spring and plunger assembly. (Courtesy Colt)*

firing; both are elements that create noise and defeat the effectiveness of silenced weapons. The Mark 2, Mod. O pistol had a stainless-steel frame and slide. It used special 9mm Parabellum ammunition—a 158-grain (10.2-gram) projectile that traveled at 900 feet per second (274 meters per second), which is well below the speed of sound and capable of being silenced. Smith & Wesson's experimental department delivered these special guns in June 1969.

Given the success with the basic pistol portion of the Hush-Puppy program, Smith & Wesson decided to expand their 9mm Parabellum pistol line. A small lot of Model 59 prototypes was released for field evaluation in June 1971. The frame of the Model 59 is made of the same high-strength aluminum alloy used in the Model 39. In comparing the two guns, the Model 59 has a thicker (.985 inches [25mm] compared to .730 inches [19mm]), but straighter, pistol grip than the Model 39. Unloaded, the Model 59 weighs only 2 ounces (.057 kilogram) more than the Model 39, a minor price to pay for doubling the magazine capacity. Once again a military project helped to bring about a new commercial combat handgun, but the U.S. armed forces has yet to benefit in a big way from these experimental activities.

U.S. Air Force 9mm Handgun Program, 1977

In August 1977, the U.S. Air Force Armament Laboratory at Eglin Air Force Base began to study the feasibility of substituting a 9mm Parabellum automatic pistol for the Smith & Wesson Model 15 .38 Special revolvers and M1911A1 automatic pistols carried by Air Force ground personnel. In a letter to the major handgun manufacturers, Dale M. Davis, Technical Director, Guns, Rockets, and Explosives Division, told the pistol community:

> Currently, the Air Force side arm is an S&W M15 .38 special revolver, many of which are worn and require replacement or rebuilding. Stocks of .38 special ball ammunition are depleted. In addition, there has been considerable user dissatisfaction expressed with respect to maintaina-

Top to bottom: *Model 39 "Hush-Puppy" silenced pistol, designated the 9mm Pistol WOX–13A* (Courtesy U.S. Navy); *U.S. Navy Mark 2, Mod. O Silenced Pistol developed by Smith & Wesson* (Courtesy U.S. Navy); *and production version of Smith & Wesson Model 59 pistol.* (Courtesy Smith & Wesson)

*Smith & Wesson Model 15 Combat Masterpiece, the standard U.S. Air Force side-
arm.* (Courtesy Smith & Wesson)

bility, fire power and lethality of this weapon and cartridge. It is therefore an opportune time to consider
replacement with a more suitable item. (Dale M. Davis to
addressees, "Air Force Side Arm," 12 August 1977)

In response to this solicitation for weapons, the following
handguns were submitted for test and evaluation (all in 9mm
Parabellum):

1. Beretta Model 92S–1
2. Colt Stainless Steel Pistol (SSP)*
3. Fabrique Nationale Browning Hi-Power M1935
4. Fabrique Nationale Fast Action (Modified Hi-Power)*
5. Heckler & Koch P9S
6. Heckler & Koch VP-70 (selective fire pistol)
7. Heckler & Koch PSP*
8. Smith & Wesson Model 459 and 459A (Improved M59
with different extractor, new firing-pin safety device, and
modified rear sight.)*
9. Star M28 (New, experimental, double-action automatic with ambidextrous safety and fourteen-cartridge-
magazine capacity.)*

---

*These handguns are not commercially available.

With the exception of the FN Hi-Power and the FN Fast Action, all of these pistols are double-action. The Hi-power is single-action, and the Fast Action is a new mechanical concept midway between single-action and double-action. Fabrique Nationale's Fast Action (FA) can be cocked, and then the hammer can be pushed forward with the thumb. When the person carrying it is ready to use it, he can pull the trigger to fire. Most double-action automatics tend to pull up and to the right when the trigger is pulled for the first shot. Firing the Fast Action makes the simplicity of this new type of mechanism quickly appreciated, and the first-shot accuracy is also soon noted.

Externally, the Fast Action looks a great deal like a modernized and customized Hi-Power. It can be distinguished by its slightly longer frame, matt-gray-black parkerized finish, combat sights, and ambidextrous and enlarged safety lever. To those users who have cursed the traditional, small safety-lever of the Hi-Power, this new safety-lever will be appealing. (No photographs or drawings can be published at this time because Fabrique Nationale is still undecided about the future of the Fast Action pistol. It has been tested by Belgian and other European police organizations, but a major military or police sale will have to occur before FN will give this new handgun more widespread publicity.)

Colt's Stainless Steel Pistol will also have to be ordered in large numbers before they will manufacture this new double-action pistol. The SSP is the design of Robert E. Roy, who carried out the basic work on this gun in the late 1960s. First introduced as Colt's Model 1971 Double-Action Pistol, this weapon has lain dormant for nearly a decade while Colt's management has vacillated about its introduction. In 1977, the Air Force handgun project led Colt engineers to dust off their prototypes and submit ten of them for the trials. Again, the fate of the Colt Stainless Steel Pistol is uncertain.

The Colt Stainless Steel Pistol bears considerable design similarity to the Petter and SIG P210 designs. The slide moves on rails cut into the frame. Colt's new handgun also has an *en bloc* dismountable hammer-and-fire-control mechanism similar in concept to the Peter and SIG designs. In the

Early prototype version of Colt Stainless Steel Pistol, about 1970. (Courtesy Colt)

Stainless Steel Pistol, the *en bloc* fire-control mechanism has been improved and is covered by U.S. Patent 3,682,040 (8 August 1972). Those models of the SSP being tested by the U.S. Air Force have been altered externally somewhat. The trigger-guard has been enlarged and squared off so it looks less like the Smith & Wesson Model 39. A matted rib has also been added to the top of the slide.

As it has progressed, the U.S. Air Force 9mm handgun program has generated considerable interest within U.S. and NATO military circles. As a consequence of the creation of a Department of Defense Joint Service Small Arms Program in December 1978, the Air Force will also generate background data for evaluating the replacement of all handguns carried by U.S. military personnel. Early test results indicate that there are several excellent candidates that could eventually replace the M1911A1 automatic pistol. Those tests also indicate that the M1911A1 will be hard to beat when it comes to overall reliability, which, of course, is one of the key features of a combat handgun. Although a decision about an American Air Force or Joint Service handgun may be several years away, the German police have recently made some important decisions about new automatic handguns.

GERMAN POLICE PISTOL TRIALS

The German police pistol trials of the mid-1970s may turn out to be one of the most interesting handgun events of the past three decades. Four major German arms-makers developed handgun models that would meet requirements es-

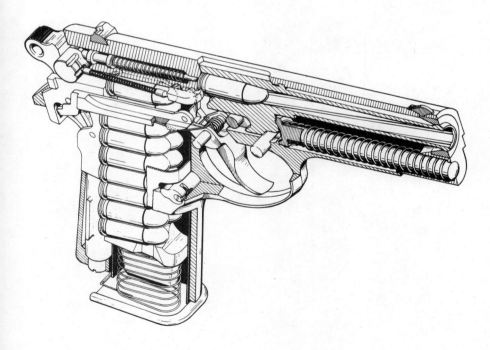

Cutaway view of Colt Stainless Steel Pistol prototype, 1970. (Courtesy Colt)

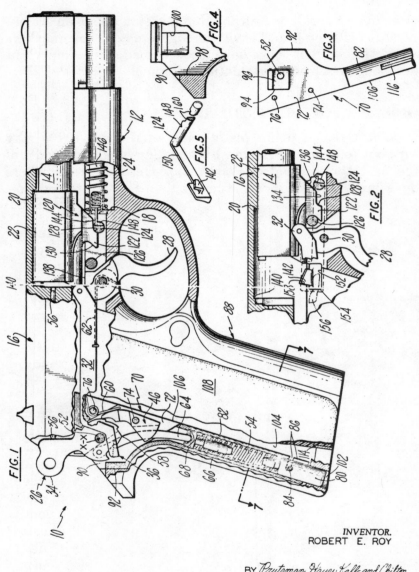

FIG.4

FIG.3

FIG.5

FIG.2

FIG.1

INVENTOR.
ROBERT E. ROY

BY *Prutzman, Hayes, Kall and Chilton*

ATTORNEYS

Patent drawing showing internal mechanism of Colt Stainless Steel Pistol. (Courtesy U.S. Patent Office)

tablished by the West German Ministry of the Interior. The Federal Republic of Germany has two basic classes of police forces—those who report to the Federal Government in Bonn, and those who are responsible to the individual German states. The Bundesgrenzshutz (border police) and Bereitschaftpolizei (Police Field Force Reserve), who fall in the Federal Government category, have traditionally carried the P1 (P38) 9mm Parabellum handgun. Local police forces have carried 7.65mm (.32 ACP) automatic pistols. In the wake of the Palestinian terrorist attack at the 1972 Olympic games in Munich, the West German government decided to standardize police handgun ammunition (9mm Parabellum) and create uniform specifications for law-enforcement handguns.

In addition to the dimensional criteria (see accompanying table), the Federal authorities required a weapon that could be safely carried and drawn from a holster with a live round in the chamber. Candidate weapons had to be capable of immediate fire without the deliberate operation of safety or cocking levers. Pistols should also be useable by either right- or left-handed shooters with minimum inconvenience. And the handgun must have a service life of at least 10,000 shots. It should be noted that no existing 9mm Parabellum handgun could satisfy all of the Federal requirements. Some new thinking had to be done.

Originally, four guns were submitted for evaluation—Heckler & Koch Polizei Selbstlade Pistole (PSP), Mauser HsP, SIG-Sauer P225, and Walther P5. After some initial trials, Mauser withdrew their gun pending further engineering. The Heckler & Koch, SIG-Sauer, and Walther pistols have been approved for purchase by German state police organizations. They were given "P" (Pistole) numbers by the government of the Federal Republic of Germany following the pattern established in the postwar period by the Bundeswehr (P1, Walther P38; P2, SIG P210; P3, ASTRA 600/43; and P4, Walther P38K (kurz)).

Most German police organizations have made their decisions on a new handgun at this writing, with the SIG-Sauer P225 (P6) being the most frequent choice. International sales of these three handguns to police forces promise to be substan-

Comparison of Federal Republic of Germany Police Handguns Specifications and Candidate Handguns

	FRG Specification	P5 (Walther)	P6 (P225)	P7 (PSP)
Method of operation:		Falling block (modified P38)	Browning type	Blowback with gas-piston retardation
Caliber:	9 x 19mm Parabellum	9 x 19mm Parabellum	9 x 19mm Parabellum	9 x 19mm Parabellum
Magazine capacity:	8-shot minimum	8	8	8
Muzzle energy:	500 joules minimum (369 ft-lbs)	ca. 500 joules (369 ft-lbs)	ca. 500 joules (369 ft-lbs)	518 joules (382 ft-lbs)
Overall length:	180mm (7 in) maximum	180mm (7 in)	180mm (7 in)	166mm (6.54 in)
Overall height:	130mm (5.13 in) maximum	129mm (5.08 in)	131mm (5.16 in)	125mm (4.92 in)
Width:	34mm (1.34 in) maximum	32mm (1.26 in)	34mm (1.34 in)	28mm (1.1 in)
Barrel length:		90mm (3.54 in)	97.6mm (3.84 in)	105mm (4.13 in)
Sight radius:		134mm (5.28 in)	145mm (5.71 in)	147mm (5.79 in)
Frame material:		Aluminum	Aluminum	Steel
Weight:	1 kg (35.27 oz) maximum	.795 kg (28.04 oz)	.82 kg (28.92 oz)	.98 kg (34.57 oz)

tial during the next decade. As a consequence, it will be some time before any of these guns are available on the commercial retail market. The following table presents the German police organizations and the handguns they have adopted:

New Model Handgun Adoption by Federal Republic of Germany Police Organizations

Bundesgrenzschutz	P6 (SIG-Sauer P225)
Bereitschaftpolizei	P6

The Mauser 9mm Parabellum HsP evolved from a short, stubby .45 ACP handgun developed by the Swiss designer Walter Ludwig. Changing the pistol from .45 ACP to 9mm Parabellum required more time and money than anticipated by Mauser. If technical and financial problems can be overcome, this pistol may be marketed in Europe and the United States. (Courtesy Mauser)

Federal Customs Police   P6
Schleswig-Holstein   P6
Hansestadt-Hamburg   P6
Lower Saxony   P7 (Heckler & Koch PSP)
Bremen   P6
North Rhine-Westphalia   P6
Hessen   P6
Rhineland-Palatinate   P5 (Walther)
Baden-Wurttenberg   P5 and P7
Bavaria   P7
Saarland   P9S (Heckler & Koch)
West Berlin   P38 made in France by Manurhin
                                (due to treaty restrictions)

Grenzschutzgruppe
(Anti-terrorist commandos)   P7

All three of the new police handguns have one feature in common—none have a traditional manually operated safety. Because of the instant, quick-draw-readiness requirement levied by the German Ministry of the Interior, the designers at the three arms companies had to develop alternative means of creating a safe, but loaded, handgun.

The P5 is essentially a new generation P38. Starting with the basic operating mechanism of that World War II handgun, the people at Walther created a new and much improved design. The most interesting aspect of the P5 is its safety arrangement. When the pistol is uncocked and carried in the holster, the firing pin rests in such a position that it matches up to a hole counter-bored into the face of the hammer. In this position, the striking surface of the hammer cannot touch the firing pin. As the double-action trigger is pulled to the rear, the trigger-bar (which connects the trigger to the hammer assembly) rotates both the hammer and the firing-pin safety lever to the rear. The rearward motion of the firing-pin safety lever brings a cam to bear against the base of the firing pin, raising it so that it is in the proper relationship with the hammer face to permit firing. The single-action cycle is similar, but in that case the hammer is cocked. Only when the trigger is pulled does the firing-pin safety lever raise the firing pin so it can be struck by the hammer. When the

The Walther P5 9mm Parabellum pistol. (Courtesy Walther)

decocking lever is used to lower the hammer, the firing pin is already in the down position. Thus, even with a fast-falling hammer, the cartridge in the chamber cannot be fired.

The Walther P5 and SIG-Sauer P6 (P225) firing-pin safeties are similar in principle, but differ in exact details. In function, they serve the same purpose as the transfer-bar in modern revolvers. Both mechanical devices eliminate accidental discharge of the gun by introducing a mechanical linkage that must be consciously activated to permit firing. Although these firing-pin safety systems are virtually fail-safe, long-time handgun users may wish to experiment with these new mechanisms before they are convinced that they are as safe as the older type of mechanical safeties that lock the moving parts in such a way that they will not function until the safety is mechanically released. Future combat handguns will probably incorporate systems similar to the Walther and SIG-Sauer firing-pin safety because of the increased speed with which the gun can be brought into use.

SIG-Sauer's P6 (P225) is essentially a small version of the

Walther P5 Firing-pin Safety System

Pistol uncocked: Firing pin (38) held in safe position by spring. Note counterbored hole in face of hammer (5).

Pistol cocked: Firing pin still held in safe position prior to pulling trigger.

Pistol fired: Upon pulling trigger, firing-pin safety lever (4) raises the firing pin so that it can be struck by the hammer.

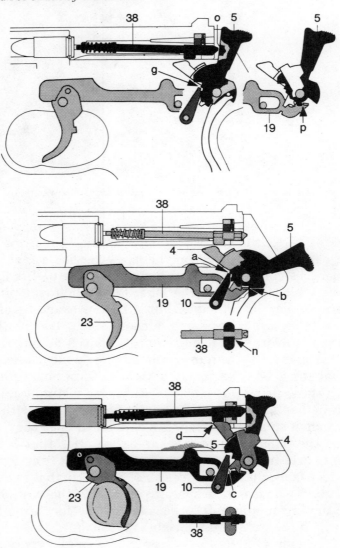

SIG-Sauer P220 and P225 Firing-pin Safety System

Firing-pin safety catch. For maximum safety, the firing pin is locked. Quick readiness is assured since this safety catch is released automatically by pulling on the trigger. The catch is not released until the trigger is consciously pulled.

Decocking lever: This lever permits the hammer to be lowered without danger. The firing pin is blocked during and after decocking.

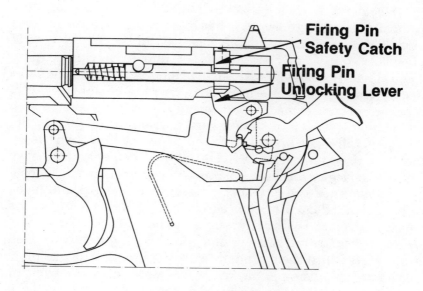

**Firing Pin
Safety Catch**

**Firing Pin
Unlocking Lever**

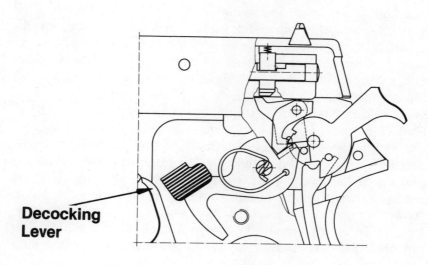

**Decocking
Lever**

P220 introduced in 1975. The P6 version is only .3 ounce (.01 kilogram) lighter than the P220, but it is nevertheless significantly smaller in size, as indicated by the accompanying photographs. It is also significant that the P6 has a magazine capacity of only eight shots instead of the nine in the P220 magazine.

Heckler & Koch's Polizei Selbstlade Pistole has the most radically new design. First, it has a gas-retarded blowback action. This operating principle was used in the World War II German Volksturm Gewehr VG1-5 and in a Swiss experimental handgun developed during that war at the Eidgenossische Waffenfabrik, Bern. Second, cocking of the Heckler & Koch gun is performed by squeezing the cocking lever, which runs the full length of the forward portion of the pistol grip.

Generally, gas pressure is used to unlock and open the action of a firearm. In the PSP, Heckler & Koch engineers have employed a gas-actuated piston to keep the breech mechanism shut until the chamber pressure drops to a safe level. When a loaded cartridge is seated in the PSP's chamber, the gas-piston port is directly beneath the mouth of the case. When the cartridge is fired, a portion of the gases generated are diverted into the cylinder below the barrel. The gas pressure acts upon the piston, which is attached to the front of the slide, retarding the rearward motion of the slide until the chamber pressure drops to a safe level. Afterwards, the PSP acts like any other blowback pistol. Utilizing gas pressure to retard the movement of the slide eliminates the need for complex mechanical-locking systems or excessively heavy slides and springs. Thus, a lightweight pistol was possible—34.57 ounces (.98 kilogram) with a steel frame.

Cocking the PSP is simple, but it takes some thought at first. The pistol is cocked by squeezing the grip to compress the cocking lever located beneath the trigger-guard and hinged at the bottom of the forestrap. Cocking requires about 15 pounds (67 newtons) of pressure, which is not difficult because three fingers of the shooting hand grasp the lever. After the pistol has been cocked, only 1.25 pounds (6 newtons) of force are required to keep it cocked. The PSP firing pin protrudes from the rear of the slide and thus acts as a

Top, *SIG-Sauer P225 Police Pistol.* Bottom, *SIG-Sauer P220 Military Pistol. Note the differences between these two handguns. The P225 has a shorter barrel and slide, and the pistol grip is also shorter; thus, the magazine holds eight rather than the nine cartridges held in the P220 magazine. Observe also the reshaping of the hammer and pistol grip in the P225. The P225 has the M1911A1-type button magazine release, but it can be supplied with the magazine release mounted at the base of the pistol grip as shown in the P220.* (Courtesy SIG)

Actual-size Heckler & Koch PSP (P7). (Courtesy Heckler & Koch)

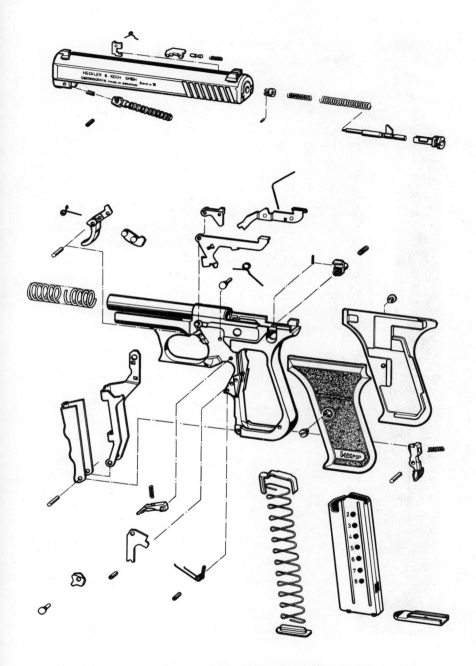

Disassembled view of Heckler & Koch PSP. (Courtesy Heckler & Koch)

cocking indicator. When the PSP is fired, it is recocked automatically as long as the cocking lever is held in the rear position. When that lever is released, the firing pin is lowered to the uncocked position. The PSP may, of course, be carried safely with a loaded chamber. A butt-mounted, magazine-catch release (a typically German feature) may be one of the few design drawbacks to this otherwise excellent handgun.

OTHER COMBAT HANDGUNS OF THE 1970s

Benelli Model 76 Pistol. This excellently made 9mm Parabellum pistol is constructed entirely of machined parts, with the exception of two minor parts, which are castings. The design is unusual for a high-power pistol because the barrel is mounted directly to the frame and because it is a hesitation-lock-breech system. A small, hinged, locking toggle at the rear of the separate breech block delays the opening until the bullet has left the muzzle, and chamber pressure has dropped to a safe level. The principal advantage is in the greater accuracy possible from a fixed barrel. Movable barrels are inherently less accurate because they jump around from shot to shot. This handgun feels good, and the grip angle is superior to many other contemporary autoloaders. The Benelli 76 is marketed in the United States by Sile Distributors.

Detonics .45 Caliber Automatic Pistol. The Detonics .45 Associates firm was established in the early 1970s to produce a reduced version of the M1911A1 .45 automatic pistol. It is primarily sold to police officers looking for an easily concealed off-duty gun. Much shorter, both front-to-back and top-to-bottom, than the M1911A1, the Detonics .45 is only 6.75 inches (171.5mm) long and 4.5 inches (114mm) high. It weighs 29 ounces (.82 kilogram), about 10 ounces (.28 kilogram) less than the standard M1911A1. In modifying the M1911A1 design, the grip safety was eliminated.

Built upon a new—not cut down—investment cast frame (a modern, precision-casting technique) and slide provided by Essex Arms, the Detonics .45 is a production model and not a limited-edition, customized handgun. The traditional, remov-

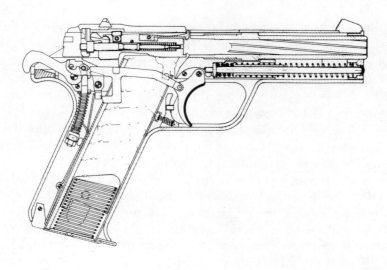

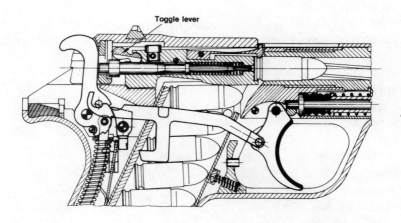

Toggle lever

The Benelli Model 76 9mm Parabellum Pistol. Top, *the pistol cocked and ready for single-action firing.* Bottom, *the pistol uncocked and ready for double-action firing. Note the toggle lever, which is the key to the Model 76 operation. When the slide is held forward by the recoil spring, the rear of the breech bolt drops slightly to engage the locking surface in the top of the frame. When the pistol is at rest, the slide can be pulled to the rear, and it unlocks from the frame by the interaction of the locking surfaces. When the gun is fired, it does not unlock because the toggle lever pivoted to the upper rear of the breech bolt is held by the slide's inertia at such an angle that the bolt cannot rise. The toggle lever only keeps the bolt locked to the frame during the peak pressures. After the pressure drops, the bolt unlocks, and the slide can travel to the rear.* (Courtesy Benelli)

able, barrel bushing has been discarded, and a conical muzzle enlargement has been added to the barrel, which seats directly into the slide. The recoil-spring assembly is a self-contained unit—two springs, inner and outer, around a full-length guide. A recoil-spring cap holds the springs onto the guide. As noted in the discussion of the U.S. Army M15 General Officer Pistol, the recoil spring is critical to the proper operation of very short automatic pistols, and the Detonics people seem to have created one good solution to that problem.

In shortening the standard .45 barrel, Detonics had to sacrifice some projectile velocity and energy. Recoil and muzzle jump are not uncomfortable, but both are greater than that experienced with the standard M1911A1 or the Colt Commander. Also, people with large hands will find this little .45 difficult to hold. This gun should be considered only as a secondary weapon—not as a primary combat handgun.

Navy Arms Mamba Automatic Pistol. Named after an aggressive, lethal snake of southern Africa, the Mamba is

The Detonics .45 Associates Automatic placed on top of a standard M1911A1 Colt Browning automatic pistol. (Courtesy Detonics)

another of the new generation of all-stainless-steel automatics. It originally was a joint venture of West German and South African interests and was marketed by Gear Ratio Engineering (pty.) Ltd. doing business as Sandock-Austral Small Arms. The Mamba was developed to meet the needs of the armed forces of the Republic of South Africa. The Americanized Mamba will be built from imported investment castings that will be finished and assembled in the Navy Arms New Jersey factory. Essentially, this weapon is a modernized Browning Hi-Power with a modified Smith & Wesson Model 39 double-action mechanism. The latter was modified to permit use of a Browning-type manual safety.

Other significant design features of the Mamba include an ambidextrous safety lever and a specially designed slide that eliminates the need for a barrel bushing. The barrel has a patented, self-cleaning, rifling system; and the trigger mechanism can be removed from the pistol as a single unit. Although the pistol grip was designed to enhance pointability, the distance to the trigger is a bit too long for users with small hands. This is only a minor shortcoming in an otherwise excellent handgun.

Sterling Arms Model 450. Sterling Arms Corporation started in the handgun business in the 1960s, and at first the firm produced only .22, .25, and .380 caliber pocket pistols. By the mid-1970s, they introduced a double-action automatic pistol that fires the .45 ACP cartridge. Of all-steel construction, the Model 450 has a frame wide enough to permit a slight staggering of cartridges in the magazine for a total capacity of eight shots.

Locking of the Model 450 is after the Browning/Colt-type, but much modified. Most significant is the fact that the barrel bushing can be adjusted to compensate for wear. There are also two sets of guide rails on the frame. The rear set is of the conventional type, with a second set lower and ahead of the trigger to better support the front of the slide.

A hammer-blocking, firing-pin safety is incorporated into the slide. This manual safety, which does not affect the movement of the sear or trigger, allows the Model 450 to be carried

Top, *Nonte photograph of 9mm Parabellum experimental Husqvarna gas-operated pistol.* Bottom, *preproduction model of Wildey gas-operated stainless-steel pistol.* (Courtesy Wildey)

cocked and locked for single-action fire or hammer-down for a double-action first-shot capability. The manual-safety lever is ambidextrous insofar as it can be moved from the left side to the right side for left-handed shooters with very little effort.

The double-action lockwork is of the simplest type, rugged, and durable. Everything about this handgun seems large and sturdy. It may not be as pleasing to look at as other contemporary automatics, but it should provide the user with good service.

Wildey Firearms Automatic Pistol. Wildey J. Moore began development of this handgun in March 1973, and Moore would be the first to acknowledge his design debt to the Swedish engineers at the Husqvarna factory. Husqvarna displayed 9mm-Parabellum-prototype pistols in the early 1970s, but the project was later dropped. The basic design of the Husqvarna and Wildey pistols uses an annular (ring) piston, which surrounds the barrel. The barrel has a number of small gas ports (six in the Wildey pistol). The piston moves to the rear when the gasès drive it. The piston strikes the slide to provide the momentum necessary to unlock the pistol. As the slide moves to the rear, cams rotate, causing the bolt to unlock; the bolt and slide continue to the rear.

The Wildey gas-operated, stainless-steel pistol is an interesting and very well-made weapon, but it is chambered for two new, very powerful cartridges—the 9mm and .45 caliber Winchester Magnums. Ballistic performance can be summarized as follows:

	9mm Winchester Magnum	.45 Winchester Magnum	9mm Parabellum JHP
Projectile weight:	115 grains (7.5 grams)	230 grains (15 grams)	90 grains (5.8 grams)
Muzzle velocity:	1475 fps (450 mps)	1400 fps (427 mps)	1475 fps (450 mps)

The kinetic energy developed by the full-metal-jacket, round-nose bullet is very great, and, as explained in chapter 8, these projectiles will pass through human targets. The Wildey pistols, with the correct ammunition, may be appropriate for hunting big game, but it is unlikely that this handgun will be used for military or police purposes.

3

Selection Criteria

MOST HANDGUNS ARE bought and used for recreation, on a par with golf clubs and tennis racquets. While such sporting handguns do have some defensive and offensive capabilities, that aspect of the pistols is only incidental to their primary use as target shooting or hunting pieces. The combat handgun, however, is an entirely different matter. Its sole purpose is to provide maximum defensive and offensive advantage to professional gun carriers—law-enforcement officers, military personnel, or members of quasi-military intelligence and security agencies. The combat gun will normally retain some sporting potential, and it can certainly provide recreation to the owner who enjoys shooting in general, but that is merely incidental to its primary mission—saving lives by incapacitating or killing those who have broken the law or threatened life.

To be efficient in that role and give the user maximum survival probability in a gunfight, the combat gun must have some characteristics necessarily different from other firearms.

Attributes sportsmen seek in target and hunting weapons can be inappropriate for a handgun that might be used in an armed encounter. Likewise, some of the characteristics suitable for military sidearms can be undesirable in handguns used in urban combat and interfere with their effectiveness. While many standard-model handguns are used daily as combat arms, the firearms industry has yet to give us the ideal model. In fact, many models advertised and sold for combat use are seemingly so far from ideal that they severely handicap the officers using them. The ideal combat handgun should be neither sporting nor military, but a combination of the two with additional essential characteristics and capabilities.

IDEAL CHARACTERISTICS

Lightweight. Lightness is an important consideration, but it is not as essential as some other characteristics, especially when a trade-off is necessary with other desirable features, such as limited recoil and muzzle jump. In virtually all calibers through .45 ACP, a weight of 32 ounces (.91 kilogram) will keep recoil and jump within the tolerances of the average semitrained shooter. Thus, a maximum weight of 32 ounces (.91 kilograms) for the combat handgun provides a gun that can be carried for long periods without fatigue. In calibers of less recoil, such as 9mm Parabellum and .38 Super, the weight could be reduced to as little as 22–25 ounces (.62–.71 kilograms) without introducing serious recoil problems. Highly experienced shooters seldom experience difficulty with these calibers in guns weighing as little as 20–22 ounces (.57–.62 kilograms), and exceptional gun users can handle heavily-loaded .45 ammunition in guns weighing a mere 22 ounces (.62 kilograms).

The desirability of a lightweight weapon to the user is, of course, to reduce carrying fatigue and the bulk of the handgun. But there is a related side issue. An individual who is aggravated by carrying an unnecessarily heavy gun through an eight-hour working shift will probably want to exchange it for a lighter arm after duty hours, often leading to the use of inadequate and unsafe handguns (such as .25 and .32 auto-

My Dream Autoloader

By Maj. George C. Nonte, Jr.

George Nonte developed his criteria for the ideal combat handgun during the course of three decades of pistol shooting. The autoloader illustrated above represents what his ideal handgun would have been in 1969. During the decade that followed, his thoughts were refined somewhat, but this drawing is still a reasonable representation of the type of handgun that would result from applying Nonte's "ideal characteristics." (George C. Nonte drawing, courtesy Shooting Times)

matics or snub-nosed revolvers) when off duty. However, if the duty gun is a light 24–32 ounces (.68–.91 kilogram), the user is far more likely to continue carrying it after duty and thus be armed with a more potent gun with which he is very familiar. Ideally, the same gun should be carried at all times so that its proper use under stressful conditions becomes as instinctive as the application of the brake pedal when a pedestrian darts in front of one's car.

Compactness. Compactness serves many purposes, not

the least of which is concealment for undercover use. Compactness is also relative. What is compact in a .45 caliber pistol is not necessarily so in the smaller 9mm, .380, or .32 automatics. In the largest calibers, a triangular envelope approximately 6.5 x 4.75 x 1.25 inches (165 x 121 x 32 millimeters) represents the minimum size that will enclose an adequate, reliable mechanism. Of course, compactness can be overdone, as it is in all .25 automatics. The frame of the gun must be large enough for a specific cartridge, with a barrel long enough to allow development of the cartridge's ballistic potential. The pistol grip must be of adequate size to allow a firm hold for both rapid-fire controllability and accuracy. Reliability is also related to the size and weight of moving parts; beyond a certain point reduction in size reduces the functional reliability of key components, such as trigger mechanisms and the like.

Compactness, too, is an item subject to trade-offs. The size envelope allows for the essential mechanical elements to be contained in the weapon but still permits a reasonable degree of concealment. It is also small enough to permit the user to ride in a car with the gun in a belt holster without jamming the muzzle into seat cushions, which might prevent his getting out of the vehicle and into action quickly.

Cartridge capacity. Magazine capacity is important, but it should not be allowed to override other considerations. Within a given butt size, the smaller the cartridge the more the magazine will hold. To make a comparison, the seven-shot, .45 caliber Government Model magazine (or rather, the space it occupies) can be made to hold over twice as many .32 ACP cartridges, but most users will agree that seven .45 rounds have more stopping power and lethality than fifteen to seventeen .32 rounds. Firepower, in terms of the lethality of the first two or three shots, is generally more important than a large number of cartridges. Few gun battles involve the expenditure of more than a handful of cartridges.

Generally speaking, a grip circumference larger than that produced by a double-column 9mm magazine cannot be comfortably accommodated by any but the largest hands. A grip longer than that of the Browning Hi-Power or the Smith & Wesson M59 is unnecessarily bulky. The practical limits are thirteen to fifteen rounds in 9mm and .38 Super and seven to eight rounds in .45. These capacities are often reduced by shortening gun butts and magazines to facilitate conceal- ment, but even then double-column 9mm magazines will hold ten to eleven rounds and the single-column .45 five to six rounds.

Mechanical safety. Total freedom from accidental dis- charge from any cause cannot realistically be achieved. How- ever, the incorporation of a Walther-type firing-pin block (freeing the firing pin only when the trigger is pulled); a Browning-type-inertia firing pin; large, strong sear/hammer- engagement surfaces; intercept or safety-hammer notch or lever; and a robust, manual-safety-system hammer notch or lever should prevent such discharges except under the sever- est instances of abuse. The older Browning-type manual safety is far less reliable than the Smith & Wesson or Star hammer- blocking types; and the narrow, thin, sear-and-hammer- engaging surfaces of Colt target guns are not especially reliable under situations of mechanical stress. The Walther

This Smith & Wesson Model 59 double row magazine holds 15 cartridges. For a 9mm handgun this is about the largest practical magazine.

P5 and SIG P6 firing-pin safeties described in chapter 2 are alternatives to the more common mechanical safeties. Incorporating these types of safety mechanisms will prevent firing if a slip should occur during cocking, if the trigger finger should slip during double-action fire, or if the gun should be dropped a moderate distance on a hard surface in any attitude. The ideal combat handgun must be mechanically safe.

Mode of fire. Several popular authorities on pistolcraft condemn double-action (DA) automatics, while at least as many praise them. The principal objection to double-action lockwork appears to be the fact that the first shot requires .5 inch (12.7 millimeters) or more of trigger travel, but subsequent shots need only about .0625 inch (1.6 millimeters) or so. The opponents of double-action automatic pistols contend that these two different sets of conditions for the first two consecutive shots are ruinous to individual accuracy. While others have not found this to be true, it is a situation that can be corrected by a redesigned manual safety that can be engaged without automatically dropping the hammer and can be quickly and easily manipulated from either hammer-down (for double-action first shot) or cocked-and-locked (for single-action first shot) positions.

Disassembly without tools. Disassembly without using any tools should be possible and is not intended, as it is in military weapons, to allow for user repair while in action. Instead, it is incorporated into the design to encourage users to conduct frequent cleaning, lubrication, and preventative maintenance—leading them to greater familiarization with the arm's inner workings and more confidence in the weapon. An additional benefit of easy disassembly is that less-skilled and modestly-equipped armorers can perform routine repairs when they do become necessary, thus avoiding costly and time-consuming trips to a gunsmith or shipment of the gun back to the factory. Ideally, no tools at all should be required for disassembly, but a small combination screwdriver/punch of the type originally issued with the M1911 .45 automatic pistol is quite acceptable, if incorporated into the gun—

perhaps clipped inside the magazine well or fit into some other part of the gun.

Light recoil. Low levels of recoil and muzzle jump permit greater rapid-fire accuracy and a higher rate of aimed rapid fire. Further, light recoil reduces the time and cost required to develop acceptable levels of marksmanship during training, especially of recruits who have little or no previous handgun experience. Savings is one of the principal reasons that revolver-armed departments for so many decades have trained new officers with so-called mid-range, or reduced-load, ammunition. But achieving low recoil through the use of lightly loaded ammunition gives the trainee false confidence in his abilities, especially when he subsequently switches to full-charge service ammunition.

Obviously, low recoil should be achieved through the design of the handgun mechanism without sacrificing ammunition performance. This can be accomplished by incorporating the muzzle-brake/compensator characteristics of the Mag-Na-Port system into barrels and slides and by using other known design features and characteristics.

Fast sights. The finest target sights made are of little value in a gunfight if they cannot be instantaneously aligned on the target under widely varying light conditions. Sights on a combat handgun must be low in profile and free of sharp corners and edges that snag on clothing or equipment and must be especially sturdy and resistant to damage or shifting caused by rough-and-tumble action. Ideally, combat sights—both front and rear—should be integral with the gun slide, protected after the fashion of modern, military-rifle sights. Combat sights should also make use of color or low-level luminosity inserts for added visibility in poor light.

Provision, of course, must be made for calibrating the sights with the service load and for subsequent change if necessary, but beyond that adjustments become more a liability than an asset for they increase the probability of built-in inaccuracy. For this reason, the ideal combat gun should employ something similar to the commercial, single-unit Seventrees

Guttersnipe, with its luminous, tapered, rectangular sighting groove.

Functional reliability. The necessity for 100 percent functional reliability needs no explanation. A combat gun may be used against a determined antagonist only once in a lifetime, or it may never be used at all. But if that one time does occur, the individual must be able to draw and fire his weapon in absolute confidence that the gun will unhesitatingly function for the necessary number of shots. Even the slightest malfunction or hesitation can be fatal; and if the gun has a history, either factual or rumored, of occasional malfunctions, it may well create in the mind of the user a lack of trust that can be fatal in itself. Absolute reliability is essential in the ideal combat handgun.

Ammunition tolerance. Autoloader tolerance for different types of ammunition can never be as great as it is for revolvers simply because self-loading handguns require a minimum level of recoil energy in order to function properly. This is not a major worry since only full-power ammunition should be considered for either service or training use. There is no substitute for the power of full-charge cartridges in an encounter, and maximum proficiency with a handgun can only be achieved by using the service cartridge in combat training and marksmanship qualification. Therefore, the tolerances referred to here concern different types of ammunition, all being full-charge. This means reliable functioning with standard ball cartridges, high-performance/expanding-bullet loads of various profiles and bullet weights, and training ammunition that may approximate either of the other types. The gun must operate with factory and handloaded cartridges assembled to various lengths and with bullets of semi-wadcutter, round-nose, truncated-cone, and other shapes. The weapon must also be designed specifically to handle the high chamber pressures that accompany the maximum velocity of high-performance ammunition.

Operating ease and convenience. Reliability, accuracy, and power are of little use if the handgun handles awkwardly and is slow to put into action and reload. Ideally, every operation (drawing, firing, and quick reloading) should be performed easily, without shifting one's hold on the gun. Only the insertion of a loaded magazine should require a second hand.

Such smoothness requires a grip that fits naturally in the user's hand and a trigger location suited to the trigger finger. There must not be any adjustment of one's hold required between drawing and firing. Also, the manual safety must be shaped and located so that it may be disengaged by the shooting thumb without shifting one's grip; if manual cocking is desired, this, too, must be possible without altering the grip. The hammer, if exposed, and the slide in recoil must not pinch or cut the shooting hand, and the slide must automatically lock open after the last shot is fired from the magazine.

The magazine release must be readily accessible to the shooting-hand thumb without significant change of grip, and the empty magazine must either fall out freely or be provided with an automatic means of forcible ejection. The magazine-well mouth must be funneled to permit quick and easy insertion—even unseen—of a loaded magazine by the off hand. There must be a stop that will resist hard-ramming of the magazine, and the magazine must engage positively under all conditions. Once a fresh magazine is in place, the slide stop must be located so that it can be easily and quickly depressed by the shooting thumb (again without shifting the grip) to allow the slide to run forward, chamber a round, and ready the gun for continued firing.

The awkward and unfamiliar operating procedures evident in some recent designs must be avoided. One example of this is the use of a trigger-pull to disengage the slide stop after reloading, after which the trigger must be released and pulled again to fire a shot. In the stress of combat, such unusual operating procedures are fraught with danger not only to the user but to innocent bystanders as well. Operation must be kept simple and obvious, and that operation must be learned fully through regular handling of the pistol. No existing production gun meets all of these requirements, nor do many conversions. However, it would appear that further development of work done by many combat pistolsmiths would allow a production gun to meet these desirable features.

Maintenance. Although parts interchangeability is not especially important to the user working in an urban environment, the isolated rancher, state trooper, or game warden must be able to replace a broken extractor or firing pin immediately. The one-gun man cannot afford to wait weeks or months for a factory or gunsmith repair.

Complete interchangeability also allows quick, low-cost repair and maintenance by police armorers—and users can resort to cannibalization (borrowing parts from other pistols of the same model) in an emergency. Parts interchangeability of this level exists now in some makes and models, so its application to new guns should not represent an insurmountable design problem.

Accuracy. Accuracy is a relative term. Although the following specifications may be criticized by some, they represent one line of thought about combat-handgun use. At 25 yards (22.9 meters), five consecutively fired shots should fall within a 2.5-inch (63.5-millimeter) target area; at 50 yards (45.7 meters), five shots should fall within a 5-inch (127-millimeter) target area. It is well known that most gunfights involving law-enforcement officers occur at ranges of less than 20 feet (6.1 meters). Only rarely is a shot required or taken beyond that range, and anything beyond 25 yards (22.9 meters) is usually intended as suppressive fire not really expected to hit a precise target. With that in mind, it would seem that even the above modest requirements are excessive.

Secure grip. A no-slip grip is essential; a steady grip must remain so even when perspiration, water, grease, or dirt are on the gun or user's hand. All of the popular grip materials (wood, plastic, nylon, ivory, metal) are less than satisfactory in this respect, even when combined with stippled, checked, or grooved front and backstraps.

Of the materials currently used, sharply checkered, unfinished (no varnish or other coating) wood is best, but there is a better material available to a limited extent. It is a semisoft rubber compound used in the Pachmayr Signature .45 Auto wraparound grips and in the Mershon line of revolver

This type of accuracy is more than acceptable for any normal combat requirements. Target shot by Colt .45 Automatic. (Courtesy Armand Swenson)

grips (also a Pachmayr product). These grips are molded in a checkered pattern and have a slightly tacky feel that persists even when wet or greasy. Further, there is just enough give to the material that it conforms to every irregularity of the hand and provides the securest of holds. The ideal combat

Pachmayr "Signature" wrap-around grips for the Colt Government Model .45 automatic pistol. These grips are moulded with a checkered pattern, and they have a tacky feeling that improves the shooter's grip when his hands are slippery with sweat, grease, or other substances.

gun should be fitted with a variation of the Pachmayr Signature grips.

No-snag outline. Reaching for a conventional, target-sighted automatic pistol from under a coat in a hurry can be an unpleasant experience if the sights or other protuberances rip into clothing and skin and hang there for an instance before tearing free. The time lost can be fatal for the combat shooter.

Front sights should slope forward, and rear sights should be rounded on all corners. Magazine bases should be rounded after the fashion of the Seventrees ASP, and hammer spurs should be rounded off and polished smooth. All other protrusions, such as slide stops and safeties or exposed pin ends, need similar treatment to avoid this hazard. The sharp, rear corners of slides and frames should also be finished smoothly. Thus modified, the ideal combat automatic will come out of pocket, waistband, or holster smoothly and unimpeded.

Caliber. The best caliber for combat use is a controversial subject and is discussed at length in the chapter devoted to ammunition. However, no cartridge with a bullet diameter of less than 9mm, or producing less muzzle energy than the 9mm Parabellum, should be considered worthwhile, except possibly in a second or spare gun. In any case, only high-performance, expanding-bullet loads should be considered. The 9mm Parabellum and the .45 ACP are considered by some to be excessively bulky, while the .38 Super is thought by many to be the optimum choice. The .38 Super would be an excellent cartridge for the ideal combat handgun if it were more widely utilized by police organizations. The 9mm Parabellum is probably the best compromise.

Pointability. Under stress, pointability can be more important than sights and accuracy combined. There are instances when a shot must be taken without regard to position, sights, or any accepted rules of shooting. The user must pull, point, and shoot as fast as possible in the hope of avoiding a bullet. In this situation, the gun must point as precisely as

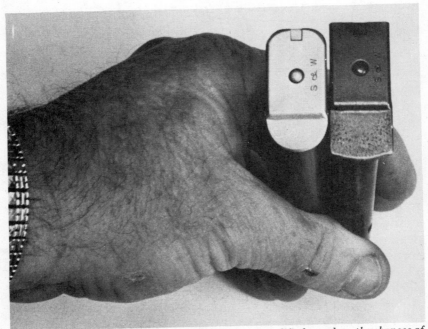

The Smith & Wesson magazine on the left has been modified to reduce the chances of it snagging when drawn from the holster.

the user's forefinger. The ability of the bullet to hit where the shooter points is the result of a combination of factors—barrel-grip angle, grip profile, trigger reach, and even recoil and jump. It will not be the same for everyone or for every gun. Assorted shapes and sizes of grips combined with adjustable trigger reach, will make the ideal gun point well for most users.

These criteria for an ideal gun reflect the conditions encountered by professional handgunners in urban areas today. They differ a good deal from the requirements recognized in the 1950s, 1930s, or earlier. Until quite recently, many departments and individuals considered the sidearm more an ornament than a tool and training in combat-style shooting an absolute waste of time. In earlier decades, officers seldom encountered armed antagonists in the city, and when they did one or two warning shots usually ended the affair. Today, however, armed, aggressive criminals in far greater numbers are the rule.

Today's urban situation makes it essential that the officer have a specialized weapon of high power and lethality and that he be well-trained in its use. The days when a patrolman could be handed a small-caliber revolver and cartridges, shown how to load it, and sent on duty are long past.

There are many guns available to the potential user that are not suitable as combat handguns, but these unsatisfactory weapons are often chosen when departmental regulations allow. Unfortunately, many officers choose guns based on aesthetic appeal or for some factor not associated with its genuine utility.

In the many unacceptable categories are, first, the very small pistols in .25 and .32 caliber. The low lethality of their cartridges rules them out, and further, their small size makes them quite difficult to shoot accurately. They are also often of very poor quality, design, and material; and many models are long out of production—with the result that spare parts and reliable service are unavailable. In the second category of unacceptable guns are the larger guns of .380 ACP caliber. Guns of this type of modern design and current manufacture are suitable as second guns with high-performance ammuni-tion but not as primary armament. Older model guns usually have little to recommend them in even the second-gun category for basically the same reasons that disqualify .25 and .32 pistols. The third category contains the vast number of souvenir and surplus military sidearms from World War II and earlier. With a few exceptions, such guns are not good urban combat weapons. Of the dozens of models usually available on the open market, only the Browning FN Hi-Power and the Colt M1911A1 .45 Government Model may be considered worthwhile. Even the more sophisticated and modern, double-action Walther P38 makes a less-than-ideal combat arm, but may be considered as acceptable as the Colt and Browning.

Chapter 5 will present a number of currently produced automatic pistols and will evaluate them against the criteria presented for the ideal combat handgun. For most individuals who cannot afford a custom handgun or who do not want to worry about creating a personalized handgun, the problem is basically one of choosing the best off-the-shelf automatic pistol.

4

Testing and Evaluation

THE TESTING OF any device or system can generally mean two different things—the examinations an individual might undertake to determine if the item in question is suitable for his personal needs, or the professional, laboratory and shooting-range examinations that determine if a product will be satisfactory and reliable for a wide audience. An individual's tests are often no more sophisticated than determining if a mechanism functions satisfactorily and promises to provide the type of performance characteristics for which it is needed. Professional, in-house or department-level testing of combat handguns is, however, a more complex process. In either individual or professional testing, the examiner must first establish what the handgun is expected to accomplish and then determine what tests must be conducted to determine if it will meet the established requirements. In accomplishing this, quite possibly no two test designers will produce exactly the same test procedures, but all should consider carefully every aspect of the gun's performance—durability, reliability, cost, user training, and maintenance.

Consider the tests an individual can conduct. Assume that you are in need of a new combat autoloader. Perhaps you have just taken employment as a law-enforcement officer and will be living with this new gun for years. At some time, your life and survival may depend upon its performing properly for you. Some of your tests will be conducted before you ever examine a single gun. The cost of the weapon, for example, will be limited to the price range ($150–$400) of the standard production handguns on the market, unless you are interested in obtaining a custom-built handgun for $450–$600. If you are limited by the money you have to spend, obviously a custom piece will not pass your first test. Caliber is another prepurchase test. This can be a subjective issue, based upon your own personal prejudices, experiences, and preferences. If, for instance, you are enthusiastic about the big .45 ACP cartridge, then obviously the ultracompact, double-action 9mm pistols cannot pass your test. Or if you are a devotee of the highest velocity obtainable, then even the best .45 available cannot meet your requirements. A series of physical and mechanical tests will help you determine if the handgun you want meets your personal requirements.

Functional reliability. This is the most important aspect of all, and it is absolutely essential that you establish an acceptable level of reliability. No matter how finely made or aesthetically appealing a handgun might be in all other respects, if it is not functionally reliable it can get you killed in a combat situation. One first step in determining functional reliability is simply to retire to the pistol range with a minimum of 200 rounds of ammunition and fire all that ammunition as quickly as possible. Simply load the magazines (you may use inexpensive ball rounds of lower quality), charge the gun, and run the cartridges through as fast as you can pull the trigger. Do not worry about accuracy or any other factor. During the early stages of this test firing, it is quite likely that you will encounter occasional malfunctions in the feeding, extraction or ejection, recoil, or lock. In the beginning, pay no attention to these problems other than to clear them and continue firing. A new gun requires break-in shooting, just like a new automobile requires a certain amount of use before it will function at its best.

Most likely, by the time you have completed the 200 rounds, the gun will have smoothed out, firing the last 100 rounds without a malfunction. If at round 200, the gun has not produced a minimum of 100 consecutive, trouble-free shots, it is not yet ready to protect your life. At this point, two alternatives are open to you—fire an additional 100 to 200 rounds, in which case the gun is quite likely to smooth out by itself and deliver the desired reliability, or have the handgun tuned to overcome the problems. You can do this yourself or have it done by a professional (see chapter 10). Before undertaking any mechanical work, determine how the handgun performs with the high-quality ammunition you expect to use normally.

Accuracy. This means practical accuracy in your hands, rather than mechanical accuracy. Any new, modern autoloader suitable for combat use may normally be expected to deliver perfectly adequate accuracy—at 25–30 feet (7.6–9.1 meters), five consecutively fired shots should fall within a 2.5–3-inch (63.5–76.2-millimeter) target area. This accuracy should be obtained by one-hand and two-hand point shooting without the use of sights, not deliberately aimed fire.

Begin on the range with a combat-style silhouette target with scoring rings at a distance of either 15 or 25 yards (13.7 or 22.9 meters). All accuracy shooting must be done with the cartridges you will carry on duty. Fire several five-shot groups of deliberately aimed fire from the standing, two-hand position. It will be worthwhile to target the gun by making whatever sight shifts are necessary to place the group on point-of-aim during this shooting, but this is not essential in evaluating the gun's accuracy. Be concerned with group size and consistency at this point. Assuming you are a competent marksman and have developed some familiarity with the particular gun involved, maximum acceptable group size at 15 yards (13.7 meters) should be 3 inches (76.2 millimeters). If the gun will not deliver this under the condition described, have another marksman of known ability check the gun, too.

If the first target test produced acceptable accuracy, repeat the exercise with one-hand and two-hand, five-shot groups fired both slowly and rapidly without sights at 7–12 yards (6.4–10.9 meters). Accuracy requirements become more subjective here, and rather than place a precise dimensional limit upon group size, keep in mind that the gun should keep all shots within the vital area of the silhouette target. Again, if the gun does not produce for you, have an expert check it.

Pointability. In unaimed fire, pointability becomes a significant factor in practical accuracy. A gun that will shoot one-hole groups in deliberately aimed fire may produce totally unacceptable groups when fired instinctively. For many individuals, the relatively straight and squarish grip of the original Colt M1911 (characteristic in the combat Commander) causes instinctive shots to go consistently low, sometimes plowing the dirt in front of the target. At the other extreme, the Mauser Parabellum with its more angled, differently shaped grip may well cause some shooters to go high. A grip that is either too small or too large may make firm control impossible, resulting in very large, inconsistent groups. Excessive recoil (a function of both the cartridge loading and gun weight, as well as several other factors) may cause rapid-fire groups to be strung vertically over as much as 2 feet (.61 meters). Regardless of the reason, if the gun you are testing does not permit you to place consistent, homogenous, five-shot, rapid-fire groups in the kill zone without sights, the gun simply is not passing the test as far as you are concerned.

Often failure to point satisfactorily does not mean that a particular gun is unacceptable, however. Numerous modifications may be made to both gun and grips to improve pointability—altering grips, replacing parts, reshaping butt, modifying trigger or trigger guard. This is covered in detail in chapter 7.

Handling. Handling is an all-inclusive term, difficult to define. Perhaps a more sophisticated word would be anthropomorphics, the study of the adaptability of a particular mechanism, or system, to manipulation and control by the user. Automobile and aircraft designers and manufacturers spend millions of dollars on anthropomorphic studies to ensure that all controls may be quickly, easily, and efficiently operated by the driver or pilot, and that the possibility of improper operations or mistaken operations is held to the absolute minimum. The autoloading pistol is a much simpler mechanism than an F–4 Phantom fighter aircraft, but its controls are no less essential to the performance of its mission.

Quite simply, this means that the safety, slide stop, hammer, trigger, magazine catch, and other components must be shaped and positioned so that they may be manipulated by the user's gun hand with maximum speed and convenience. Likewise, the number of controls that must be manipulated to perform a given function must be held to a minimum. An example of poor handling is a magazine catch located at the butt, requiring more movement and nearly twice as much time to replace a magazine than a side location behind the trigger guard. A double-action automatic may be drawn and fired with one less movement (that of disengaging the safety or cocking the hammer) than a single-action automatic. A gun with an open slide runs home automatically when a loaded magazine is inserted, making it ready for continued firing a split second more quickly than a gun with a manual slide stop that must be depressed to chamber a round after the magazine is inserted. In addition, protrusions from the body of the gun, particularly those with sharp corners and edges, can snag and cause delay in getting the gun into action from a holster or from beneath clothing.

There are many, many other aspects of handling. To simplify evaluation, please consult the following list:

1. **Ambidextrous use:** Is it reasonably practical to manipulate and fire the gun with the left (or right) hand in the event that the gun hand becomes disabled?

2. **Butt frame:** Are there large areas of smooth, slick metal that prevent a secure hold?

3. **Clogging:** Is the gun free from excessive clearances, openings, or protrusions and gaps through which foreign

material or lint from clothing may enter and cause malfunctions? Could a sliver of leather scraped from the holster by protrusions intrude and cause a malfunction?

4. **Cocking, hammer spur, or cocking lever:** Can cocking be accomplished quickly and easily with the gun hand without shifting the grip or hold on the butt of the gun?

5. **Concealability:** If this is a factor, is the shape, weight, and size of the gun such that it does not make its presence obvious by bulging or trapping clothing during normal body movements such as walking, sitting, turning, reaching into pockets, etc.? Often, a gun that appears to be concealed perfectly while one is standing straight or walking becomes very obvious when stooping, crouching, twisting, or sitting.

6. **Disassembly:** Can the gun be quickly disassembled and reassembled for repairs or cleaning without tools?

7. **Ejection hazard:** When fired from any reasonable combat position and attitude, does the gun hurl fired-cartridge cases in a direction or pattern that will distract the shooter?

8. **Flash, blast, recoil:** Is the flash, blast, or recoil unusually uncomfortable? Do they distract or startle the user during firing?

9. **Grasping surfaces:** Does the slide possess sufficiently deep and sharply defined grasping surfaces to allow positive retraction for loading under all conditions, including when the user has wet hands or is wearing gloves?

10. **Grips:** Do the grips interfere in any way with manipulation of the various controls, or do they in any way damage the hand under recoil? Do the grips provide a secure, non-skid hold during the successive recoil of rapid fire, even when the hand and gun are wet?

11. **Holstering:** Does the gun have any particular characteristics of shape or design that make it difficult to fit into a conventional holster?

12. **Integrity:** When loaded and ready for action, can the gun be inserted fully into its holster or other carrying place or position without displacing the slide, safety, slide stop, or any other movable part or control? As an example, some custom combat conversions are so set that the mere act of holstering the gun retracts the slide slightly; the slide might

not return to battery as the gun is drawn and, therefore, not allow a shot to be fired until the slide is manually shoved forward.

13. **Magazine:** Does the magazine enter its seat in the gun smoothly and easily and engage the magazine catch quickly and positively? Can the magazine be easily and quickly reloaded, even under dirty, wet, or cold conditions? Are there any protrusions on the floorplate or elsewhere that interfere with holstering and drawing or that can snag on clothing or hands?

14. **Magazine catch:** Is the magazine catch located where it may be quickly and easily manipulated by the shooting hand without changing one's hold to eject the empty magazine while the off hand is securing and preparing to insert a fully-charged magazine?

15. **Manual safety:** Is the safety lever located and shaped so that it may be manipulated as the gun is drawn without requiring any significant effort, additional movement, or time? Is the safety located and designed so that friction and impact developed in carrying it in a holster or waistband are likely to disengage it prematurely?

16. **Moving parts clearance**: Do any of the moving parts (slide, hammer, grip safety) strike the shooting hand when the gun is fired from any reasonable position or attitude? Are there any movable controls, such as slide stop or safety, that strike the hand during normal functioning?

17. **Sights:** If adjustable, are the sights designed so that adjustments will not be inadvertently changed by contact with other objects or by carrying the gun in holster or clothing? Are the sighting elements sufficiently large and wide and clearly defined to allow immediate alignment on the target?

18. **Slide stop:** Does the slide stop function automatically to lock the slide rearward after the last round is fired from the magazine, thereby signifying that the gun is empty and facilitating rapid reloading? Can the slide stop (if not fully automatic as in some recent designs) be easily reached and manipulated by the thumb of the shooting hand without changing the hold to run the slide forward when a freshly charged

magazine is inserted? If the slide stop is automatic, is its functioning absolutely reliable, and does it introduce any time-lag in opening fire from a freshly inserted magazine?

19. **Trigger clearance:** Is the trigger guard of sufficient size and adequate shape forward of the trigger to allow the finger to enter freely without interference and without snagging fingernails or gloves when the gun is drawn hurriedly?

20. **Trigger reach:** Particularly in a double-action design, does the trigger, when in the ready position, fall in a position where it may be readily engaged by the finger and moved through its full travel without clamping or undue effort?

21. **Uncocking:** Can the hammer or striker be safely lowered on a chambered cartridge without undue effort or the danger of the hammer "getting away" and causing an inadvertent firing?

The average user will not be terribly concerned with extreme temperature and climate tests, but it is still a good idea to check the ability of a particular gun to function reliably under abnormal conditions. A few individuals might have an environmental chamber available for these tests, but a fair approximation of two of these tests can be conducted without any special equipment.

Low temperatures reduce chamber pressure and velocity. A cold-weather test is easy to conduct and requires only that you cold-soak the gun in the freezer compartment of your refrigerator. Degrease the gun thoroughly by rinsing in solvent and place it loaded and cocked (if a single-action design) in the freezer, unprotected by any wrapping or covering. Place with it an additional twenty to thirty rounds of service ammunition, preferably loaded in spare magazines. Let the gun and ammunition "soak" for a minimum of twenty-four hours, remove from the freezer, and fire the ammunition as quickly as possible. It is essential that the firing be conducted before the gun and ammunition have an opportunity to thaw, so if the shooting range is some distance away, keep the gun and ammunition cold en route in a cooler lined with dry ice. Wear gloves during this test firing, and do not attempt to scrape frost or ice from the gun. Shoot it just the way it came from the freezer. Run the first magazine through as quickly as possible, reload, and continue firing until you have shot all the cold-soaked cartridges or the gun fails. If the gun does not function reliably after cold-soaking, it is not a dependable combat arm at extremely low temperatures. If its behavior is marginal, improvement can be made by using a special low-temperature lubricant sparingly at all friction points. Conventional oils and greases are not suitable since they stiffen and become solid at very low temperatures.

If extremely wet weather concerns you, you can conduct a simple rain test. Hang the loaded and cocked gun on a convenient post and expose it to a moderate but steady water spray for several hours. This spray will slowly wash away the lubricants, producing the same effect as long exposure to heavy rain. After a minimum of three to four hours of exposure, have someone direct the spray on the weapon and fire it at least twenty to thirty times. If the gun malfunctions, it will not do for full-time service during long exposure to heavy rain. An alternative wet-weather-test procedure is to rinse the gun thoroughly in solvent to remove all traces of lubricant, load and cock it, submerge it for two to three minutes in a bucket of water, remove, and fire immediately. It is not the water that causes the trouble, but the absence of lubricant brought about by the washing action of rain or spray.

Military high-temperature tests are normally combined with sand and dust tests. An individual cannot conduct such an examination without damaging the weapon, since deliberately filling and covering a loaded and cocked gun with sand or mud will cause some deterioration, especially when the particles are ground between the moving parts during attempted firing. Generally speaking, the basic designs currently available have already been thoroughly proved in this fashion, and you need not run any further tests.

A law-enforcement department or agency wishing to test a particular make or model of combat handgun can conduct essentially the same tests as the individual user. However, a department employing a large number of armed personnel who will all be utilizing the same weapon must approach the tests somewhat differently. When the individual tests a gun, he is testing it to suit only himself. A department must con-

duct its tests to ensure that a particular handgun will suit a
large number of individuals with widely varying physiques,
backgrounds, and levels of ability. For example, a gun found
to be entirely satisfactory in handling for an officer with
small hands might be totally unsuitable for an individual
with large hands. Such a weapon would probably not be satisfactory for departmental use where glove sizes might range
from fourteen to seven.

For department-level testing, a test board or committee
is usually selected. Five or six members is an optimum size
for the test group, and they should represent the different
physical sizes and levels of dexterity present in the department. The members should also be selected for having a typical level of training—they should not be raw recruits, nor
should they be top-level marksmen. The test group should examine several specimens of each of the handguns under consideration, putting them through those tests and checks the
department considers essential, with the individual results
being carefully tabulated and recorded. The raw data produced
by the several individuals each testing several specimens of
the same gun can be examined, and a valid determination
made as to its overall suitability.

There is one other unique aspect of department testing
that can assume great importance—the effect a particular
handgun model has on marksmanship and gun-handling
training. Is the model under consideration suitable to the
training needs of the law-enforcement organization that is
evaluating it? Will the average officer be able to learn how to
shoot it accurately and safely in a reasonable length of time?

These are very important considerations, and the tests
that will help answer these questions should be conducted
with several groups of new recruits. Each group should complete its handling and marksmanship training with one of the
handgun models under consideration. The instruction and
training conditions for all groups must be as nearly alike as
possible. Generally, by the completion of firearms training,
differences will be noted in the rate of progress and the proficiency level attained by the different groups. A typical example of this is the test conducted by the South Pasadena,

California, Police Department. Traditionally armed with revolvers, this department wanted to switch to autoloading pistols for their improved firepower and so ran two recruit committees through their firearms training, one with the revolver and one with the Smith & Wesson Model 39 autoloader. Early it was noted that those recruits using the Model 39 were progressing more rapidly; at the end of the training program they had achieved a substantially higher level of marksmanship proficiency. When this obvious advantage was coupled with the other positive characteristics of the autoloader, it became quite clear to the department that switching to the Smith & Wesson Model 39 would be quite advantageous.

Tests for large departments can often be accomplished more economically by an outside agency, such as a firearms consultant or a testing laboratory. In fact, by querying manufacturers or government agencies with an interest in the subject, a group can often determine if a particular weapon has already been tested by some other department, agency, or military branch, in which case the results of those tests might be obtained and a proper evaluation made without running separate examinations.

Every weapon intended for use as a combat arm should be tested at least to the degree necessary to ensure the user that it will meet his particular needs and circumstances. Most handgun designs are, of course, thoroughly tested before the item is mass-produced, and each gun is proof-fired before it is sent to a dealer; but each individual weapon should be submitted to some kind of testing program before the user invests money in its purchase or risks his life on its dependability. One of the greatest mistakes an individual or department can make is to come to an arbitrary decision about a service weapon based only on advertising, a salesman's pitch, personal preference, or hearsay.

Evaluation of Current Production Models

THIS CHAPTER EVALUATES some of the major combat handguns available in the United States and Europe in mid-1979. The evaluations presented here are based upon a handgun's suitability for combat, based upon the criteria established in chapter 3. The reader may wish to refer back to the chapter when examining these evaluations. For reasons more fully developed in chapter 8, handguns firing cartridges less powerful than the 9 x 19mm Parabellum are not included because of their limited lethality. Some mechanically excellent handguns and some extremely powerful ones receive low marks in the following evaluations because they are not particularly suited for combat use. In reviewing these grade reports, bear in mind that combat suitability is the basic concern.

Although this book is devoted primarily to automatic pistols, a sample of current revolvers has been included for purposes of comparison. Should your favorite handgun not be listed, apply the criteria outlined in chapter 3 and evaluate it yourself. By that process, you should be able to determine if it will meet your needs. Do not feel shy about disagreeing with the evaluations; they represent the collective wisdom of a small group of experts. Look at each gun in terms of the evaluative criteria and make your own decisions. A few evaluation forms have been left blank at the end of this chapter to permit you to do your own handgun rating.

For current prices and information on what models are currently available, consult the latest issue of *The Gun Digest* or Stoger's *Shooter's Bible*.

BENELLI MODEL 76 AUTOMATIC PISTOL

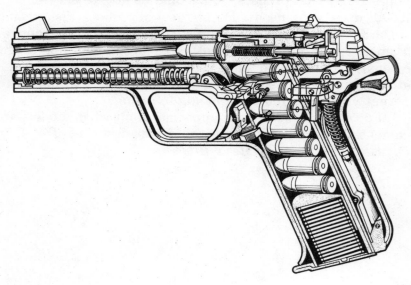

Characteristics	Excellent	Adequate	Poor
Weight	X		
Compactness		X	
Mode of fire (double or single action)	DA		
Ease of disassembly		X	
Recoil		X	
Sights			
Front		X	
Rear		X	
Pointability	X	X	
Accuracy	X		
Functional reliability		X	
Ammunition tolerance			*
Operating ease and convenience		X	
Maintenance		X	
Grip	X		
No-snag outline		X	
Caliber		*	

*Some problems have been reported with the Model 76's tolerance to soft-nosed or hollow-point projectiles when six or more such cartridges are loaded into the magazine. There have been no problems with full-metal, jacketed bullets.

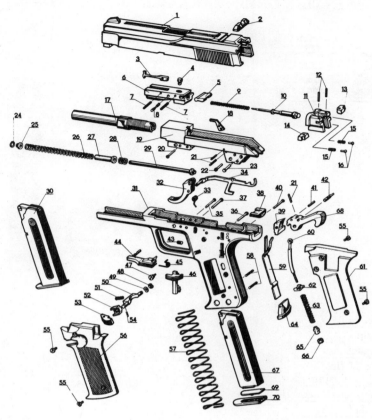

Specifications	English	Metric
Caliber	9mm Parabellum	9 x 19mm
Overall Length	8.07 in	205mm
Weight, Empty	34.2 oz	.97 kg
Barrel Length	4.25 in	108mm
Method of Operation	Recoil operated	
Method of Locking	Fixed barrel, inertia-locked bolt and slide	
Feed-Device Capacity	8 cartridges	

BERETTA MODEL 92 DOUBLE-ACTION PISTOL

Characteristics	Excellent	Adequate	Poor
Weight		X	
Compactness			X
Mode of fire (double or single action)	DA		
Ease of disassembly	X		
Recoil	X		
Sights			
Front		X	
Rear		X	
Pointability		X	
Accuracy		X	
Functional reliability		X	
Ammunition tolerance		X	
Operating ease and convenience		X*	
Maintenance	X		
Grip		X	
No-snag outline		X	
Caliber	X		

*This version of the Model 92 has a manual safety that locks the trigger mechanism.

Specifications	English	Metric
Caliber	9mm Parabellum	9 x 19mm
Overall Length	8.54 in	217mm
Weight, Empty	33.50 oz	.95 kg
Barrel Length	4.92 in	125mm
Method of Operation	Recoil operated	
Method of Locking	Falling block driven down to disengage the slide and stop the barrel.	
Feed-Device Capacity	15 cartridges	

BERETTA MODEL 92S DOUBLE-ACTION PISTOL

Characteristics	Excellent	Adequate	Poor
Weight		X	
Compactness			X
Mode of fire (double or single action)	DA		
Ease of disassembly	X		
Recoil	X		
Sights Front		X	
Rear		X	
Pointability		X	
Accuracy		X	
Functional reliability		X	
Ammunition tolerance		X	
Operating ease and convenience		X*	
Maintenance	X		
Grip		X	
No-snag outline		X	
Caliber	X		

*This version of the Model 92 has a manual safety that locks the firing pin.

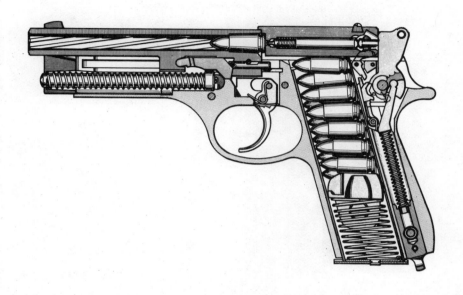

Specifications	English	Metric
Caliber	9mm Parabellum	9 x 19mm
Overall Length	8.54 in	217mm
Weight, Empty	34.50 oz	.95 kg
Barrel Length	4.92 in	125mm
Method of Operation	Recoil operated	
Method of Locking	Falling block driven down to disengage the slide and stop the barrel	
Feed-Device Capacity	15 cartridges	

CESKA ZBROJOVKA MODEL 75
DOUBLE-ACTION PISTOL

(Courtesy Masami Tokoi)

Characteristics	Excellent	Adequate	Poor
Weight		X	
Compactness		X	
Mode of fire (double or single action)		DA	
Ease of disassembly		X	
Recoil		X	
Sights Front		X	
Rear		X	
Pointability		X	
Accuracy		X	
Functional reliability	X		
Ammunition tolerance	Unknown		
Operating ease and convenience		X	
Maintenance		X	
Grip		X	
No-snag outline		X	
Caliber	X		

Specifications	English	Metric
Caliber	9mm Parabellum	9 x 19mm
Overall Length	8.0 in	203mm
Weight, Empty	35.2 oz	1.0 kg
Barrel Length	4.72 in	120mm
Method of Operation	Recoil operated	
Method of Locking	Modified Colt/Browning locking system	
Feed-Device Capacity	15 cartridges	

CHARTER ARMS UNDERCOVER .38
SPECIAL REVOLVER

Characteristics	Excellent	Adequate	Poor
Weight	X		
Compactness	X		
Mode of fire (double or single action)	DA		
Ease of disassembly		X	
Recoil		X	
Sights Front	X		
Rear		X	
Pointability		X	
Accuracy		X	
Functional reliability		X	
Ammunition tolerance		X	
Operating ease and convenience		X	
Maintenance	X		
Grip		X	
No-snag outline		X	
Caliber		X	

Specifications	English	Metric
Caliber	.38 Special	9 x 29mm R
Overall Length	6.25 in	159mm
Weight, Empty	16 oz	.45 kg
Barrel Length	2.0 in	51mm
Method of Operation	Charter Arms-type revolver	
Method of Locking revolver	Charter Arms-type	
Feed-Device Capacity	5-cartridge cylinder	

COLT COMBAT COMMANDER AUTOMATIC PISTOL

Characteristics	Excellent	Adequate	Poor
Weight		X	
Compactness		X	
Mode of fire (double or single action)		SA	
Ease of disassembly	X		
Recoil	X		
Sights			
Front		X	
Rear		X	
Pointability		X	
Accuracy		X	
Functional reliability	X		
Ammunition tolerance	X		
Operating ease and convenience		X	
Maintenance	X		
Grip		X	
No-snag outline		X	
Caliber	X		

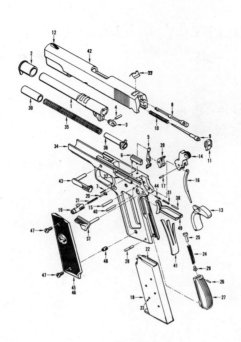

Specifications	English	Metric
Caliber	9mm Parabellum .38 Colt Super .45 ACP	9 x 19mm 9 x 23mm SR 11.43 x 23mm
Overall Length	7.875 in	200mm
Weight, Empty	36 oz (9mm and .38) 37 oz (.45 ACP) 27.5 oz (.45 ACP)	1.02 kg 1.05 kg 0.78 kg (aluminum frame)
Barrel Length	4.25 in	108mm
Method of Operation	Recoil operation	
Method of Locking	Colt/Browning link- type locking system	
Feed-Device Capacity	9 cartridges (9mm and .38) 7 cartridges (.45 ACP)	

COLT GOVERNMENT MODEL MK IV/SERIES '70
AUTOMATIC PISTOL

Characteristics	Excellent	Adequate	Poor
Weight		X	
Compactness			X
Mode of fire (double or single action)		SA	
Ease of disassembly	X		
Recoil	X		
Sights Front		X	
Rear		X	
Pointability		X	
Accuracy		X	
Functional reliability	X		
Ammunition tolerance	X		
Operating ease and convenience		X	
Maintenance	X		
Grip		X	
No-snag outline		X	
Caliber	X		

COLT GOVERNMENT MODEL AUTOMATIC PISTOL
CALIBER .45

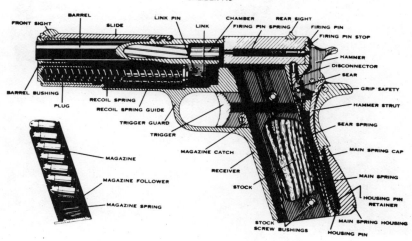

Specifications	English	Metric
Caliber	9mm Parabellum .38 Colt Super .45 ACP	9 x 19mm 9 x 23mm SR 11.43 x 23mm
Overall Length	8.5 in	216mm
Weight, Empty	40 oz (9mm and .38) 39 oz (.45 ACP)	1.13 kg 1.11 kg
Barrel Length	5 in	127mm
Method of Operation	Recoil operation	
Method of Locking	Colt/Browning link-type locking system	
Feed-Device Capacity	9 cartridges (9mm and .38) 7 cartridges (.45 ACP)	

COLT PYTHON REVOLVER

Characteristics	Excellent	Adequate	Poor
Weight		X	
Compactness			X
Mode of fire (double or single action)		DA	
Ease of disassembly		X	
Recoil		X	
Sights Front		X	
Rear		X	
Pointability		X	
Accuracy	X		
Functional reliability	X		
Ammunition tolerance	X		
Operating ease and convenience		X	
Maintenance	X		
Grip		X	
No-snag outline		X	
Caliber	X		

Specifications	English	Metric
Caliber	.357 Magnum	9 x 29mm R
Overall Length	7.75 in 9.25 in 11.25 in	197mm 235mm 286mm
Weight, Empty	33 to 43.5 oz	0.94 to 1.23 kg
Barrel Length	4.125 in 5.625 in 7.625 in	105mm 143mm 194mm
Method of Operation	Colt-type revolver	
Method of Locking	Colt-type revolver	
Feed-Device Capacity	6-cartridge cylinder	

DETONICS .45 ASSOCIATES AUTOMATIC PISTOL

Characteristics	Excellent	Adequate	Poor
Weight		X	
Compactness	X		
Mode of fire (double or single action)		SA	
Ease of disassembly		X	
Recoil			X
Sights			
Front			X
Rear			X
Pointability		X	
Accuracy		X	
Functional reliability		X	
Ammunition tolerance		X	
Operating ease and convenience		X	
Maintenance		X	
Grip			X
No-snag outline	X		
Caliber		X	

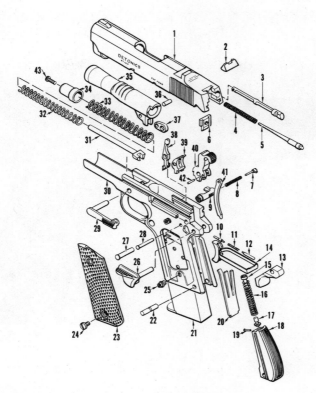

Specifications	English	Metric
Caliber	.45 ACP	11.43 x 23mm
Overall Length	6.75 in	171.5mm
Weight, Empty	29 oz	.82 kg
Barrel Length	4.5 in	114mm
Method of Operation	Recoil operation	
Method of Locking	Modified Colt/ Browning locking system	
Feed-Device Capacity	Special 6-cartridge magazine, or standard M1911A1 7-cartridge magazine	

FN BROWNING HI-POWER (M1935)
AUTOMATIC PISTOL

Characteristics	Excellent	Adequate	Poor
Weight	X		
Compactness		X	
Mode of fire (double or single action)		SA	
Ease of disassembly		X	
Recoil	X		
Sights			
Front		X	
Rear		X	
Pointability	X		
Accuracy	X		
Functional reliability	X		
Ammunition tolerance	X		
Operating ease and convenience		X	
Maintenance	X		
Grip	X		
No-snag outline	X		
Caliber	X		

STA 139

Specifications	English	Metric
Caliber	9mm Parabellum	9 x 19mm
Overall Length	8 in	203mm
Weight, Empty	32 oz	.91 kg
Barrel Length	4.75 in	121mm
Method of Operation	Recoil operation	
Method of Locking	Browning-type locking system	
Feed-Device Capacity	13 cartridges	

HECKLER & KOCH P9S AUTOMATIC PISTOL

Characteristics	Excellent	Adequate	Poor
Weight		X	
Compactness		X	
Mode of fire (double or single action)	DA		
Ease of disassembly		X	
Recoil		X	
Sights			
Front	X		
Rear	X		
Pointability	X		
Accuracy	X		
Functional reliability	X		
Ammunition tolerance		X	
Operating ease and convenience	X		
Maintenance	X		
Grip	X		
No-snag outline	X		
Caliber	X		

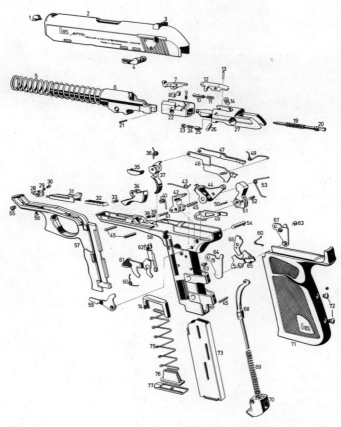

Specifications	English	Metric
Caliber	9mm Parabellum	9 x 19mm
Overall Length	8.5 in	216mm
Weight, Empty	32 oz without magazine	.91 kg
Barrel Length	5 in	127mm
Method of Operation	Retarded blowback	
Method of Locking	Roller-locked-breech system	
Feed-Device Capacity	9 cartridges	

HECKLER & KOCH POLICE
SELF-LOADING PISTOL (P7)

Characteristics	Excellent	Adequate	Poor
Weight	X		
Compactness	X		
Mode of fire (double or single action)	DA		
Ease of disassembly	X		
Recoil	X		
Sights Front	X		
Rear	X		
Pointability	X		
Accuracy	X		
Functional reliability	X		
Ammunition tolerance	X		
Operating ease and convenience	X		
Maintenance	X		
Grip	X		
No-snag outline	X		
Caliber	X		

* Special squeeze lever for cocking described in chapter 2.

Specifications	English	Metric
Caliber	9mm Parabellum	9 x 19mm
Overall Length	6.54 in	166mm
Weight, Empty	34.57 oz	.98 kg
Barrel Length	4.13 in	105mm
Method of Operation	Blowback	
Method of Locking	Blowback with gas-piston retardation	
Feed-Device Capacity	8 cartridges	

NAVY ARMS COMPANY MAMBA 9MM PARABELLUM PISTOL

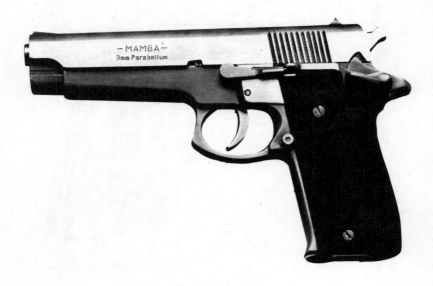

Characteristics	Excellent	Adequate	Poor
Weight		X	
Compactness		X	
Mode of fire (double or single action)	DA		
Ease of disassembly	X		
Recoil		X	
Sights			
Front		X	
Rear		X	
Pointability	X		
Accuracy	X		
Functional reliability		X	
Ammunition tolerance		X	
Operating ease and convenience		X	
Maintenance	X		
Grip		X	
No-snag outline	X		
Caliber	X		

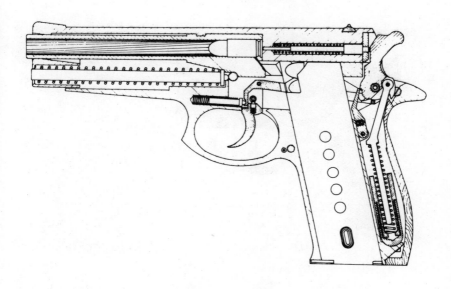

Specifications	English	Metric
Caliber	9mm Parabellum	9 x 19mm
Overall Length	8.6 in	218mm
Weight, Empty	42 oz	1.19 kg
Barrel Length	5.0 in	128mm
Method of Operation	Recoil operation	
Method of Locking	Modified Colt/Browning locking system	
Feed-Device Capacity	15 cartridges	

RUGER SECURITY-SIX REVOLVER

Characteristics	Excellent	Adequate	Poor
Weight		X*	
Compactness		X	
Mode of fire (double or single action)		DA	
Ease of disassembly		X	
Recoil		X	
Sights Front		X	
Rear		X	
Pointability		X	
Accuracy		X	
Functional reliability		X	
Ammunition tolerance		X	
Operating ease and convenience		X	
Maintenance		X	
Grip		X	
No-snag outline		X	
Caliber	X		

*Evaluation based upon 2.75-inch-barrel model.

RUGER.
SECURITY-SIX
DOUBLE ACTION REVOLVER

CYLINDER CENTER PIN SPRING
CYLINDER CENTER LOCK PIN
CYLINDER
CYLINDER CENTER PIN ROD
FRONT SIGHT CROSS PIN
FRONT SIGHT BLADE
REAR SIGHT ASSEMBLY
FRAME
EJECTOR ROD
BARREL
RECOIL PLATE CROSS PIN
RECOIL PLATE
HAMMER
FIRING PIN
FIRING PIN REBOUND SPRING
CYLINDER RELEASE BUTTON
TRANSFER BAR
FRONT LATCH SPRING
FRONT LATCH CROSS PIN
HAMMER DOG PIVOT PIN
FRONT LATCH
HAMMER DOG SPRING
EJECTOR SPRING
HAMMER DOG SPRING PLUNGER
EJECTOR ROD WASHER
HAMMER PIVOT ASSEMBLY
CRANE/CRANE PIVOT ASSEMBLY
HAMMER DOG
CYLINDER LATCH SPRING
HAMMER STRUT
MAINSPRING
GRIP PANEL BOSS
CYLINDER LATCH PLUNGER
TRIGGER GUARD PLUNGER CROSS PIN
EJECTOR
TRIGGER GUARD PLUNGER
CYLINDER LATCH
TRIGGER GUARD PLUNGER SPRING
TRIGGER BUSHING
MAINSPRING SEAT
TRIGGER PIVOT PIN
GRIP PANEL SCREW
TRIGGER SPRING
GRIP PANEL
PAWL SPRING
GRIP PANEL DOWEL
TRIGGER
FRAME
PAWL
TRIGGER GUARD
PAWL PLUNGER

CROSS SECTION VIEW

Specifications	English	Metric
Caliber	.357 Magnum	9 x 29mm R
Overall Length	8.0 in	203mm
	9.25 in	235mm
	11.25 in	286mm
Weight, Empty	33.25 oz (4-in barrel)	.94 kg
Barrel Length	2.75 in	70mm
	4.0 in	102mm
	6.0 in	152mm
Method of Operation	Ruger-type revolver	
Method of Locking	Ruger-type revolver	
Feed-Device Capacity	6-cartridge cylinder	

SIG-SAUER P220 AUTOMATIC PISTOL

Characteristics	Excellent	Adequate	Poor
Weight	X		
Compactness		X	
Mode of fire (double or single action)	DA		
Ease of disassembly	X		
Recoil	X		
Sights			
Front	X		
Rear	X		
Pointability	X		
Accuracy	X		
Functional reliability	X		
Ammunition tolerance	X		
Operating ease and convenience	X		
Maintenance	X		
Grip	X		
No-snag outline	X		
Caliber	X		

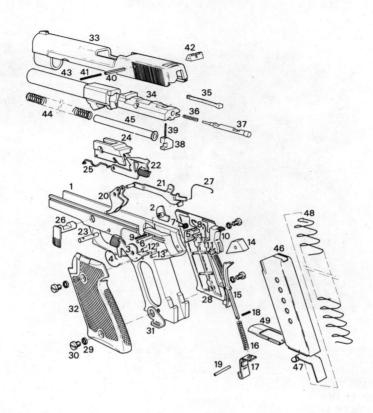

Specifications	English	Metric
Caliber	9mm Parabellum	9 x 19mm
Overall Length	7.8 in	198mm
Weight, Empty	29.3 oz	.83 kg
Barrel Length	4.4 in	112mm
Method of Operation	Recoil operation	
Method of Locking	Modified Colt/Browning locking system	
Feed-Device Capacity	9 cartridges	

SIG-SAUER P225 AUTOMATIC PISTOL (P6)

Characteristics	Excellent	Adequate	Poor
Weight	X		
Compactness	X		
Mode of fire (double or single action)	DA		
Ease of disassembly	X		
Recoil	X		
Sights			
Front	X		
Rear	X		
Pointability	X		
Accuracy	X		
Functional reliability	X		
Ammunition tolerance	X		
Operating ease and convenience	X		
Maintenance	X		
Grip	X		
No-snag outline	X		
Caliber	X		

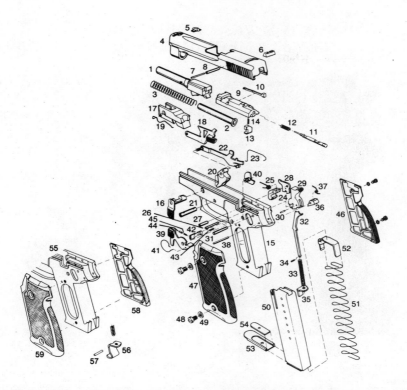

Two variations of SIG-Sauer P225. On the right is the model with the magazine catch on the left side of the frame behind the trigger (42). On the left is the model with the magazine catch at the bottom of the frame (56).

Specifications	English	Metric
Caliber	9mm Parabellum	9 x 19mm
Overall Length	7.09 in	180mm
Weight, Empty	29 oz	.82 kg
Barrel Length	3.84 in	97.6mm
Method of Operation	Recoil operation	
Method of Locking	Modified Colt/Browning locking system	
Feed-Device Capacity	8 cartridges	

169

SMITH & WESSON MODEL 19 .357
COMBAT MAGNUM REVOLVER

This model has a 2.5-inch barrel.

Characteristics	Excellent	Adequate	Poor
Weight		X	
Compactness		*	
Mode of fire (double or single action)		DA	
Ease of disassembly		X	
Recoil		X	
Sights Front		X	
Rear		X	
Pointability	X		
Accuracy	X		
Functional reliability	X		
Ammunition tolerance	X		
Operating ease and convenience	X		
Maintenance	X		
Grip	X		
No-snag outline			X
Caliber	X		

*Compactness is only satisfactory with the 2.5-inch (64mm) length barrel. See chapter 1.

This model has a 4-inch barrel.

Specifications	English	Metric
Caliber	.357 Magnum	9 x 29mm R
Overall Length	7.5 in	191mm
	9.5 in	241mm
Weight, Empty	31 oz (2.5-in barrel)	88 kg
	35 oz (4.0-in barrel)	99 kg
Barrel Length	2.5 in	64mm
	4.0 in	102mm
Method of Operation	Smith & Wesson-type revolver	
Method of Locking	Smith & Wesson-type revolver	
Feed-Device Capacity	6-cartridge cylinder	

SMITH & WESSON MODEL 39 AUTOMATIC PISTOL

Characteristics	Excellent	Adequate	Poor
Weight	X		
Compactness	X		
Mode of fire (double or single action)	DA		
Ease of disassembly	X		
Recoil	X		
Sights			
Front	X		
Rear	X		
Pointability	X		
Accuracy	X		
Functional reliability	X		
Ammunition tolerance	X		
Operating ease and convenience	X		
Maintenance	X		
Grip	X		
No-snag outline	X		
Caliber	X		

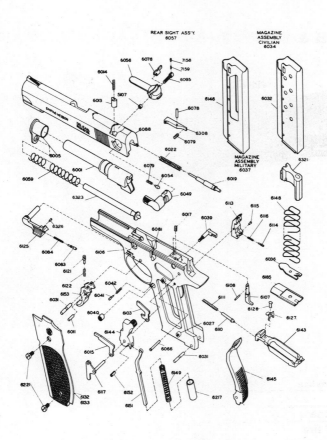

REAR SIGHT ASS'Y
6057

MAGAZINE
ASSEMBLY
CIVILIAN
6034

MAGAZINE
ASSEMBLY
MILITARY
6037

Specifications	English	Metric
Caliber	9mm Parabellum	9 x 19mm
Overall Length	7.44 in	189mm
Weight, Empty	26.5 oz	.75 kg
Barrel Length	4.0 in	102mm
Method of Operation	Recoil operation	
Method of Locking	Modified Colt/Browning locking system	
Feed-Device Capacity	8 cartridges	

SMITH & WESSON MODEL 59 AUTOMATIC PISTOL

Characteristics	Excellent	Adequate	Poor
Weight	X		
Compactness	X		
Mode of fire (double or single action)	DA		
Ease of disassembly	X		
Recoil	X		
Sights			
Front	X		
Rear	X		
Pointability	X		
Accuracy	X		
Functional reliability	X		
Ammunition tolerance	X		
Operating ease and convenience	X		
Maintenance	X		
Grip		X	
No-snag outline	X		
Caliber	X		

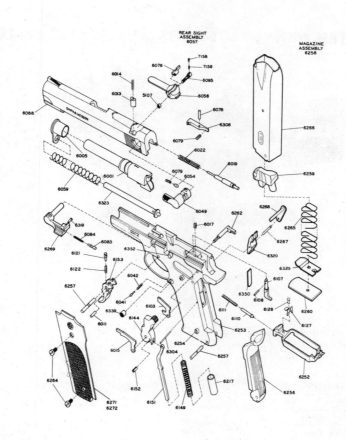

Specifications	English	Metric
Caliber	9mm Parabellum	9 x 19mm
Overall Length	7.44 in	189mm
Weight, Empty	27 oz	.77 kg
Barrel Length	4.0 in	102mm
Method of Operation	Recoil operation	
Method of Locking	Modified Colt/Browning locking system	
Feed-Device Capacity	14 cartridges	

175

STAR BKS "STARLIGHT" AUTOMATIC PISTOL

The 9mm Parabellum BKS "Starlight" is in the center between the Model SM in .380 ACP and the Model PS in .45 ACP.

Characteristics	Excellent	Adequate	Poor
Weight		X	
Compactness		X	
Mode of fire (double or single action)		SA	
Ease of disassembly		X	
Recoil		X	
Sights			
Front		X	
Rear		X	
Pointability		X	
Accuracy		X	
Functional reliability		X	
Ammunition tolerance		X	
Operating ease and convenience		X	
Maintenance		X	
Grip		X	
No-snag outline		X	
Caliber	X		

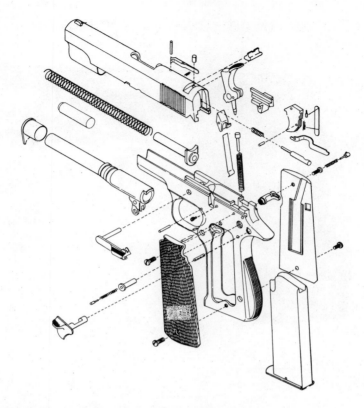

Assembly of Star automatic pistols, Models A, P, and B.

Specifications	English	Metric
Caliber	9mm Parabellum	9 x 19mm
Overall Length	7.68 in	195mm
Weight, Empty	26 oz	.75 kg
Barrel Length	4.3 in	110mm
Method of Operation	Recoil operation	
Method of Locking	Modified Colt/Browning locking system	
Feed-Device Capacity	8 cartridges	

STAR PD AUTOMATIC PISTOL

Characteristics	Excellent	Adequate	Poor
Weight	X (very light)		
Compactness	X		
Mode of fire (double or single action)		SA	
Ease of disassembly		X	
Recoil		X	
Sights Front		X	
Rear		X	
Pointability		X	
Accuracy		X	
Functional reliability		X	
Ammunition tolerance		X	
Operating ease and convenience		X	
Maintenance		X	
Grip		X	
No-snag outline		X	
Caliber		X	

George C. Nonte, Jr. firing the Star PD automatic pistol.

Specifications	English	Metric
Caliber	.45 ACP	11.43 x 23mm
Overall Length	7.0 in	178mm
Weight, Empty	24 oz	.68 kg
Barrel Length	3.8 in	97mm
Method of Operation	Recoil operation	
Method of Locking	Modified Colt/ Browning locking system	
Feed-Device Capacity	7 cartridges	

STERLING ARMS MODEL 450
DOUBLE-ACTION PISTOL

Characteristics	Excellent	Adequate	Poor
Weight		X	
Compactness		X	
Mode of fire (double or single action)		DA	
Ease of disassembly		X	
Recoil		X	
Sights Front		X	
Rear		X	
Pointability		X	
Accuracy		X	
Functional reliability		X	
Ammunition tolerance		X	
Operating ease and convenience		X	
Maintenance	X		
Grip		X	
No-snag outline		X	
Caliber		X	

Specifications	English	Metric
Caliber	.45 ACP	11.43 x 23mm
Overall Length	7.5 in	191mm
Weight, Empty	36 oz	1.02 kg
Barrel Length	4.25 in	108mm
Method of Operation	Recoil operation	
Method of Locking	Modified Colt/ Browning locking system	
Feed-Device Capacity	8 cartridges	

WALTHER P1 (P38) AUTOMATIC PISTOL

Characteristics	Excellent	Adequate	Poor
Weight		X	
Compactness			X
Mode of fire (double or single action)		DA	
Ease of disassembly		X	
Recoil		X	
Sights Front		X	
Rear		X	
Pointability		X	
Accuracy		X	
Functional reliability	X		
Ammunition tolerance	X		
Operating ease and convenience	X		
Maintenance	X		
Grip	X		
No-snag outline			X
Caliber	X		

Specifications	English	Metric
Caliber	9mm Parabellum	9 x 19mm
Overall Length	8.5 in	216mm
Weight, Empty	33.6 oz (steel frame) 28 oz (aluminum frame)	.95 kg .79 kg
Barrel Length	4.94 in	.125mm
Method of Operation	Recoil operation	
Method of Locking	Falling block driven down to disengage the slide and stop the barrel	
Feed-Device Capacity	8 cartridges	

WALTHER P5 AUTOMATIC PISTOL

Characteristics	Excellent	Adequate	Poor
Weight	X		
Compactness	X		
Mode of fire (double or single action)	DA		
Ease of disassembly	X		
Recoil	X		
Sights Front	X		
Rear	X		
Pointability	X		
Accuracy	X		
Functional reliability	X		
Ammunition tolerance	X		
Operating ease and convenience	X		
Maintenance	X		
Grip	X		
No-snag outline	X		
Caliber	X		

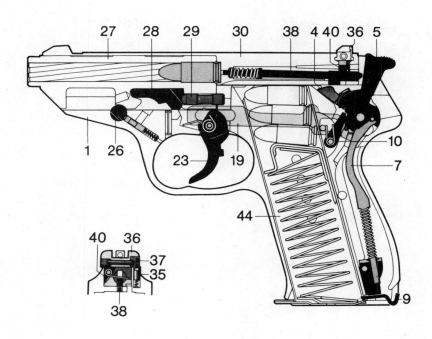

Specifications	English	Metric
Caliber	9mm Parabellum	9 x 19mm
Overall Length	7.09 in	180mm
Weight, Empty	28.04 oz	.795 kg
Barrel Length	3.54 in	90mm
Method of Operation	Recoil operation	
Method of Locking	Falling block driven down to disengage the slide and stop the barrel (P38-type)	
Feed-Device Capacity	8 cartridges	

WILDEY GAS-OPERATED PISTOL

Characteristics	Excellent	Adequate	Poor
Weight			Too heavy
Compactness		X	
Mode of fire (double or single action)		DA	
Ease of disassembly		X	
Recoil	X		
Sights			
Front		X	
Rear		X	
Pointability		X	
Accuracy	X		
Functional reliability		X	
Ammunition tolerance		X	
Operating ease and convenience		X	
Maintenance		X	
Grip		X	
No-snag outline			X
Caliber			X*

*This gun is chambered for cartridges which are better suited for big game hunting than the type of combat situations envisaged in this book.

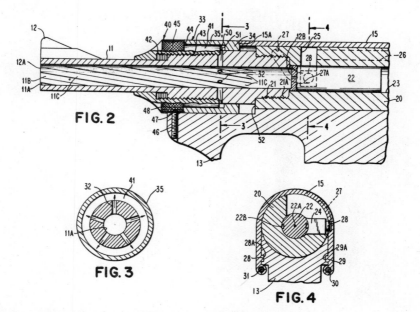

Patent drawing for the Wildey Magnum Automatic Pistol. Key numbers in this illustration are: (11) barrel; (13) frame; (15) slide; (20) receiver mounting barrel; (22) bolt; (32) gas ports; (34) gas piston; (35) forward portion of pistol. When gas flows through the ports (32) it fills the area shown in figure 3. The expanding gases force piston (34) to rear, which in turn forces slide (15) to rear to begin the unlocking cycle. (Courtesy U.S. Patent Office)

Specifications	English	Metric
Caliber	9mm Winchester Magnum	9 x 29.5mm
	.45 Winchester Magnum	11.43 x 30.4mm
Overall Length	Not available	
Weight, Empty	51 oz	1.45 kg
Barrel Length	5–10 in	127 to 154mm
Method of Operation	Gas-operated piston and bolt	
Method of Locking	Rotating bolt with bolt-carrying slide	
Feed-Device Capacity	9 cartridges (9mm)	
	15 cartridges (.45)	

HANDGUN DESIGNATION

Rudger Speed-Six Revolver

Characteristics	Excellent	Adequate	Poor
Weight		X	
Compactness		X	
Mode of fire (double or single action)		DA only	
Ease of disassembly	X		
Recoil	X		
Sights Front		X	
Rear		X	
Pointability	X		
Accuracy		X	
Functional reliability	X		
Ammunition tolerance	X		
Operating ease and convenience	X		
Maintenance		X	
Grip	X		
No-snag outline	X		
Caliber	X		

Specifications	English	Metric
Caliber	9mm Parabellum	9 x 19
Overall Length	8.0 in	
Weight, Empty	<33 oz	
Barrel Length	2.75 in	
Method of Operation		
Method of Locking		
Feed-Device Capacity		

HANDGUN DESIGNATION

Characteristics	Excellent	Adequate	Poor
Weight			
Compactness			
Mode of fire (double or single action)			
Ease of disassembly			
Recoil			
Sights Front			
Rear			
Pointability			
Accuracy			
Functional reliability			
Ammunition tolerance			
Operating ease and convenience			
Maintenance			
Grip			
No-snag outline			
Caliber			

Specifications	English	Metric
Caliber		
Overall Length		
Weight, Empty		
Barrel Length		
Method of Operation		
Method of Locking		
Feed-Device Capacity		

HANDGUN DESIGNATION

Characteristics	Excellent	Adequate	Poor
Weight			
Compactness			
Mode of fire (double or single action)			
Ease of disassembly			
Recoil			
Sights Front			
Rear			
Pointability			
Accuracy			
Functional reliability			
Ammunition tolerance			
Operating ease and convenience			
Maintenance			
Grip			
No-snag outline			
Caliber			

192

Specifications	English	Metric
Caliber		
Overall Length		
Weight, Empty		
Barrel Length		
Method of Operation		
Method of Locking		
Feed-Device Capacity		

HANDGUN DESIGNATION

Characteristics	Excellent	Adequate	Poor
Weight			
Compactness			
Mode of fire (double or single action)			
Ease of disassembly			
Recoil			
Sights Front			
Rear			
Pointability			
Accuracy			
Functional reliability			
Ammunition tolerance			
Operating ease and convenience			
Maintenance			
Grip			
No-snag outline			
Caliber			

Specifications	English	Metric
Caliber		
Overall Length		
Weight, Empty		
Barrel Length		
Method of Operation		
Method of Locking		
Feed-Device Capacity		

195

HANDGUN DESIGNATION

Characteristics	Excellent	Adequate	Poor
Weight			
Compactness			
Mode of fire (double or single action)			
Ease of disassembly			
Recoil			
Sights Front			
Rear			
Pointability			
Accuracy			
Functional reliability			
Ammunition tolerance			
Operating ease and convenience			
Maintenance			
Grip			
No-snag outline			
Caliber			

Specifications	English	Metric
Caliber		
Overall Length		
Weight, Empty		
Barrel Length		
Method of Operation		
Method of Locking		
Feed-Device Capacity		

6

Custom Combat Handguns

SOME USERS OF combat handguns desire modifications and additions to their weapons that require major changes to standard production models. To accomplish this, some gunsmiths have specialized in altering production pistols to the specialized demands of shooters. Three points should be kept in mind when considering custom combat handguns. The extent of modification can vary greatly. The complexity ranges from the simple addition of new sights or the changing of the barrel of a revolver to changes that require substantial redesign and remanufacture of the handgun. Also, revolvers are more easily modified than self-loaders. Changing the barrel length of a revolver is a relatively simple process. Altering the length of an automatic-pistol barrel can require extensive welding and machining. Finally, during the last decade, the custom-gunsmithing profession has developed some "standard-pattern" custom handguns to meet the high-quantity demand for custom products and to keep the price down. Whereas a standard custom handgun usually costs at least three times the price of the basic production model, an individualized custom pistol might run as much as five to six times the original factory price. Since most individuals cannot afford the luxury of a one-of-a-kind custom handgun, this chapter will concentrate on the standard custom models that have appeared in recent years.

A decision that the consumer should make before he enters the custom-handgun market is how much customizing is really essential. The journal articles that have been published about combat handguns over the last fifteen years seem to promote the idea that a high degree of customizing is not only desirable but perhaps essential if the combat shooter is to be equipped with a first-class weapon. Actually, the most common mistake is not too little customizing, but too much.

Aside from the disadvantage of the high cost, there is a real danger in overcustomizing a gun. The basic characteristics that make it a good handgun in the first place can be compromised. For example, excessive weight reduction in a handgun can make it difficult to control when using high-performance ammunition. Excessive shortening of the butt of an automatic in the interest of concealability will have an equally negative impact on control. The current trend of producing short, big-bore autoloaders quite often results in decreased functional reliability, loss of accuracy, and loss of velocity. The fitting of extra-long or extra-heavy slides and barrels can make the gun clumsy and unwieldy. Pistolsmiths and users sometimes lose sight of the axiom that too much of a good thing can be bad. Customizing should have a purpose and not be done just for its own sake.

The term "combat conversion" appears to have first been applied to the modified and shortened Colt M1911A1 automatic pistols developed by Armand Swenson. This leading pistolsmith begins this conversion operation by making the standard commercial Colt Government Model or Colt Commander a more accurate weapon. The tuning process (described more fully in chapter 10) is the first step. Essentially, this consists of deburring and polishing all of the slide, frame, barrel, and magazine surfaces that come in contact with the

This Colt M1911A1 Government Model was reworked by Armand Swenson in the early 1970s. Note his external modifications: new sights, long tang safety lever, checkered forward portion of hand grip, and squared-off trigger guard to aid two-handed holding of the pistol. Dr. William Baker, owner of the Swenson Colt, notes that after more than 30,000 shots, the pistol provided the pictured five-shot target group at twenty-five yards (twenty-three meters). Jokingly he wrote: "Armand, don't you think I should get a refund on this old gun?" After 30,000 rounds, such accuracy is amazing. (Courtesy Swenson)

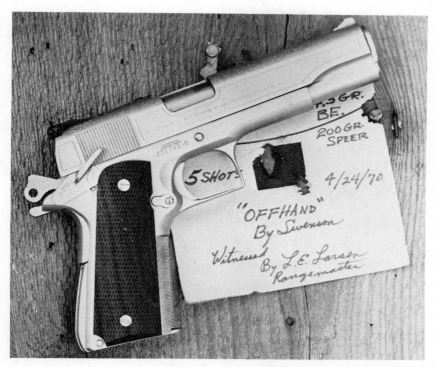

Right-hand view of Swenson/Colt Combat Conversion built in 1970. (Courtesy Swenson)

cartridge at any time during the feeding cycle. A slight polishing of the slide-breech face and extractor may also be required. In addition, it may be necessary to chamfer or bevel the perimeter of the chamber mouth or reshape part of the feed ramp. Modification of the ejection port is another common change made to improve functional reliability.

Once the pistol fires standard and high-performance ammunition without any problems, Swenson turns his attention to those elements that affect accuracy. New combat sights (Smith & Wesson Model 39) are installed. The barrel bushing is checked for proper fit, and a long guide for the recoil spring is installed. The result is an automatic pistol that shoots well and functions reliably. The accompanying photographs help tell the story of the Swenson .45 Pistol. (Photos 1 through 9)

A pair of Swenson/Colt Combat Conversions. Top, a Colt Commander; bottom, a Government Model. (Courtesy Swenson)

James W. Hoag also specializes in Colt M1911A1 combat conversions. In addition to tuning for accuracy, Hoag prepares guns for both match target and combat work. Among his offered modifications are installation of combat sights; ambidextrous, thumb-safety levers; bobbed hammers; checkered front straps; wider-grip safety tangs; beveled magazine

A shortened M1911A1 Colt by Armand Swenson. (Courtesy Swenson)

A Swenson/Colt Commander. Note the checkered, but flat, back strap and the leather-covered base plate on the magazine to protect it when it is dropped from the gun. The leather-covered base plate was a Swenson original. (Courtesy Swenson)

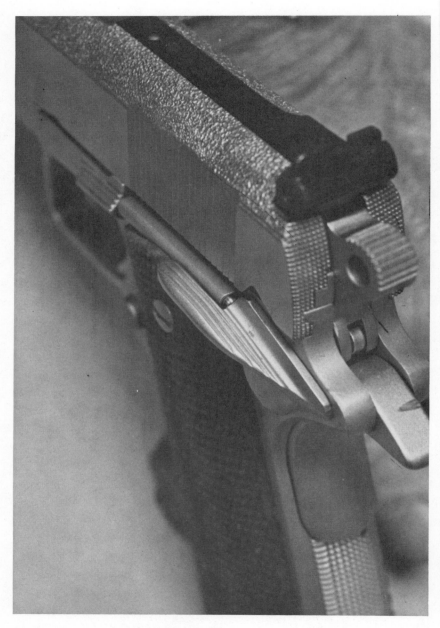

This Smith & Wesson Model 39 has combat conversions by Swenson. There is a new rear-sight mount and the top surface of the slide has been stippled (note the large tang safety lever). (Courtesy Swenson)

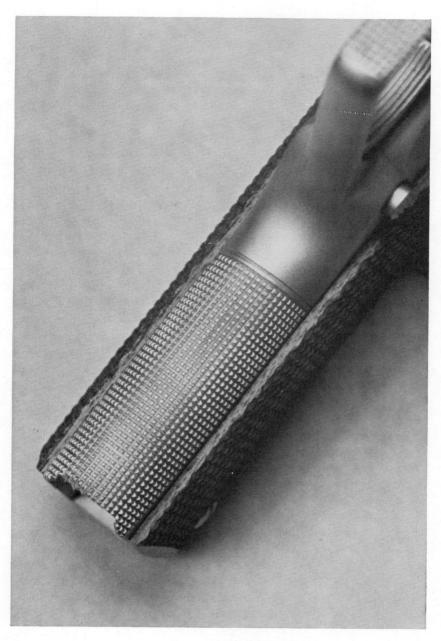

Another Swenson conversion. The Smith & Wesson Model 39 shows the checkered front strap of the pistol handgrip. (Courtesy Swenson)

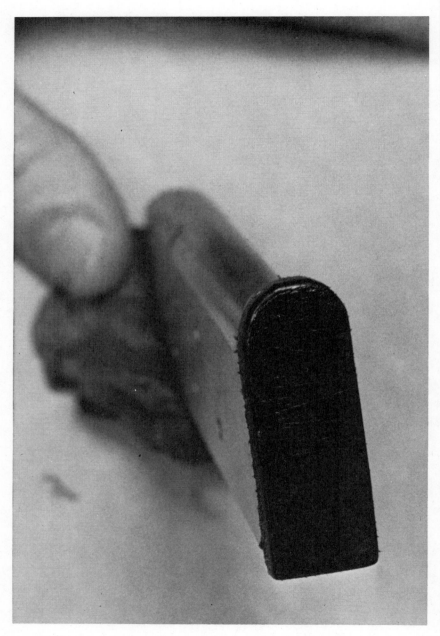

The Swenson combat conversion includes a leather-covered magazine base. (Courtesy Swenson)

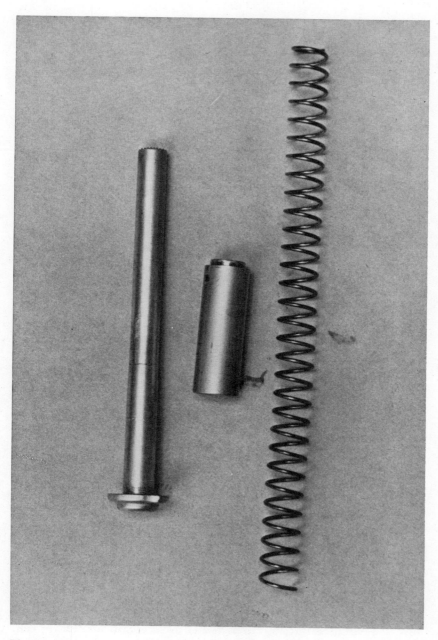

The Swenson conversion lengthens the recoil-spring guide, which prevents spring kinks. (Courtesy Swenson)

The range of James W. Hoag Colt .45 conversion. From top to bottom: *long slide model with an 8-inch (203-millimeter) barrel; 6-inch (152-millimeter) barrel; standard 5.5-inch (140-millimeter) barrel; and the combat version with a 4.5-inch (108-millimeter) barrel. Only the 4.5-inch (108-millimeter) is suitable for combat use.* (Courtesy Hoag)

wells; squared trigger guards; extended slide stop levers; and enlarged (lowered) ejection ports. Hoag provides his custom .45 Colts in barrel lengths ranging from 4.25–8 inches (108–203 millimeters). The 4.25-inch (108-millimeter) is intended for combat use, while the longer guns were created for target shooting.

Hoag has also made an FN Browning Hi-Power combat conversion, which is tuned for better feeding. The forestrap is checkered, and the trigger guard is squared and checkered. The magazine well is beveled for quicker reloading, the thumb-safety lever is enlarged, and Smith & Wesson Model 39 rear and front sights are installed.

Recently Don McNabb of M-S Safari Arms introduced an

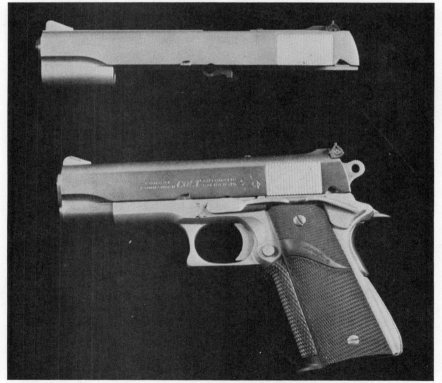

Lindsey Alexiou, working under the name Trapper, has been tuning and customizing combat handguns for many years. (Courtesy Tom Wagster)

More customized guns by "Trapper" Lindsey Alexiou. (Courtesy Tom Wagster)

The M-S Safari Arms Enforcer. This .45 caliber pistol is basically a shortened M1911A1-type handgun with a newly manufactured frame. Note the finger grooves, squared trigger guard on the frame, and the checkered forestrap and flat back strap. The beavertailed grip safety, ambidextrous safety, Commander-type hammer, and Model 39 Smith & Wesson rear sight are also readily apparent. (Courtesy M-S Safari)

Enforcer combat version of the Colt M1911 Mark IV automatic pistol. In addition to the basic tuning, M-S Safari Arms shortened the frame, slide, and barrel. The following comparison with the standard M1911A1 and the Colt Commander is illuminating:

Handgun Characteristics

	M-S Enforcer	Colt Commander	M1911A1
Overall length	7.5 in (191mm)	7.875 in (200mm)	8.5 in (216mm)
Barrel length	3.8 in (97mm)	4.25 in (108mm)	5.0 in (127mm)
Weight	35 oz (.99 kg)	37 oz (105 kg) steel frame	39 oz (1.11 kg)
Magazine capacity	6	7	7

The M-S Safari Enforcer uses a new frame with finger grooves incorporated into the pistol grip and a squared-off trigger guard to improve holding and firing in a two-handed position. In addition, M-S Safari has introduced some inter-

Close-up view of Enforcer beavertailed grip safety. (Courtesy M-S Safari)

esting components in the Enforcer model that can also be purchased as accessories for standard M1911A1 pistols. First, and most useful, is the long, ambidextrous, thumb-lever safety. Like those incorporated on other combat conversions of single-action Colt automatics, this modified safety is a positive addition to this type of handgun since it speeds the combat-readiness of the weapon. The extended lever for the slide release is also a utilitarian modification. Less essential, but still useful, is the beavertail-grip-safety assembly. This modified tang helps to spread the recoil of the weapon over a greater area, while eliminating the possibility of the hammer pinching the web of the shooter's hand during firing.

Close-up view of Enforcer padded-base magazine and beveled magazine well. (Courtesy M-S Safari)

Other nice touches in the M-S Safari Arms Enforcer design include the beveled magazine well, padded magazine base, modified barrel bushing, and recoil-spring assembly. The Enforcer can be fitted with Smith & Wesson Model 39-type or Behlert rear sights and a front blade sight with red plastic insert for improved aiming. This gun is available in two basic finishes. One model is entirely coated (inside and out) with Du Pont Teflon to eliminate lubrication problems; the other version is finished with Armoloy. Armoloy, developed by Armoloy, Inc., consists of an electrochemically bonded, rather than mechanically bonded, finish. This finish does not crack and peel the way regular hard chrome or nickel plate can, and it is a handsome silver grey matte. The Enforcer is fitted with either Pachmayr neoprene Signature grips or Herrett wooden grips.

The Seecamp double-action conversion of the Colt

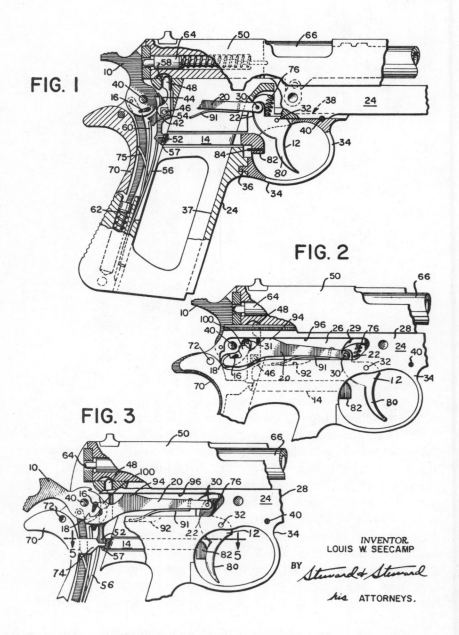

Patent drawings for the Seecamp double-action-conversion system for the Colt
M1911A1-type automatic pistol. (Courtesy U.S. Patent Office)

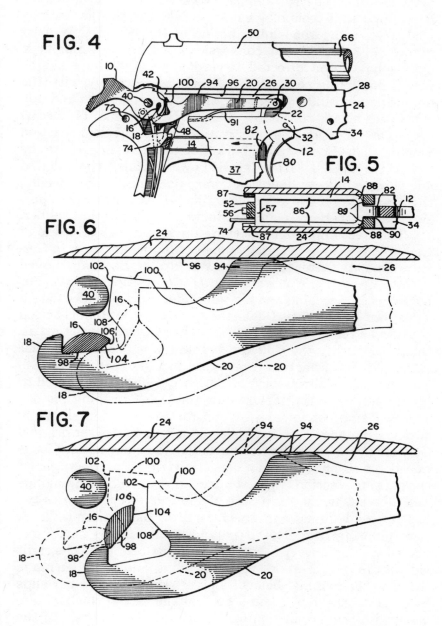

FIG. 4

FIG. 5

FIG. 6

FIG. 7

M1911A1 and the Browning Hi-Power automatic is one of the most important technological steps taken in the last twenty years. Since the 1954 introduction of the Smith & Wesson Model 39, most combat conversions of Colt/Browning-type pistols have been directed toward improving those single-action handguns so that they compare favorably with the double-action Model 39. Long, thumb-lever safeties and holsters with straps that allow the Colt/Browning to be carried cocked are questionable substitutions for a true double-action handgun. The Seecamp double-action mechanism permits the Colt M1911A1 and Browning Hi-Power pistols to be updated and used as modern double-action combat guns. Additionally, the conversion made a double-action .45 ACP automatic possible before there were any production models in that caliber.

The Seecamp double-action conversion is the work of Louis W. Seecamp, a certified master gunmaker born in Germany in 1901. After the Second World War, Seecamp moved first to Canada (1952) and then to Connecticut (1959). For many years, Seecamp and his son Luder (Larry) made custom rifles, but in the late 1960s they created the double-action conversion for the Colt M1911A1. Theirs was not the first attempt to modify the Colt for double-action. There are other M1911A1 double-action prototypes in the experimental collection at the Colt factory, but other designers attempted to build special cocking devices for the Colt/Browning pistols. The Seecamp conversion, by contrast, is very simple. Only two new moving parts have been added, and all of the original Colt lockwork has been retained. The original trigger is reduced in size, and a new double-action trigger presses against the old single-action trigger to fire the weapon. The Seecamps mill a recess in the right side of the frame that exposes the base of the hammer and gives the draw bar a place to lie. A new, pivoting trigger is fitted and pinned into a newly machined pivot point. A hardened pin protrudes from the right side of the trigger above its pivot point, and a similar pin is fitted to the hammer below its pivot point. A draw bar slips over the trigger's pin, and a hook at the rear of the bar coincides with the hammer's pin. A spring forces the rear of the bar upward so that its hook engages the hammer pin.

Colt Lightweight Commander in .45 caliber. (Courtesy Colt)

When the trigger is pulled in the double-action mode, the upper part of the trigger rotates forward, pulling the draw bar with it, which in turn pulls the foot of the hammer forward, and thus brings the hammer to the cocked condition. As the trigger pull continues, the draw-bar hook and hammer pin reach a point where the hook is cammed downward, allowing the hammer to fall. Simultaneous with hammer release, the new trigger contacts the old trigger and pushes it rearward to move the original sear out of the hammer's path. The hammer is thus free to stroke the firing pin.

During recoil, the lockwork functions normally, leaving the hammer cocked when the cycle is completed. When the trigger is released after firing, the first shot is rotated forward

Top, *Seecamp Double-Action Conversion.* Bottom, *the same Seecamp converted pistol with side plate removed to show the draw bar.* (Courtesy Seecamp)

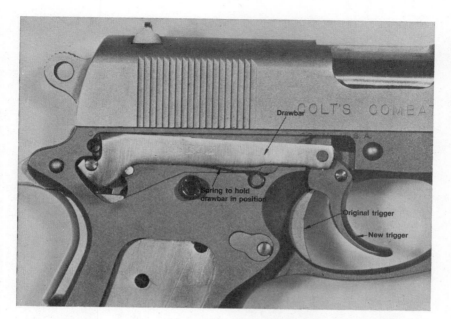

Top, *Seecamp Double-Action Conversion ready for double-action firing.* Below, *same pistol ready for single-action use.*

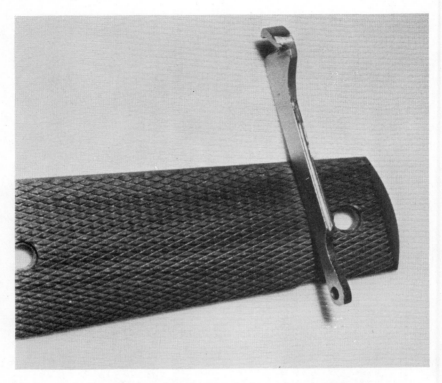

A view of the Seecamp draw bar. Note its thickness; it is a sturdy piece.

to the single-action position. The next pull of the trigger disengages the sear as the new trigger presses on the old one. Accompanying photographs provide a clear picture of how this conversion system works.

Two other conversion kits available are the Allan Speed-Cock and the Double-Ace by Caraville Arms. The Speed-Cock is built around a much modified safety system. The Double-Ace replaces the grip safety, mainspring housing and contents, and the hammer strut of the original pistol. When assembled, it acts as a squeeze-cocking unit. When the shooter grasps the handgun in the normal manner and squeezes the Double-Ace unit, the internal mechanism acts to cock the hammer, and the pistol is ready to fire. These conversions, of course, are not true double-action systems.

The Smith & Wesson Model 39 has also been the focus of

The Armament Systems and Procedures ASP is the original combat conversion of the Smith & Wesson Model 39 pistol. (Courtesy V. L. Fox)

combat conversions. Unlike the vintage single-action Colt automatic, the Model 39 is an almost perfect double-action combat automatic, but many users want to reduce its size so that it can be more easily concealed.

In the mid-1960s, combat handgun users like George C. Nonte, Paris Theodore, and others began to work on cutting the size of the Model 39. Over a several-year period, Theodore sold a total of 300 modified Model 39s under the name Seventrees ASP, but this company was unable to make deliveries and eventually closed its doors. In 1976, a new company,

Armament Systems and Procedures Inc. of Appleton, Wisconsin, purchased a license to manufacture the patented ASP combat pistol. This firm has agreed to fill all back orders for ASPs, some of which date to 1971. The current production ASP features Teflon-S coating for protection from corrosion, see-through injection-molded Lexan grips to permit monitoring of cartridge supply, and the guttersnipe sight.

More recently, Charles C. Kelsey, Jr. and his associates at Devel Corporation have introduced a Model 39 conversion that follows in the tradition of the Seventrees ASP. The major features of the Devel conversion are:

1. See-through window in grip to permit quick monitoring of magazine capacity
2. Flutes in slide to reduce weight
3. Redesigned barrel bushing to produce greater accuracy
4. Roll pin added to frame to aid feeding of cartridges
5. Custom-spring package that replaces all original Smith & Wesson springs
6. Ramp-type front sight with bright red insert
7. Special magazines
8. Removal of frame spur on backstrap of pistol grip
9. Removal of hammer spur
10. Magazine well beveled for quicker loading
11. Modified magazine release
12. Squared-off trigger guard for two-hand holding
13. Ambidextrous safety lever
14. Removal of magazine disconnector.

Model 39 Conversions

	Smith & Wesson Model 39	Devel	Seventrees ASP
Overall length	7.44 in (189mm)	6.75 in (171mm)	5.75 in (146mm)
Barrel length	4 in (102mm)	3.5 in (89mm)	2.5 in (64mm)
Weight	26.5 oz (.75 kg)	23.1 oz (.65 kg) w/o magazine	24 oz (.68 kg) loaded
Magazine capacity	8	7	7

Austin F. Behlert of The Custom Gunshop has also developed a cut-down Model 39, as illustrated in the accompanying photographs. In addition, Behlert has made an FN Browning

The Devel Corporation combat conversion of the Smith & Wesson Model 39 shortens the overall length of the pistol by 0.69 inch (18 millimeters), while decreasing its height by 0.5 inch (12.7 millimeters). The Devel pistol weighs 3.9 ounces (.1 kilogram) less than the standard Model 39. (Courtesy Devel Corporation and Smith & Wesson)

Two Behlert Model 39 Mini combat automatics. The top view is the Economy Model 39 Mini, and the bottom view is the Delux Mini. The Delux has finger grooves cut into the frame, a squared-off trigger guard, Behlert sights, and a Behlert screw-in barrel bushing. (Courtesy Behlert)

Three combat conversions of the FN Browning Hi-Power Pistol. (Courtesy Behlert)

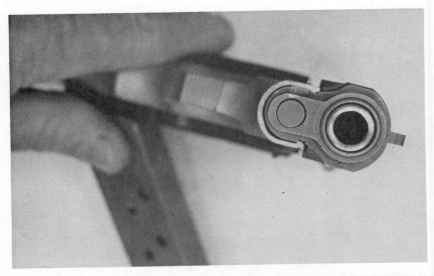

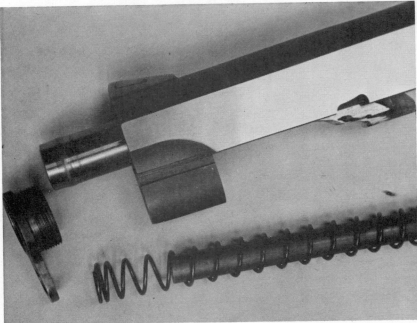

Two views of the Behlert screw-in barrel bushing as installed on the Smith & Wesson Model 39 automatic pistol. The muzzle end of the slide must be bored and threaded to use this new bushing. A circumferential bead that seats the bushing must be added at the muzzle end of the barrel. (Courtesy Behlert)

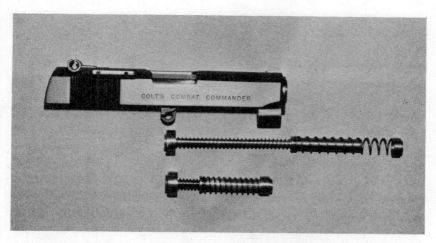

The slide on this Combat Commander has been shortened by .70 inch (17.8 milli-meters). A Spring Extendor is shown at full extension and also as it appears on installation.

Hi-Power pistol that is reduced in size and weight, called the Mini. Behlert is also well known for his general custom work. He has produced an excellent, combat-type, adjustable rear sight; his own extended-tang, thumb-safety lever (both regular and ambidextrous); and a screw-in barrel bushing, which improves accuracy considerably. The barrel bushing works on the same principle as the muzzle bushing used on the Smith & Wesson .38 Special caliber Model 52 automatic pistol (a variant of the Model 39). Behlert is a top-flight machinist whose speciality is handguns. If you have need for a customized combat handgun, seek such a professional whose work has been described in this chapter or who is otherwise well known.

In closing this chapter, some words of caution should be given about trying to shorten the barrels and slides of automatic pistols. Certainly, more is involved than making a few cuts with a hacksaw. Once the slide and barrel have been shortened, and a new barrel bushing installed by a professional, there is still the question of adapting the recoil spring and perhaps eliminating the forward locking lug of the barrel so that there will be sufficient clearance for the bushing when the gun is unlocking. These are critical operations.

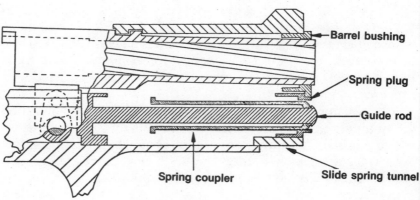

Barrel bushing

Spring plug

Guide rod

Slide spring tunnel

Spring coupler

The Seecamp Spring Extendor is shown as it appears at battery position in the left-side photo view and the right-side sketch view. (In the photograph, the left side of the frame front has been milled away to provide an unobstructed look at the system.)

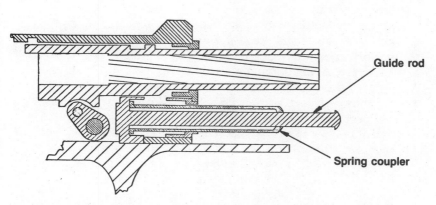

Guide rod

Spring coupler

The Seecamp Spring Extendor is shown as it appears at the recoil position in the left-side photo view and right-side sketch view. (In the photograph, the left side of the frame front has been milled away for a clearer view of the system.)

This photo shows the comparative size of the SIG-Sauer P220 .45 caliber automatic pistol (Browning BDA and a Seecamp Colt Combat Commander, which has been shortened and converted to double-action).

The recoil spring can present a special challenge. Some remarks on this subject by Larry Seecamp follow.

Under the development of our patent pending Seecamp Spring Extender, we did not accept requests to shorten the slides of Colt M1911A1-type pistols. Reliability has always been our primary concern, and reduction of the length of the slide reduces the energy of the recoil spring, which is also shortened in the process. Since the performance of the recoil spring is critical to the reliable performance of the pistol, slide length should be reduced with care. A smaller and more compact handgun is of little value if dependability has been sacrificed.

The Seecamp Spring Extender allows us to maintain the necessary spring energy to reliably operate the pistol, and it allows us to shorten the M1911A1 slide by 1.125 inch (28.575mm) and the Commander slide by 0.6875 inch (17.4625mm). In the Seecamp Spring Extender, two springs, joined by a coupling sleeve, act in tandem to supplying the equivalent performance of a much longer spring than the available space would normally allow. The inner spring urges the coupler forward, thereby providing added compression to the outer spring when the slide is at battery

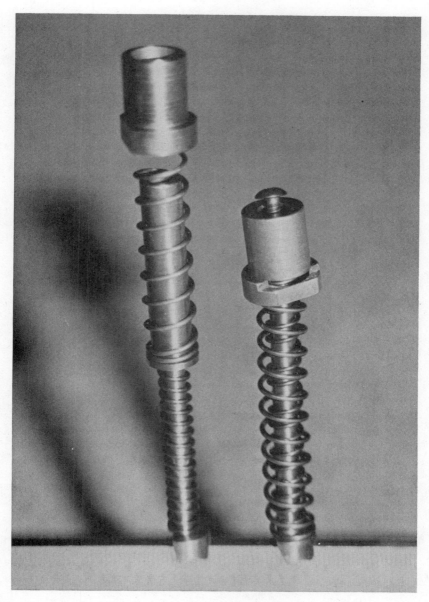

On the right is a standard Detonics dual-spring arrangement. Note the gap between the head of the screw and the spring bushing. This gap exists when the screw is removed and rests on the front of the guide rod, demonstrating how little spring compression is available at battery. On the left is a Seecamp Spring Extendor adapted for the Detonics. Both are shown in full extention.

232 closed The battery load

(i.e., closed). The battery load of the spring is thus increased considerably. As the slide is retracted, both springs share in compression.

The Seecamp Spring Extender offers tremendous flexibility within the severely limited space. While the space available for the outerspring on full compression is restricted to the confines of the spring tunnel—as is normal—the inner spring is allowed to telescope out beyond the slide face on recoil along with the coupling sleeve within which it is housed. By experimenting with different coupler lengths and spring wire sizes, the optimum Spring Extender for a particular handgun type can be devised. Perhaps the most remarkable thing about the Spring Extender is that such a simple concept has not been used before. We believe that this new device will present the opportunity for new improvements in handgun design.

While the foregoing reflects only one approach, it does indicate that one should not approach even the most simple aspect of handgun modification lightly. Such custom work should be done only when it is necessary and when it enhances the performance of the combat handgun.

7

Customizing Your Own Autoloader for Combat

HIGHLY SOPHISTICATED, extensively modified, costly combat conversions are quite acceptable for the few individuals who can afford them and who can wait several months or longer for their completion by one of the few artisans who do this kind of work (the user may have to acquire another gun for the interim). This is obviously not practical for thousands of users who still want to affect some changes to their autoloaders. With a few hand tools and a thorough familiarity with the mechanics of their sidearms, most users can make several modifications on any good gun that will further improve its performance and raise the shooter's level of confidence in it.

The following tools will be useful for the home gunsmith: small- or medium-size machinist (ballpeen) hammer; small set of good, Swiss-pattern, needle files; 12-inch (304.8-millimeter), flat, mill file, 6-inch (152.4-millimeter) round file, pin punches to fit gun; high-quality screwdrivers to fit gun; set of hard Arkansas stones; prick punch or centerpunch; portable electric drill, preferably with a drill-press stand; brass or hard-fiber drift; and a small sharp knife. In addition, a small, high-speed hand grinder such as the Dremel Moto-Tool would be a great time and labor saver; and a propane torch would allow silver soldering to be done.

If you have a Colt Government Model or Commander, there are several so-called bolt-on accessories and replacement parts you can consider, which are offered by a number of manufacturers who claim they will improve the perform-ance of your gun. One of the most important things you can do to any service autoloader is to install a rear sight, adjust-able for both windage and elevation to allow precise targeting with the particular load being utilized. Such a sight is espe-cially useful if you are using high-performance ammunition, which generally impacts substantially lower than conven-tional hard ball.

Installing the MMC Combat Sight, which provides en-tirely adequate latitude of windage and elevation adjustment yet is compatible with the existing front sight, requires vir-tually no modification of the slide. You need only a small file, hammer, and drift to install it. Remove the slide and fix it solidly in a vise. With a soft drift and hammer, drive the exist-ing rear sight out of its dovetail to the right. Following the in-stallation instructions and diagram, use a small file to cut a slight clearance at the center front of the dovetail. Remove any burrs in the dovetail as well as any grease or dirt. Insert the MMC sight from the right into the dovetail as far as it will go with hand pressure. It should enter only slightly—if it enters a quarter or more of its width, it probably will be too loose to withstand recoil after installation. If it is loose, raise ten to twelve small dimples in the bottom of the dovetail with a prick punch, insert the sight, and tap it into the dovetail with the soft drift. Take care to strike squarely and do not batter the sight's edges. As accurately as you can, align the sight laterally, centering it from side to side in the slide. Check the movement of both windage and elevation screws, reas-semble the gun, and target it. Once you are certain it is tar-geted, use a prick punch or centerpunch to stake the dovetail centrally, directly in front of the sight base. Even though the sight may seem perfectly tight, this additional bit of security should be applied.

Another product in this line is a complete rib-sight unit called the Quick-Draw Rib supplied by BoMar for the Colt, Browning, and Smith & Wesson automatics. It consists of a massive rib the length of the slide with full-house, target, rear sight, and massive front sight. To install this unit, first drive out the original sight and punch out or file off the front sight. Position the rib unit on top of the slide, paying particular attention to note whether there are any burrs or bumps that prevent it from making smooth contact throughout. If there are any, dress them off with files. Clamp the rib securely to the slide after you are sure that it is centered on the slide and that the ejection cutout is aligned with the port. Select a pointed punch that is a slip fit in the screw holes through the rib and carefully centerpunch the location of each attaching screw on the top of the slide. Alternatively, if you do not have a punch that will fit, select a twist drill the same size as the holes in the rib and spin it just enough in each hole to cut a small, conical depression in the slide. Remove the rib. On a drill press, very carefully drill those holes located ahead of the ejection port through the slide roof with the correct-size drill. The holes behind the ejection port should be drilled approximately ³⁄₁₆ inch (4.76 millimeters) deep. Pay close attention so that the holes do not break through into the firing-pin tunnel or any other recess inside the rear of the slide. Follow this by carefully tapping those holes with a tap and removing burrs from both ends of the holes. Place the rib back on the slide and turn the installation screws tight. If the rear screws are too long and reach bottom in the holes without drawing up tight, shorten them. Likewise, if the front screws protrude inside the slide, shorten them. Since the screws might loosen under recoil, it is a good idea to remove each screw one at a time and thoroughly clean it and its hole with acetone and coat the threads of the screws with Loc-Tite. Drive the screws in as tightly as possible. The rib will be on the slide to stay. To target the gun, chose one of several models of target-type sights available. Most of these, however, require extensive gunsmithing for proper fit, and you should not install one yourself unless you have better-than-average skills and tools.

Replacement grips can be a most useful accessory. Available in a wide variety of materials, shapes, and sizes, they are simply screwed in place after the originals are removed. The most common mistake with grips is to choose a pattern too large and bulky. Combat use generally requires a minimum amount of grip material. While both smooth and checkered wood grips are favored by many, the Pachmayr Signature rubber-like grips made for the Colt Government Model are considered by some experts to be the best available for combat use. Their shape and texture produces a very secure hold.

Many shooters find that the Government Model hammer pinches the web between thumb and forefinger against the grip safety tang or digs into the skin as the slide slams back in recoil. The resulting bruise can interfere with smooth gun handling. If the tip of the hammer spur is digging into your hand, it may be shortened and beveled with a hand grinder to eliminate the problem. A Commander hammer with its rounded, cocking spur may be substituted with the same result. If the Commander hammer digs into your hand, grind away the part of the surface that is doing the damage. A simpler method of eliminating both pinching and jabbing-hammer damage is to replace the existing grip safety with the "spade-grip safety" offered by The Custom Gunshop. This unit is a standard grip safety to which a broad piece of metal has been welded or brazed. This lays over the web of the hand and prevents the hammer from reaching the skin. Installation requires no special effort. Remove the original grip safety and replace it.

If you are using a Colt with the arched-style, mainspring housing, instinctive pointing of the gun may be improved by replacing the housing either with the flat-style housing offered separately by Colt or surplus military parts dealers or with the modified semiarched housings available from Dan Dwyer. The latter consist of an original, military-arched housing that has been machined down to a slightly curved profile about midway between the two Colt types. Regardless of the type of replacement housing utilized, installation is simply a matter of removing the original housing and installing the new one.

If you find the narrow trigger of the Government Model a bit difficult to reach or to control properly, the addition of a trigger shoe might improve the situation. This is a slotted piece of metal fit over the original, trigger finger piece and clamped there with a pair of tiny socket-head screws. Installation is simple; however, the screws sometimes do not hold well against the smooth, hard trigger so it is a good idea to drill depressions into which their points can seat and ensure that the shoe does not bounce off.

There are several different lengths of Government Model triggers available. The so-called long trigger was originally supplied on the M1911 pistol, while the very short, deeply curved trigger was issued on the M1911A1 adopted in the 1920s. Over the years, the two types have been interchanged freely, so any vintage gun is likely to have either trigger. In addition, there have been commercial replacement and match triggers produced in recent years of a length somewhere between the two. Some of the newer triggers have steel finger pieces, while others are made of aluminum. Regardless of the type, if you are installing a new trigger, remove the old trigger and put in the new one. You should attempt to try all three lengths with and without a trigger shoe to determine which combination provides the best gun control for you.

While it is possible to become quite fast and proficient in disengaging the standard manual safety of the Government Model when drawing the gun from the cocked-and-locked position, the so-called combat safety greatly facilitates developing such a high degree of ability. Further, it provides additional leverage for actuating the safety under poor conditions or when gloves are being worn. Consequently, it is a good addition for combat use.

Combat safeties for both the Colt and Browning are available from several sources, the best known of which is probably the Armand Swenson. This safety is a new part produced by investment castings with the thumb piece enlarged and extended forward to make it easier to reach and manipulate. Installation is not quite as simple as some other replacement parts. The Swenson safety is finished externally, but the engaging surfaces that protrude inside the frame and act upon the sear have not been brought to final size and shape. These areas are marked by spots of red paint so that they may be readily recognized. Only a small amount of metal must be removed, but it must be done very carefully—with fine needle files—first using the original safety as a pattern and, finally, carefully fitting and trying the new safety until it functions correctly. Once it has been made to work by careful filing, its smoothness of operation may be somewhat improved by polishing all rubbing surfaces with a hard Arkansas stone. An alternative to the Swenson safety is one supplied by The Custom Gunshop, which is not a completely new part. It is a serviceable or new, original safety to which an extended thumb piece has been brazed. Consequently, it may normally be installed by simply substituting it for the original safety without any fitting or gunsmithing.

For left-handed users, carrying the Colt or Browning cocked and locked on the left hip becomes a problem. The existing safety cannot be manipulated as fast or as well as one might wish, even though some users have developed a technique for brushing the safety down and out of engagement with the trigger finger as the gun is drawn. This condition can be improved by installing an ambidextrous safety supplied by Swenson. This component is actually the basic, Swenson combat safety with its internal shaft shortened and notched to receive a correspondingly notched end on another shaft entering from the right side of the gun frame and carrying a similar thumb piece for manipulation by the left thumb. Installing this unit is not difficult. Fit the left half of the safety as already outlined and insert the right half so that the mortice and tenon joint of the two shafts meets squarely inside the frame. Cut a shallow relief in the upper rear corner of the right-hand grip so that the grip will lay over the new thumb piece but have adequate clearance for it to rotate smoothly when the grip is screwed solidly in place.

While the recoil of even the .45 automatic should normally not be considered objectionable, the effect one feels can be reduced somewhat by the installation of a recoil buffer available from a number of manufacturers in lengths to suit both the Government Model and the Commander. This device consists of a standard, recoil-spring guide that has been drilled out to accept a plunger and powerful backing spring. The plunger extends forward from the guide and contacts the inside of the recoil-spring plug during the last portion of the slide's rearward travel. As this occurs, the slide is decelerated rapidly by compressing the buffer spring, reducing the impact of the slide halting against the frame. Although the recoil buffer was developed to reduce recoil, its primary value lies in the fact that when the slide begins to move forward, the additional power of the compressed buffer spring acts to accelerate the slide more rapidly than the recoil spring alone. This results in far more power for feeding, chambering, and locking the gun in preparation for the next shot. Guns that produce marginal or unsatisfactory functioning can often be upgraded by replacing the recoil-spring guide with a recoil buffer. That added forward flip given the slide by the buffer spring overcomes feeding resistance. Such an added margin of functional reliability is invaluable to any combat autoloader.

The original recoil spring can also be replaced by a magnum, or high-speed, spring sold by several companies. This is a slightly more powerful recoil spring, which can be exchanged directly for the original. It provides more power for feeding and probably produces less recoil.

It has generally become accepted in recent years that two-hand gun control is vastly superior to the traditional one-hand style. While any gun can be steadied substantially by placing the left hand over the right, the amount of steadying influence exerted can be improved when the front of the trigger guard is reshaped to form a seat or pocket for the off-hand forefinger. Until recently, the only method of achieving this was by extensively forging or welding and reshaping the front of the guard. There is now available a simple, steel, investment casting to seat upon the lower forepart of the guard. In some cases it may require a small amount of file work to obtain a close fit, but once that has been accomplished it may be attached in only minutes with an epoxy compound.

For all practical purposes, this makes a permanent installation if the joint areas are first cleaned thoroughly with acetone. Instead of using epoxy, however, you could drill a hole through the casting and the guard and use a small screw to tie the two solidly together. Alternatively, if you have a torch, either soft or silver solder could be used for a very secure and somewhat neater installation. Regardless of the method, this guard spur looks like a triangular piece of metal added as an afterthought. Certainly, it is not as graceful and elegant as the more costly gunsmithing jobs, but, as far as performance is concerned, it is equal to the best.

Another bolt-on accessory that can be considered practical and worthwhile is the Caraville Arms Double-Ace squeeze-cocking conversion unit. This is a system of cranks and levers that connects to the hammer, entirely replacing the original mainspring housing, grip safety, and mainspring and hammer strut. It is installed on the gun quite easily. First remove the parts mentioned above, then pin the original hammer to the new hammer strut protruding from the Double-Ace unit. The entire assembly is pinned into the rear of the frame by means of the thumb safety and the original, mainspring-housing pin. The rear surface and main frame of the unit is pivoted at the top around the grip safety, and in its at-rest position the lower end is swung slightly rearward, thus making the butt of greater fore-and-aft length than previous. Squeezing the butt of the gun pivots the lever inward, which acts through a series of cranks and rollers to pull the hammer to the full-cock position. The gun can then be carried with the hammer down on a chambered round and cocked by squeezing the butt as it is drawn, after which squeezing the butt will first raise and then lower the hammer to fire the gun.

There are other variations of some of the devices mentioned in this chapter on the market, and all of the items considered here have been developed primarily for the Colt Government Model series of pistols. As indicated, some may be adapted to the Browning Hi-Power and fewer still to the Smith & Wesson Model 39. Further, there is some interchangeability of accessories possible between the Llama pistols (copies of the Colt) and the much-modified Star Colt. There are also a number of minor modifications and alterations that can be made to further customize the combat autoloader, and most can be performed with simple hand tools.

Roughening the front strap—and, in the case of the Browning, the backstrap as well—will make the gun seat more solidly in your hand and thereby improve control. This can be accomplished by checkering or serrating the metal, which is done with either files or machine tools by someone skilled in their operation. Some individuals utilize stippling for this purpose; and with some experience, this may be applied with a hammer and sharp punch.

To stipple the gun, strip the piece and clamp the frame solidly in a vise with the front strap up and relatively level. Take a piece of white chalk and outline the area you would like roughened. Generally, this comprises the entire area from the trigger guard to the butt, but a neater appearance may be achieved without any reduction in effectiveness by giving this area rounded ends and moving its boundaries in about $1/16$ inch (1.59 millimeters) from the ends of the frame. Grind the point of a centerpunch to a square-section with a very sharp, 45-degree pyramid point. Polish the four faces of the point smooth with Arkansas stone, removing all the grinding marks so that it will form clean, sharp dimples in the metal of the frame. With the punch in your left hand held firmly between thumb and forefinger, position its point about ¼ inch (6.35 millimeters) above the surface to be stippled. Rest your wrist across a solid support. Tense the muscles of hand and wrist so that when the head of the punch is tapped with a hammer your hand acts as a spring to withdraw the punch after it strikes the frame. Do not attempt to set the point of the punch down on the frame and then strike it; to do so will cause skidding and irregular dimples.

Starting in the center of the area to be stippled, strike the punch with a medium-sharp blow, and note the size and depth impression it makes. Adjust the force of the blow to obtain the texture you want and move outward over the face of the area with successive blows, each overlapping the last dimple by about one-third. Take care when moving along the edges or borders of the pattern to produce a uniform line. As you progress, examine the punch point frequently; if it begins to become dull and rounded, reshape it. A dull punch does not produce the same impression as a sharp one, and you can obtain a uniform surface only by keeping it sharp. If the punch dulls too quickly, you will have to reharden it. Rub your fingers over the surface that has been stippled. You may wish to retain the many minute burrs that you feel because they make the grip even more secure as they dig into the skin of the gun hand. If this is not desirable, the stippled area can be burnished with a wire brush to remove the sharp edges. The stippled area may then be spot blued.

Your first stippling job should probably be done with the punch held at right angles to the gun surface. However, you might want to experiment on scrap metal with different angles to produce different textures and a different direction of the burrs than an angled punch will make. If the punch is angled, its point will throw up a sharp burr leaning away from the punch pit. Advantage can be taken of this to produce a much sharper and more abrasive surface. Some pistolsmiths do not overlap the stippling dimples. Instead, they hold the punch at a very acute angle and form each dimple completely separate with a very pronounced burr turned up by the point.

If stippling seems like too complicated a process but you would still like to roughen the front strap to improve your grip, there is a temporary alternative. Remove the grips and cut a piece of coarse or medium sandpaper or abrasive cloth that will wrap around the front strap and lap back over the sides of the frame about ¼ inch (6.35 millimeters). Carefully fold and crease this piece of paper to fit properly and reinstall the grips, using them to clamp the abrasive strip tightly in place. If you have difficulty in clamping the abrasive tightly enough, cut the piece longer so that it extends back over the full width of the frame sides and punch holes in it to lay over the grip-screw bushings. A bit of rubber cement applied thinly to the front strap will also help.

Another way to roughen the front strap without any permanent alteration to the gun involves the use of a pimpled rubber sheet, such as found on the faces of ping-pong paddles. Cut a piece that just fits the front strap and clean the metal thoroughly with acetone. Apply good-quality rubber cement sparingly and carefully press the pebbled rubber snugly into place. If you encounter difficulties in making it adhere over the entire curved surface, spot it in place and wrap the entire butt of the gun snugly with a bandage or strips of cloth until the cement has cured thoroughly. This pebbled rubber sheet has a unique, flexible feel and provides a very good hold once one becomes accustomed to it.

Since the advent of the Smith & Wesson Model 39 automatic, many shooters of other handguns have wanted the narrow, flat surface that the Model 39 possesses on the top of its slide. Theoretically, this flat has somewhat the same effect as a rib, but there is no proof that it actually improves sighting. Without much difficulty, the same effect can be achieved on a Colt or Browning. If you intend to retain the original sights, remove the slide from the gun, clamp it in a vise, and drift out the rear sight. Leave the front sight, but with a small C-clamp attach two strips of hardwood or metal astride the slide just rearward of the front sight to prevent your files from inadvertently striking the front sight in subsequent operations. Scrub off the top of the slide with solvent. The flat can vary in width, but ³⁄₈ inch (9.5 millimeters) is a good size. This will not require the removal of an excessive amount of metal nor weaken the locking-lug area of the slide. Carefully mark the outline of the flat on the slide with two strips of masking tape applied and burnished against the metal so they will not slip or peel.

Lay a 12-inch (304.8-millimeter) file across the top of the slide perpendicular to its longitudinal axis and grab both ends of it firmly. Pressing down only lightly, push and pull the file from the front sight to the rear. If you have it positioned correctly, fine slivers of steel will roll off with every stroke. After a few strokes, rub the working surface of the file with white chalk to prevent the teeth of the file from clogging. Vary the pressure of your stroke, if necessary, to ensure that the flat develops the same width throughout its length. As the flat becomes wide enough, check with a small square placed against the side of the slide to ensure that you are forming it perpendicular to the sides. Continue to file until the flat has reached the width you want and finish by polishing the filed surface with abrasive cloth on a flat stick or piece of steel, removing any burrs around the edge of the flat. Apply cold blue to the filed surface to darken it, reinstall the rear sight, and retarget the gun. If the rear sight does not fit as tightly as it should, turn up a few burrs in the bottom of the dovetail to make it tight enough for targeting. When targeting has been completed, stake the sight securely in place at both front and rear of the dovetail with a centerpunch.

Shooters with large hands sometimes have some difficulty in getting their trigger finger into the guard in a hurry. The most practical alteration to help this situation is to reshape the front of the guard, removing no more than half its width and flaring the remaining portion smoothly into the rest of the gun. Cutting away the entire front of the guard is not advised as this eliminates all protection to the trigger. To achieve this alteration, begin at the upper front of the guard using a ¼-inch (6.35-millimeter) or smaller round file to cut a semicircular groove even with the edge of the frame and to a depth of half the original guard width. Drop down to the bottom of the guard, and just forward of the foremost trigger position do the same thing again. Follow this by roughening off the surplus metal between the two notches. You can do this with an assortment of files or abrasive wheels and rotary files in a Moto-Tool. On steel frames, the abrasive coarse wheels are preferable; while on aluminum frames such as the P38 and the Smith & Wesson, a rotary file does the best job. It is a good idea to adhere several layers of masking tape over the frame to protect the gun from scratches where the files might run into it. Once the metal between the two notches has been roughed out, take needle files or a hand grinder and smooth up the cut surfaces. Flow the upper end of the cut smoothly into the underside of the frame and taper the lower cut so that there is no sharp transition point. Smooth all edges and remove file or grinding marks with narrow strips of fine abrasive cloth applied bootblack fashion through and over the guard.

There is one other slight addition you might wish to add if you are very concerned about snagging your trigger finger.

Carefully bend the narrowed portion of the guard to the left, bowing it leftward and forward a bit more to provide additional finger clearance. This is not a job for the amateur, however. The chances of spoiling the guard are too great if you are not extremely skilled, but a pistolsmith can do it easily with heat-and-formed punches.

Recharging an empty automatic in the middle of a gunfight is immeasurably faster and easier than reloading a six-gun under identical conditions. However, the typical production gun still leaves a bit to be desired in this area. Assuming that magazines fit correctly and fall free easily when the magazine catch is disengaged, you can perform one alteration that will make quick insertion of replacement magazines much easier. With small, round, flat files, file a 45-degree bevel completely around the mouth of the magazine well. The thickness of the frame metal around this well is adequate in most guns for beveling, or funneling, to increase the mouth a full $1/16$ inch (1.59 millimeter) on all sides. This makes it much easier to get the replacement magazine started into the butt in times of stress. The bevels should be filed at approximately 45-degree angles. They should flow smoothly together at the corners. All burrs should be removed, and the inner and outer edges of the bevels can be improved slightly rounding them off. Once the shape has been established, with abrasive cloth around a stick or piece of metal, polish the filed areas perfectly smooth.

Most autoloaders possess a number of protrusions and sharp edges that can snag on flesh or clothing and interfere with getting into action quickly. Almost any corner or edge of a gun is capable of causing this problem if it is sharp or burred, and some guns are shaped and finished in certain areas so that they can damage clothing in normal carrying. The sharply serrated hammer spur on the Smith & Wesson Model 39 is one example. This problem can be solved by rounding off the outer edges of the hammer and knocking the sharp tops off the serrations with a hand grinder. Any other sharp edge can be eliminated similarly, and many gun owners habitually bevel, or round off, all sharp corners on the entire rear portion of any big autoloader. It takes only a few moments to file a shallow, 45-degree bevel around the rear edge of the slide and bevel the sharp, bottom rear corners of the slide at the guide grooves. Upper, outer corners of rear sights can be beveled, too, as can sharp corners and edges on the butts. The job is quick and easy and requires only abrasive cloth and a small file. Once it is done, you will need a refinish job or some touch-up bluing.

For over sixty years, the grip safety of the Colt Government Model has been publicized as a great advantage, and perhaps it was in the days when individual soldiers with little mechanical knowledge had to be trained hurriedly in its use. Today, however, the grip safety is considered by many to be superfluous, considering the manner in which th big gun is used for personal defense and law enforcement. The Government Model must be carried in the locked-and-cocked position to be prepared for immediate action. Under these conditions, the grip safety is not necessary and can even be a hazard if the user must grab the gun and fire hurriedly from an unconventional position. The simplest way to avoid this is to block the safety in the disengaged position. The simplest, quickest, and cheapest method of blocking the safety is to wrap friction tape around the butt to hold the safety down at all times. A neater method is to remove the grips, depress the grip safety with tape, and drill a $\frac{1}{16}$-inch (1.59-millimeter) hole through both frame and safety at a point where it will not interfere with the functioning of any other parts. The outer edge of the hole in the frame is then opened up a bit with a countersink, and a short pin with a countersunk head to match is made from a screw or nail and cut just long enough to reach through the frame and one side of the grip safety. The pin is then put in place, the tape removed, and the grips reinstalled. The grip prevents the pin from coming out, and the head on the pin prevents it from moving inward to interfere with other functioning. In this fashion, the grip safety is permanently locked out of action. Removing the pin restores all of its original functions if for some reason that should be desired.

You can probably think of other minor modifications to a particular gun that can be accomplished with hand tools, and there are certainly many not mentioned here. The suggestions made in this chapter are restricted to those modifications that have proven practical to the working handgunner. Many other simple alterations you can make may be more cosmetic than functional, but anything you do that will improve the handling, reliability, or accuracy of the gun with which you defend your life is certainly worthwhile.

For additional information, read George C. Nonte, Jr.'s *Pistolsmithing*. (Harrisburg, PA: Stackpole Books, 1974). See also the discussion of accessories in chapter 11.

8

Combat Handgun Ammunition: Good and Bad

A FIREARM, WHATEVER the type, is merely a vehicle by which the projectile is aimed and launched. The desired result on the target is produced by the projectile, not the gun. Of course, the projectile owes some of its performance characteristics (accuracy and velocity, for example) to the gun, but, in the main, the projectile does the work. Ammunition is as important to combat shooting as the weapon. In fact, the ammunition should be chosen for the effect desired, and the gun choice determined by the ammunition.

This chapter was written from notes, tapes, and numerous interviews with Lee E. Jurras. Jurras is widely recognized for his development of Super Vel ammunition, which set the standard now followed by all manufacturers of high-performance handgun ammunition. In fact, almost all contemporary, American, high-performance, handgun ammunition is the result of development work conducted by Jurras in the 1950s and 1960s.

Traditionally, autoloading pistols have been designed to

utilize cartridges loaded with metal-jacketed bullets of a round-nose configuration. These are bullets composed of a lead core around which is wrapped a moderately thick envelope of soft metal, usually an alloy of copper called gilding metal. This envelope is open at the base of the bullet, exposing the lead core. It usually wraps unbroken around the point, or nose.

The reason for this type of bullet design and construction is often misunderstood. The widely held belief that this so-called hard-ball bullet design was due to terms of the Hague Convention of 1907 is not true. The Hague Convention, which the United States signed, prohibited the use of "dum-dum" (soft-nosed, expanding) bullets for military small arms use, but the basic design of autoloading-pistol ammunition had been developed and more or less standardized a full decade before the delegates in Hague considered the humanitarian aspects of military ammunition. The state of the technology at the time the one-hand autoloading firearm was becoming a reality actually determined why autoloader ammunition developed the way it did.

In the late 1880s, the revolver—more often than not in single-action form—reigned supreme among handguns. A particular type of cartridge had evolved for use with the revolving, repeating-pistol mechanism. It had a straight-sided, cylindrical case bearing a substantial flange, or rim, around the perimeter of its head, or base. This ensured that the cartridge was in the correct position for proper ignition of the primer by the firing pin and provided a surface against which an extractor could act to remove fired cases from the chambers. In addition, the revolver cartridge was loaded with a blunt, cone-shaped bullet, which was cast (swaged) from a very soft, lead alloy and coated with lubricant to ease its passage through the barrel and prevent adherence of lead particles from the bullet to the bore surface. In revolvers, this type of cartridge performed admirably, even when loaded with black powder. Consequently, early designers of self-loading pistols utilized the same kind of cartridge.

Hopeful automatic-pistol designers encountered three serious problems in making mechanisms that would handle

Obsolete military revolver cartridges. Left to right: *9mm Danish Army Revolver, 10.6mm German Ordnance Revolver, 11mm French Ordnance Revolver, and 10.4mm Italian Ordnance Revolver.*

the rimmed, lead-bullet, black-powder cartridge. The large, cartridge-case rims interfered seriously with both loading and feeding from almost any type of magazine, and the rim made the pistol unnecessarily wide. The excessive amount of fouling generated by black powder (over 55 percent of the powder is converted to solid residue during combustion) hopelessly clogged autoloading mechanisms after the firing of relatively few rounds. And the successful operation of an autoloading mechanism required that the cartridge be stripped from the magazine and deflected by feed surfaces into the chamber with great speed and force, deforming the soft lead bullets in the process; reliable feeding was virtually impossible.

To solve the case-rim difficulty, the rim at the rear of the case was removed to allow cartridges to stack smoothly in a magazine. These rimless cartridges took less space and fed more smoothly from the magazine. In removing the rim, it was necessary to provide a seat for the extractor. An angular groove was cut around the perimeter of the case head. Some early automatic-pistol designers attempted to simplify this pattern even further by eliminating the extractor, depending solely on case projection to remove fired cases from the gun.

With the rim removed, however, there was no surface on the cartridges to form a reliable stop to control the depth to which it could enter the chamber. This was solved in two different ways. One way required eliminating the crimping of the case mouth upon the bullet, which is employed in the assembly of revolver cartridges. In this method, the bullet made a very tight fit in the case mouth, and the mouth was left uncrimped, forming a square shoulder that could seat a corresponding shoulder at the front of the chamber and properly control the depth to which the cartridge entered the chamber. The second method of controlling depth required leaving a very slight flange protruding at the rear of the case and beveling that flange. The accompanying extractor groove was also shaped so that there would be no interference with smooth feeding. With this system, the very slight rim produced arrested cartridge entrance into the chamber and allowed the case mouth to be crimped upon the bullet. This latter type of case design is referred to as semirimmed, found today in .38 ACP, .25 ACP, and .32 ACP cartridges. It was also utilized from time to time in other cartridges, now obsolete. The rimless case is found in all other modern, centerfire, autoloading-pistol cartridges. A few calibers used slightly bottle-necked cases, but the majority were more or less cylindrical with just enough taper to ease extraction.

Smokeless powder became available at the end of the nineteenth century, and it was immediately substituted for the black powder used in earlier experimental models. Smokeless powder proved to be a much more suitable propellant for autoloading-pistol cartridges. It eliminated the residue problem almost completely (thousands of rounds could be fired without any malfunctions from powder residue), but its greater energy allowed the use of smaller amounts of powder. Thus, smaller cartridge cases could be designed. Autoloading-pistol cartridges of any given bullet diameter could be

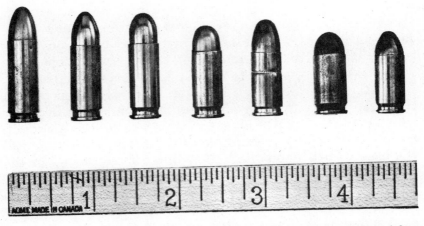

A sample of 9mm pistol cartridges. From left to right: *9mm Mauser (9 x 25mm); 9mm Largo (9 x 23mm), also called 9mm Bayard and 9mm Steyr; .38 ACP "Super Automatic" (9 x 23SR mm); 9mm Browning Long (9 x 20SR mm); 9mm Parabellum (9 x 19mm); 9mm Makarov (9 x 18mm); .380 ACP (9 x 17mm), also called 9mm Browning Short, 9mm Kurz, and 9mm Corto.* (Courtesy Jack Krcma)

half the length of existing black-powder-revolver cartridges of comparable performance.

Solving two of the basic problems left only the feeding difficulties produced by lead bullets. The solution was obvious: enclose the lead bullet in an envelope of harder metal that possessed sufficient strength to prevent deforming by the impacts experienced during feeding and chambering. Jackets were made of various materials—pure copper, brass, copper-nickel alloys, soft steel, and many other variations. Eventually it was determined that the copper-zinc alloy known as gilding metal provided the best combination of low cost, adequate strength, and ease of manufacture. It remains so today.

As the autoloading-pistol cartridge developed, assorted bullet shapes were tried. It was quickly discovered that the round-nose bullet worked best. This form became standard, though the truncated-cone developed for the Parabellum series of pistols enjoyed popularity for several years. The truncated-cone bullet was used only in ammunition for Parabellum pistols and very briefly for the Italian Glisenti. It dis-

Left to right: *Semi-wadcutter Keith-style, round-nose, and wadcutter bullets. For nearly 70 years, this was the primary range of pistol and revolver projectiles. The primary automatic projectile was similar to the round-nose lead bullet as shown above, but a gilding metal envelope covered the nose.* (Courtesy Lee Jurras)

appeared from the scene in the 1930s and did not reappear in autoloader ammunition until the 1960s.

By 1900, the autoloading-pistol cartridge had taken the basic form it would have eighty years later. For combat use this round-nose, metal-jacketed bullet is not the most efficient type. It produces less tissue damage than soft-lead bullets or modern, expanding types. The jacketed bullet driven at maximum velocities practical in conventional handguns will not deform in tissue, although it will sometimes flatten slightly or tumble if it strikes a major bone. Generally speaking, it punches a relatively clean, neat hole of its own diameter through the target. Its wounding power depends on striking a vital organ, nerve center, or an important bone structure. When the jacketed bullet fails to strike a critical point, it can still produce painful injuries (and may even produce eventual death), but in most instances it will not instantly immobilize or incapacitate the target. Bullet diameter, weight, and velocity affect the amount of damage a bullet will do to a target when it strikes a nonvital area. Certainly, a .45 caliber bullet will displace more tissue and produce more damage than one of .25 caliber. Likewise, a bullet traveling at a very low velocity may not penetrate very far, while one of higher velocity will pass completely through the target.

Designers, recognizing the inherent inefficiency of the

jacketed bullet, have attempted to improve handgun ammunition by increasing bullet diameter and velocity. Unfortunately, the practical limitations of manageable handguns have precluded the achievement of any great increase in lethality. Insofar as bullet diameter is concerned, the practical maximum seems to be .45 caliber. Certainly a larger bullet could be produced, but it would require a larger, heavier, impractical pistol. Such a cartridge would also produce excessive recoil. Increasing velocity increases lethality with jacketed bullets, but only to a point. As velocity increases, other factors being equal, chamber pressure and recoil energy also increase. The practical maximum is represented by the 7.63mm (.30 caliber) Mauser-pistol cartridge with its 86-grain (5.6-gram) bullet at approximately 1410 feet per second (430 meters per second). At this velocity, the .30 caliber bullet produces 375 foot-pounds of kinetic energy,* as compared with the 369 foot-pounds of the .45 ACP. It possesses much greater penetration than the .45 bullet, but it does not do more damage to the target except under certain unusual circumstances. A high-velocity bullet striking a major bone is more likely to deform or tumble than a lower-velocity bullet of similar construction. Likewise, the higher the velocity of the bullet, the greater velocity it will transfer to tissue or bone fragments it displaces as it passes through the target.

In tests conducted by Colonel Louis A. LaGarde and Colonel John T. Thompson for the U.S. Army in 1904 on human cadavers and live animals, it was clearly demonstrated that the 7.63mm Mauser bullet produced more extensive damage than the .45 ACP bullet when major bones were struck.** Likewise, it produced more extensive damage when cranial cavities were struck. In both cases, the increased damage was due to the higher velocity given to material displaced by the higher-velocity projectile. The results of those tests can be misleading, however. Any bullet passing through the center of the cranial cavity is absolutely certain to incapacitate and

---

*The metric unit for foot-pounds of kinetic energy is the Joule. To convert foot-pounds of kinetic energy to Joules, multiply by 1.3558179. Therefore, 375 foot-pounds of energy equals 508.4 Joules.

**For a complete discussion, see Julian S. Hatcher, *Textbook of Pistols and Revolvers* (Small-Arms Technical Publishing Company: Plantersville, South Carolina, 1935), chapter 12, pp. 401–435.

will most likely be instantly fatal. It is only of academic interest that the larger, slower projectile does not produce the massive, skull-facture pattern expected from the smaller projectile. Likewise, the fracturing of a long bone in the leg or arm will generally produce immediate incapacitation of that limb, regardless of whether the fracture is simple or compound. A similar comparison may be made of spinal-area hits.

The late General Julian Hatcher illustrated many years ago that the shape of the bullet alone had some affect on its ability to produce damage to a target. He assigned form factors to different bullet profiles, the maximum factor being applied to a flat-ended cylinder (wadcutter) and the minimum to the conventional round-nose form. A truncated-cone form is slightly superior to the round-nose, and a semi-wadcutter, or Keith-style bullet, carries a higher form factor than the truncated-cone.

The variation in lethality is due to the fact that any medium (air, water, or animal tissue) offers the least resistance to the passage of a round-nose projectile. A flat-nose cylinder meets the greatest resistance. As resistance increases, more of the speeding projectile's energy is absorbed by the medium as it penetrates; penetration depth and speed are consequently decreased. If the projectile possesses sufficient velocity and energy to completely penetrate the target or medium, then a wadcutter will transfer more of its energy to the target and exit the target at a lower velocity than will the round nose. Of course, if the projectile is not capable of completely penetrating the target, it will transfer all of its energy to that target, regardless of its shape. The jacketed, round-nose, handgun bullet possesses the greatest penetration of all types, but if the bullet penetrates the target completely it will not transfer all of its energy to the target. Such a bullet would have maximum lethality only if it traversed the full depth of the target and came to a halt at the edge of the target opposite the point of entry. This would be possible only if the target always offered exactly the same resistance.

The amount of lethality increase that can be obtained by varying the profile of a jacketed bullet is clearly limited. But several variations of the reliable round-nose form (the least lethal) have been produced successfully. However, this ammunition has been designed primarily for competitive target shooting, not combat use. Both Colt and Smith & Wesson manufacture a .38 Special caliber, and Colt makes a .45 caliber handgun for this special ammunition. They are extensive modifications of basic military- and police-handgun designs originally developed around jacketed, round-nose bullets. The conditions under which these guns are used are outlined in the rules of the National Rifle Association, which specifically makes allowance for malfunctions. The competitive shooter can, therefore, accept limited reliability without penalty—the target does not shoot back.

It is not necessary to use round-nose bullets—the most reliable, but the least lethal—to obtain 100 percent reliability. If one is willing to spend time, effort, and money, standard-production handguns can be modified to produce combat-level reliability with a wide variety of other bullet forms. This tuning process is covered in chapter 10. However, some additional steps can be taken to increase lethality.

For many years, serious handgunners have handloaded their own cartridges, even to the extent of swaging their own expanding bullets to increase performance. A number of individuals have specialized in custom handloading for those who do not have the time or facilities to load their own ammunition. Handloading became very popular in the U.S. during World War II, when ammunition for the nonmilitary consumer became difficult to find. Since it was necessary to load their own ammunition, many handgunners also took steps to improve the performance of their ammunition over the standard factory product. Consult chapter 9 for more information on handloading.

High-performance ammunition for autoloading pistols is available under a wide variety of names today in all calibers above .32 (7.65mm). True, factory-produced, high-performance, autoloading ammunition has been available since the early 1960s, when Lee Jurras, president and founder of Super Vel Cartridge Corporation, offered his first cartridges for autoloaders. Super Vel's first high-performance cartridge was the standard 9mm Parabellum case loaded with a 90-

grain (5.8-gram), jacketed, hollow-point bullet of truncated-cone form driven at 1475 feet per second (450 meters per second). This very high velocity was obtained by reducing the bullet weight (usually 112–125 grains [7.3–8.1 grams] in this caliber) and using a bullet about 0.002 inch (.05 millimeter) less in diameter than the nominal 9mm-barrel-groove diameter. Jurras found that these two elements were essential in producing maximum velocity at acceptable pressures. The .38 Special and .357 Magnum revolver cartridges and .380 ACP, .38 Colt Super Auto, and .45 ACP cartridges were subsequently added to Super Vel's line.

Velocity alone, however, does not necessarily produce any substantial increase in lethality. Jurras designed his jacketed, hollow-point bullet—designated the JHP—to produce massive expansion in animal tissue at practical, handgun velocities. The design was optimized so that it would expand at any velocity above 1000 feet per second (305 meters per second), but not disintegrate until it reached 1600 feet per second (488 meters per second).

The Super Vel 9mm was not the first expanding bullet to be offered in autoloading-pistol calibers. Nearly thirty years earlier both European and American manufacturers made .38 ACP and 9mm Parabellum loads with hollow-point and soft-point jacketed bullets. But those bullets were the standard weight for the caliber involved and were of the same basic design and construction as contemporary, rifle-caliber bullets. While they looked as if they would expand in animal tissue, in fact they would not normally do so. The early designers utilized jackets much too thick, cores too hard, and improper point design to allow reliable expansion at velocities realistic for handguns. Since recent studies* demonstrate that conventional, hollow-point, magnum cartridges generally do not produce significantly greater damage than standard-velocity, handgun ammunition, the introduction of the 9mm Parabellum Super Vel 90-grain (5.8-gram) JHP in 1968 marked the first significant step forward in autoloading-pistol ammu-

---

*The inadequacy of existing hollow-point ammunition is discussed in New York (State), Division of Criminal Justice Services, *A Special Report to the Governor of the State of New York, Hon. Hugh L. Carey, Police Handguns and Deadly Force* (State of New York, 1976), pages 73–78. See Appendix C.

Cross section of Super Vel 90-grain (5.8-gram) JHP. Note size of hollow-point cavity in relation to overall projectile size. (Courtesy Lee Jurras)

nition since the adoption of the rimless case and full-jacketed bullet in the early 1890s.

During the early 1960s, Lee Jurras experimented with many different projectile weights and shapes before he settled on the 90-grain (5.8-gram), jacketed, hollow-point bullet. He obtained abnormally high velocity using unusually light bullets (by contemporary standards) of substandard diameter. This provided the velocity necessary to obtain high kinetic energy from the projectile without exceeding acceptable chamber pressures. (These standards were established by the Sporting Arms and Ammunition Manufacturers' Institute [SAMMI].) Whereas standard, hard-ball, 9mm ammunition loaded in the U.S. produces about 345 foot-pounds of energy with a 125-grain (8.1-gram) bullet at a chamber pressure of 33,000 pounds per square inch, the Super Vel projectile produced 445 foot-pounds of energy with a much lighter bullet at the same or less chamber pressure. Jurras thus produced greater energy and obtained a slightly better form factor with the truncated-cone bullet. These two factors produced a modest increase in lethality over existing, standard, hard-ball ammunition, but Jurras realized that no significant improvement in lethality could be obtained by these two elements alone.

To produce maximum lethality, this bullet design incorporated a very thin, soft jacket; a dead-soft, pure lead core; and a nose cavity (hollow-point) that was very large by contemporary standards for hollow-point ammunition. Where previous hollow-point designs had contained simple cavities measuring barely 0.0312 inch (.792 millimeters) deep by 0.0624 inch (1.58 millimeters) in diameter, the Jurras design had a conical cavity measuring 0.125 inch (3.18 millimeters) deep and 0.185 inch (4.7 millimeters) in diameter at the front. To ensure against bullet deformation produced by feeding impacts upon feed ramp and chamber mouth—the most troublesome aspects of previous lead-bullet loads—Jurras carried the jacket forward to the mouth of the point cavity, rolling it over the lip of the cavity slightly so that when viewed in profile no lead was visible. Regardless of how the bullet impacted the barrel-feed surfaces, only the copper-alloy jacket could strike those surfaces. The jacket was made as thin as possible while still maintaining sufficient strength to resist any feeding deformation. In many guns, the jacket is very slightly deformed at the mouth of the cavity during feeding, but the amount is insufficient to affect feeding reliability.

The result of Jurras's work was a bullet design that could be considered quite fragile by previous standards, but one that would produce consistent and significant expansion in animal tissue at any velocity in excess of 1000 feet per second (305 meters per second). Considering that the factory Super Vel load propelled this bullet at 1475 feet per second (450 meters per second), it should reliably produce massive expansion (nearly explosive in animal tissue) at normal combat ranges (under 20 feet [6 meters]) and adequate expansion at ranges beyond 50–75 yards (45–70 meters).

Since animal tissue is essentially fluid interspersed with denser materials (muscle, tendon, bone, etc.), the cavity in the bullet nose causes expansion as soon as the projectile enters the target. This is a significant factor in increased lethality, essential if maximum bullet energy is to be transferred to the target. When expansion begins immediately upon target entry, the nose of the bullet mushrooms and folds back over the body, doubling or even tripling the cross-sectional area of the projectile. The resistance of the target to penetration by the bullet is proportional to the cube of the cross-sectional area of the projectile. So as expansion progresses, the bullet is slowed very rapidly by the target medium. The result is a very drastic limiting of penetration. Without expansion, this 90-grain (5.8-gram), 9mm bullet at 1475 feet per second (450 meters per second) would penetrate very deeply, but expansion reduces this penetration to a few inches. Postmortem reports indicate clearly that when this bullet makes a solid hit anywhere on the torso of a human target, it seldom exits. The result is that 100 percent of the 435 foot-pounds of kinetic energy possessed by the bullet is transferred to the target; less than 50 percent of the average 345 foot-pounds possessed by hard-ball 9mm bullets is transferred. This latter type of projectile usually maintains most of its velocity and energy after it exits the target. By limiting penetration through massive expansion of the projectile, lethality is vastly increased.

Increased energy transfer is not the only, or even the most significant, result of bullet expansion. The great increase in the cross-sectional area brought about by rapid expansion produces an equal increase in tissue displacement as the bullet penetrates through flesh. Increased tissue displacement means greater physical damage, greater neural shock, and a greater number of high-velocity secondary missiles (fragments of muscle, bone, and bullet material). The net result is a more massive wound and greater physical damage to the target, accompanied by greater hemorrhage. The greater damage-capability of Super Vel ammunition can be seen by comparing the volumes of wound cavities produced in an artificial test medium that represents animal tissue. These comparisons are conducted by firing projectiles into blocks of Dux Seal (see photograph). Test results consistently indicate that the 90-grain (5.8-gram) JHP load produces a larger cavity volume than a standard, hard-ball projectile of the same caliber (consult photographs at the end of this chapter).

Lee Jurras also applied these same principles of design to produce a jacketed, soft-point, 9mm bullet weighing 112 grains (7.28 grams) called the JSP. This bullet had the same truncated-cone profile as the JHP, but it had a slightly longer

A 10-inch by 10-inch (254-millimeter by 254-millimeter) Dux Seal block is used as a medium for comparison bullet expansion tests. Dux Seal, a Johns Manville plumbing insulation product, is similar to human tissue in consistency and is firm enough to produce expansion in projectiles that are capable of expansion. The cavity formed by the projectile is filled with water, and the water is weighed. The cavity is then filled with plaster of paris and allowed to set. The volume of the cavity is determined by immersing the cavity cast in fluid in a graduated container. These tests show expansion characteristics only. (Courtesy Lee Jurras)

jacket and no nose cavity. The JSP design expanded less rapidly and, because of its greater weight, could not be propelled to the same high velocities as the JHP. Velocity for the JSP was 1245 feet per second (379 meters per second). Compared with the 90-grain (5.8-gram) JHP load, the JSP had slightly less expansion but increased penetration. The 112-grain (7.28-gram) bullet produced a slightly longer, deeper wound cavity of slightly less diameter with approximately the same volume as wounds inflicted by the JHP. The two bullets have equal lethality in targets under 200 pounds (91 kilograms).

The 112-grain (7.28-gram) JSP bullet was designed to answer charges by some laymen and professionals that hollow-point bullets (particularly those with large nose cavities) are more inhumane than soft-point types. Former District of Columbia Police Chief Maurice L. Cullinane in a hearing before the City Council Judiciary Committee in April 1977 noted that hollow-point ammunition should be more acceptable for police use than other projectile types because there are fewer secondary injuries to bystanders from projectiles that have left their primary target. Cullinane sharply rebuked those who urged the use of bullets that would inflict less serious wounds. He told the Judiciary Committee: "I don't know what a 'humane' bullet is. A bullet is meant to kill you. That's what it's designed for. Clearly, that's what we purchase it for."

Cullinane noted that the Washington, D.C., Metropolitan Police Department has some of the most stringent regulations in the U.S. concerning the use of handguns. An officer's weapon can only be used in extreme circumstances, "but once you've unholstered it, then the rules are that you're shooting to kill." During the four-month period during which hollow-point bullets had been in use in Washington (January–April 1977), four people had been wounded with them, and all four had recovered from their wounds. The hollow-point bullet will continue to be a subject of political debate, but there is no question that it is the most effective police cartridge for close-range lethality and long-range safety.

Since the advent of Super Vel ammunition, every domestic producer of centerfire-handgun ammunition has introduced his own high-performance, improved-lethality cartridges. In some instances, these loadings have been simply copies of Super Vel bullet designs; in other cases, designs differ substantially. Most provide reliable bullet expansion and improved lethality. However, it may generally be said that the level of performance achieved by these more recent producers falls at least slightly below that of the original Super Vel loadings. In the mid-1960s, Lee Jurras closed the Super Vel factory, no longer able to compete with the larger ammunition manufacturers from whom he had to purchase cartridge cases. Still, he made an important contribution to the field. He demonstrated that a more lethal automatic-pistol cartridge was feasible.

Some discussion should also be given in this chapter to other cartridges currently in use. Three smaller calibers of interest are the .22 rimfire, .25 ACP (6.35mm Browning), and .32 ACP (7.65mm Browning). The .22 rimfire dates back to 1855. At its very best, it possesses very low energy and penetration values, and its lethality is almost nonexistent, except when a vital organ or nerve center is struck. It will not in most instances even fracture a major bone. Instead, it simply drills a neat hole or imbeds itself in the bone. Many cases have been recounted where an individual has been struck one or more times by a .22 rimfire bullet and was not incapacitated in the least; .22 caliber projectiles occasionally kill, but they are obviously not suitable for the combat handgun.

The .25 and .32 ACP calibers are probably the most widely distributed autoloading-pistol cartridges in the world. Yet they are the least developed and have undergone virtually no improvement since their original introduction at the turn of the century. Worldwide, both are loaded to very low standard velocities and energy values in a single weight of jacketed, round-nose bullets. They generally have considerable penetration and low lethality. Their strongly jacketed bullets seldom deform, even when striking major bones. When they stop inside the target and transfer all their energy to it, they are still relatively ineffective unless a vital organ or nerve center is struck. This is not to say that .25 and .32 ACP ammunition is not lethal—it is, in the same manner as is the .22 rimfire. But again, these smaller calibers are not suitable in the combat situation unless it has been handloaded in a highly specialized manner to improve its lethality.

A relatively new cartridge, the 9 x 18mm, has recently been considered suitable by some European police forces. European manufacturers designate this round 9mm Ultra or 9mm Police. It is generally the same as the 9mm Ultra cartridge developed for the German Luftwaffe during World War II and the 9 x 18mm Makarov cartridge used by the Soviet

Armed Forces. In terms of power and lethality, the 9mm
Ultra/Police ranks midway between the .380 ACP (9 x 17mm)
and the 9mm Parabellum (9 x 19mm). As the manufacturers
of the SIG P230 pistol have indicated, the 9mm Ultra cartridge case permitted them to develop more lethal loads than
were possible with the .380 ACP (9 x 17mm) case, while keeping the size of the handgun smaller than that required by the
9mm Parabellum (9 x 19mm). SIG engineers also wanted to
avoid a locked-breech mechanism. Recoil-operated (blowback)
handguns are cheaper and less difficult to manufacture.

Typical Factory Loadings

Caliber	Projectile Weight	Velocity in feet per second (meters per second)
.32 ACP (7.65 x 17mm)	71 grains (4.6 grams)	960 fps (292 mps)
.380 ACP (9 x 17mm)	95 grains (6.15 grams)	955 fps (291 mps)
9mm Ultra (9 x 18mm)	94 grains (6.1 grams)	1100 fps (335 mps)
9mm Makarov (9 x 18mm)	106 grains (6.9 grams)	1100 fps (335 mps)
9mm Parabellum (9 x 19mm)	115 grains (7.5 grams)	1150 fps (350 mps)

The 9mm Ultra/Police has only a limited improvement in
lethality over the old .380 ACP (9 x 17mm or .380 Browning),
a cartridge class with limited lethality unless specially loaded.
Current 9mm Ultra ammunition does not possess the kinetic
energy of standard, factory 9mm Parabellum and falls far
short of the lethality of Super Vel-type ammunition. The European 9mm cartridge also has none of the loading flexibility of
the 9mm Parabellum. Although, it represents one approach
to the perceived needs and requirements of some European
police forces, American police, would still be well advised to
use the 9mm Parabellum cartridge, specifically one patterned
after Jurras JHP ammunition.

Several articles and books provide additional information
on ammunition. *The American Rifleman* offers two excellent
articles by James P. Cowgill: "In Search of the Perfect Parabellum" (August 1978) and "The Newest Look at Handgun
Ballistics" (October 1975). You may also wish to consult *Defensive Handgun Effectiveness: A Systematic Approach to
the Design, Evaluation and Selection of Ammunition for the
Defense Handgun* by Carroll E. Peters (Manchester, Tennes-

see, 1977) and Stockholm International Peace Research Institute's *Anti-personnel Weapons* (Taylor & Francis, Ltd.: London, 1978). An excellent article on "Bullet Effect and Shock Power" is available in Julian S. Hatcher's *Textbook of Pistols and Revolvers* (Small-Arms Technical Publishing Company: Plantersville, SC, 1935).

The following photographs were taken on a ½-inch (12.7-millimeter) grid and show depth of penetration, general cavity size, bullet expansion, and maximum cavity diameter. Note cavity changes that result from increased velocity obtained from longer barrels.

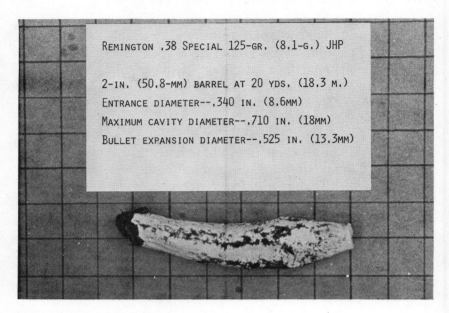

REMINGTON .38 SPECIAL 125-GR. (8.1-G.) JHP

2-IN. (50.8-MM) BARREL AT 20 YDS. (18.3 M.)
ENTRANCE DIAMETER--.340 IN. (8.6MM)
MAXIMUM CAVITY DIAMETER--.710 IN. (18MM)
BULLET EXPANSION DIAMETER--.525 IN. (13.3MM)

(Courtesy Lee Jurras)

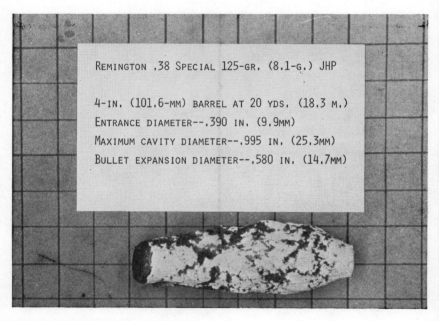

REMINGTON .38 SPECIAL 125-GR. (8.1-G.) JHP

4-IN. (101.6-MM) BARREL AT 20 YDS. (18.3 M.)
ENTRANCE DIAMETER--.390 IN. (9.9MM)
MAXIMUM CAVITY DIAMETER--.995 IN. (25.3MM)
BULLET EXPANSION DIAMETER--.580 IN. (14.7MM)

(Courtesy Lee Jurras)

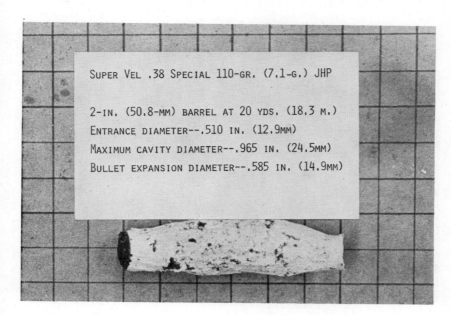

SUPER VEL .38 SPECIAL 110-GR. (7.1-G.) JHP

2-IN. (50.8-MM) BARREL AT 20 YDS. (18.3 M.)
ENTRANCE DIAMETER--.510 IN. (12.9MM)
MAXIMUM CAVITY DIAMETER--.965 IN. (24.5MM)
BULLET EXPANSION DIAMETER--.585 IN. (14.9MM)

(Courtesy Lee Jurras)

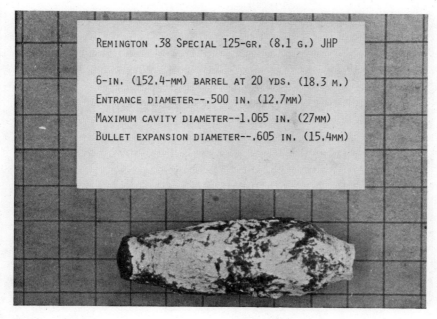

REMINGTON .38 SPECIAL 125-GR. (8.1 G.) JHP

6-IN. (152.4-MM) BARREL AT 20 YDS. (18.3 M.)
ENTRANCE DIAMETER--.500 IN. (12.7MM)
MAXIMUM CAVITY DIAMETER--1.065 IN. (27MM)
BULLET EXPANSION DIAMETER--.605 IN. (15.4MM)

(Courtesy Lee Jurras)

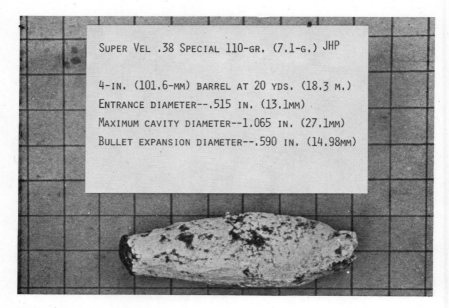

SUPER VEL .38 SPECIAL 110-GR. (7.1-G.) JHP

4-IN. (101.6-MM) BARREL AT 20 YDS. (18.3 M.)
ENTRANCE DIAMETER--.515 IN. (13.1MM)
MAXIMUM CAVITY DIAMETER--1.065 IN. (27.1MM)
BULLET EXPANSION DIAMETER--.590 IN. (14.98MM)

(Courtesy Lee Jurras)

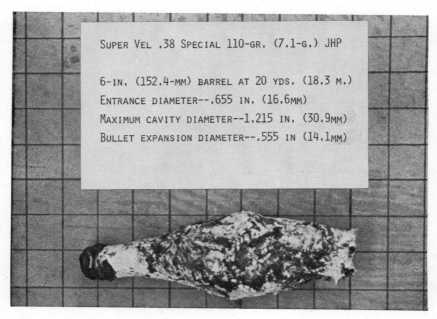

SUPER VEL .38 SPECIAL 110-GR. (7.1-G.) JHP

6-IN. (152.4-MM) BARREL AT 20 YDS. (18.3 M.)
ENTRANCE DIAMETER--.655 IN. (16.6MM)
MAXIMUM CAVITY DIAMETER--1.215 IN. (30.9MM)
BULLET EXPANSION DIAMETER--.555 IN (14.1MM)

(Courtesy Lee Jurras)

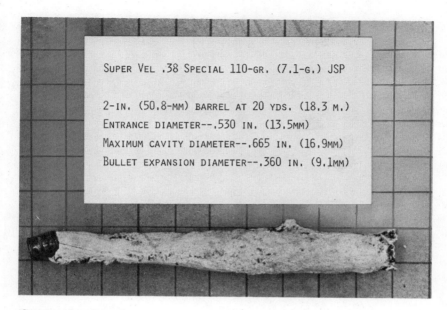

SUPER VEL .38 SPECIAL 110-GR. (7.1-G.) JSP

2-IN. (50.8-MM) BARREL AT 20 YDS. (18.3 M.)
ENTRANCE DIAMETER--.530 IN. (13.5MM)
MAXIMUM CAVITY DIAMETER--.665 IN. (16.9MM)
BULLET EXPANSION DIAMETER--.360 IN. (9.1MM)

(Courtesy Lee Jurras)

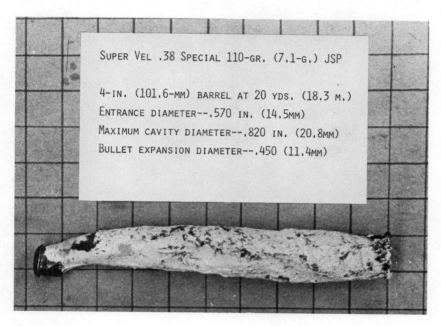

SUPER VEL .38 SPECIAL 110-GR. (7.1-G.) JSP

4-IN. (101.6-MM) BARREL AT 20 YDS. (18.3 M.)
ENTRANCE DIAMETER--.570 IN. (14.5MM)
MAXIMUM CAVITY DIAMETER--.820 IN. (20.8MM)
BULLET EXPANSION DIAMETER--.450 (11.4MM)

(Courtesy Lee Jurras)

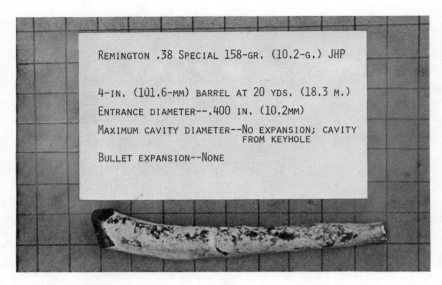

REMINGTON .38 SPECIAL 158-GR. (10.2-G.) JHP

4-IN. (101.6-MM) BARREL AT 20 YDS. (18.3 M.)

ENTRANCE DIAMETER--.400 IN. (10.2MM)

MAXIMUM CAVITY DIAMETER--NO EXPANSION; CAVITY
                               FROM KEYHOLE

BULLET EXPANSION--NONE

(Courtesy Lee Jurras)

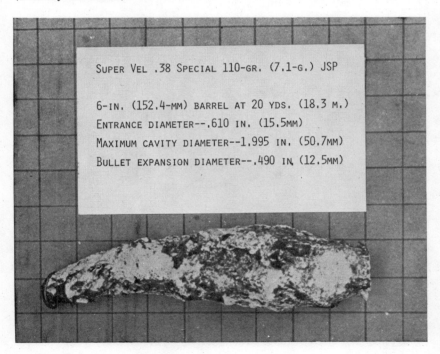

SUPER VEL .38 SPECIAL 110-GR. (7.1-G.) JSP

6-IN. (152.4-MM) BARREL AT 20 YDS. (18.3 M.)

ENTRANCE DIAMETER--.610 IN. (15.5MM)

MAXIMUM CAVITY DIAMETER--1.995 IN. (50.7MM)

BULLET EXPANSION DIAMETER--.490 IN. (12.5MM)

(Courtesy Lee Jurras)

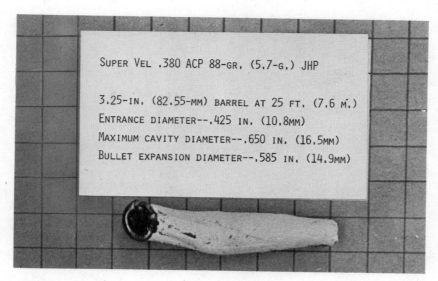

SUPER VEL .380 ACP 88-GR. (5.7-G.) JHP

3.25-IN. (82.55-MM) BARREL AT 25 FT. (7.6 M.)
ENTRANCE DIAMETER--.425 IN. (10.8MM)
MAXIMUM CAVITY DIAMETER--.650 IN. (16.5MM)
BULLET EXPANSION DIAMETER--.585 IN. (14.9MM)

(Courtesy Lee Jurras)

SUPER VEL 9MM LUGER 90-GR. (5.8-G.) JHP

4-IN. (101.6-MM) BARREL AT 20 YDS. (18.3 M.)
ENTRANCE DIAMETER--1.010 IN. (25.7MM)
MAXIMUM CAVITY DIAMETER--1.830 IN. (46.5MM)
BULLET EXPANSION DIAMETER--.615 IN. (15.6MM)

(Courtesy Lee Jurras)

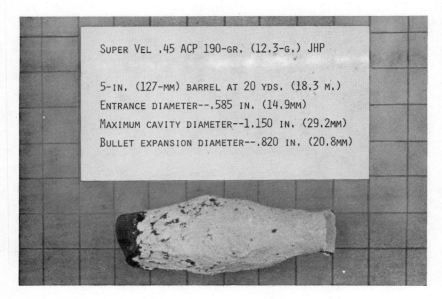

SUPER VEL .45 ACP 190-GR. (12.3-G.) JHP

5-IN. (127-MM) BARREL AT 20 YDS. (18.3 M.)
ENTRANCE DIAMETER--.585 IN. (14.9MM)
MAXIMUM CAVITY DIAMETER--1.150 IN. (29.2MM)
BULLET EXPANSION DIAMETER--.820 IN. (20.8MM)

(Courtesy Lee Jurras)

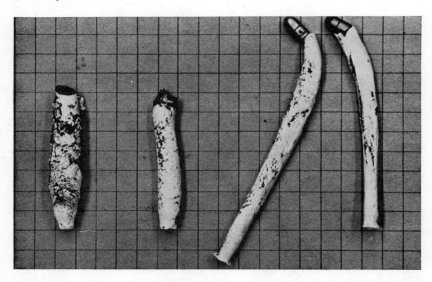

High-velocity hollow-point bullets compared to round-nose lead bullets. **Left to right:** *Speer .38 Special 140-gr. (9.1-g) JHP, 4-in. (101.6-mm) barrel at 20 yds. (18.3 m.); Speer .38 Special 140-gr. (9.1-g) JHP, 2-in. (50.8-mm) barrel from 20 yds. (18.3 m.); Remington .38 Special 158-gr. (10.2-g) round-nose lead, 4-in. (101.6-mm) barrel at 20 yds. (18.3 m); and Remington .38 Special 158-gr. (10.2-g) round-nose lead, 2-in. (50.8-mm) barrel from 20 yds. (18.3 m).*

9

Assembling Your Own Combat and Practice Loads

AMMUNITION MANUFACTURERS have devoted many decades and millions of dollars to the development of machines, materials, methods, and techniques that will produce reliable cartridges. Although factory-loaded handgun ammunition is substantially more reliable in function than typical handloads, the individual who handloads defense ammunition for his own use is by no means typical. This user has a thorough knowledge of loading techniques and ammunition functioning and pays meticulous attention to the selection and assembly of components and to the testing necessary to ensure that the desired results are achieved.

The primary purpose of handloaded, practice ammunition is to provide the shooter with a more economical means of achieving maximum weapon proficiency. It also automatically serves to increase his handloading proficiency. With a suitable amount of experience and study in loading practice ammunition, most serious shooters will develop the expertise necessary to produce reliable service ammunition. Ammunition for practice with a defensive arm should be loaded as nearly as possible to the same pressure, velocity, and recoil levels as the ammunition used for combat shooting. A practical duplication of the service load can be assembled with a cast-lead bullet of the same weight and shape and driven at the same velocity. Factors of chamber pressure, barrel time, and recoil impulse will not be precisely the same as for the service load, but they will be very close.

To load practice ammunition, begin with fired cases that are in perfect condition. Ideally they should be once-fired, but two or three times is suitable for cases to be used in an autoloader. If the ammunition is to be used in a revolver, even six firings will not present any problems as long as the cases show no evidence of damage and chamber freely after being resized full length. All autoloaders leave a small portion of the case head poorly supported where the feed ramp cuts into the chamber; the revolver chamber completely encloses the case up to the rim and sometimes the rim, as well. The result is that no significant bulges ever occur in revolver-fired cases, while autoloader-fired cases will bulge at least slightly into the unsupported area of the feedway and be weakened there. For this reason, cases for autoloaders should be very carefully inspected for any excessive feed-ramp bulge. A slight bulge is common; but when it amounts to more than about 0.01 inch (.25 millimeter), and its forward edges are sharply defined by the edge of the feed-ramp cut, the case should be discarded or used for light plinking loads.

Cases must also be inspected carefully for any other defects. Any of the following is more than adequate reason for discarding the cases: dents in the case mouth more than about 0.0625 inch (1.59 millimeter) deep; crushed case mouths; cracks or incipient cracks at the mouth; deep longitudinal scratches caused by sharp, magazine-feed lips or chamber-mouth burrs (such scratches can cause the case to split on firing); large dents in the case body or body dents containing creases or sharp edges; longitudinal cracks or splits near the head; circumferential cracks just forward of the head; deformed rims; leaking primers (indicated by sooty smudge around the primer); numerous longitudinal scratches and striations, which indicate previous reloading; or thick, greenish corrosion inside or out that has roughened the surface of the case. As cases are sorted for condition, they should be segregated by headstamp. This does not mean one make is better than another, but there will be differences in internal profile and volume, case-mouth hardness, and in other areas that will affect performance. A specific handgun may operate best and provide the greatest accuracy with a specific brand of cartridge case. If this is found to be true with your handgun, that type of case should always be used to get the best results.

The cases should be thoroughly cleaned. This is best accomplished by mechanically tumbling the cases in peanut hulls until the cases are shiny and bright outside. The insides of the cases should be scoured clean of propellant residue and mouth sealer, which is used by some factories in various loads to secure adequate bullet pull.

For a general guide to handloading procedures, refer to George C. Nonte's book *Modern Handloading* (Winchester Press: New York, 1972). The specifics of handloading combat-type ammunition are presented below.

Use a tungsten-carbide die, and verify that it will reduce the case sufficiently, so that after expanding the mouth it will still grip the bullet quite tightly. Most die makers can offer undersize dies if you have cases or bullets that make them necessary. Case lubrication is not necessary when carbide dies are used, but some handloaders prefer to use just a trace of lubricant. It eases the resizing effort slightly, and it results in a more nicely burnished finish on unplated cases. A resizing die that contains a decapping stem so that the fired primer is removed simultaneously with resizing is preferable. This does not result in a better decapping job than if done during expanding, but if you prefer to tumble the cases a second time after resizing and decapping it is more suitable. This second tumbling serves to remove all of the resizing lubricant and cleans the primer pockets. There is likely nothing to be gained by cleaning primer pockets in handgun calibers, but the result is that after resizing, decapping, and tumbling, the cases are thoroughly clean and bright inside and out, the primer pockets are clean, and there is absolutely no lubricant left to pose even the remotest possibility of primer or propellant contamination.

The next step is expanding and repriming the case. Since practice loads should be the full-charge variety, it will generate substantial recoil and be subject to heavy feeding impacts and loads. Therefore, use an undersize expander plug to obtain a very tight bullet and case assembly and to expand the mouth only to a depth slightly short of the position where the bullet base will come to rest. Thus, when the bullet is seated, the edge of its base beds itself solidly against a slight shoulder in the case. This serves no especially useful purpose in revolvers, but in autoloaders it can be essential for keeping the bullet in its proper position under feeding impacts. To accomplish this, order the expander plug to produce an inside case diameter approximately 0.004 inch (.1 millimeter) smaller than the diameter of the bullet. Generally speaking, standard-diameter expander plugs will be a bit oversize for this application, and it may be simpler to just polish one down in successively small increments until a properly tight bullet and case fit is obtained.

The expander rod must go deep enough into the case so that the conical portion of it enters the mouth slightly to produce just enough flare to allow a new bullet to enter without being shaved by the inner edge. Doing this will push the working diameter of the rod too deeply into the case, so after determining where the case shoulder must fall, alter the rod. Either cut the rod off at this point and round off the edges smoothly so that it will not scrape the brass, or polish or grind the excess rod down about 0.01 inch (.25 millimeter), leaving a shoulder on it at that point. Either operation presents a problem without power tools. If you have a hand grinder with a cutoff wheel, cutting the rod off is simple. Without such help, you will save time and frustration by taking it to a machine shop and having it done either way. Once the expander rod is properly altered, run all the cases through. Inspect each as you pluck it out of the shell holder to make sure that it has been flared sufficiently. The amount of flare will vary directly with the length of the case. Put simply, a short case will receive less flare than a longer case. If some cases are not sufficiently flared to permit a bullet to be hand-started, a simple, tapered punch can be employed to add a bit more flare so the cases can be loaded.

You can, of course, reprime the case with an on-press priming device in conjunction with the expanding operation. That method is entirely adequate, but due to the design of the priming device and the considerable amount of friction generated within the press linkage, you can not "feel" (seat) the primer into the pocket as well. A more uniform job of seating primers can be done on a bench-type priming tool as a separate operation. This will not slow down the loading process. A given number of cases can be primed more rapidly on a separate tool than on the press, but the expanding operation does require more time.

Regardless of the priming method employed, it is important to properly seat the primer. The primer should not be jammed so tightly against the bottom that the cup is deformed or the pellet is fractured, nor should there be space between the bottom of the pocket and the anvil legs. Either condition will produce ignition less consistent than when the anvil is seated solidly on the bottom of the pocket. Run your finger across each case head to make sure that the primers are seated flush or slightly below the surfaces of the case heads. Even though you think you have seated the primers solidly on the bottoms of the pockets, there is always the chance of a shallow pocket, debris in the pocket, or a primer with protruding anvil. Any of these defects can cause the primer to protrude even though it feels as if it is seated solidly. A protruding primer may cause erratic ignition by absorbing firing-pin energy as the pin drives it forward, or it may cause premature firing, known as slam firing. It also may interfere with free cylinder rotation in a revolver by binding upon the recoil shield.

With cases sized, expanded and flared, and primed, the serious work of assembling propellant and bullet is next. For the sake of economy, you will want to use a cast-lead bullet in your practice loads. This bullet should be the same shape and weight as the bullet of your service load, whether the latter be a handloaded or a factory product. Usually it is not possible to precisely duplicate the shape of the jacketed service bullet because molds to do so are not available; however, a bullet of approximately (plus or minus 5 grains [.324 grams]) the same weight as the service bullet and of approximately the same shape will do. The similar shape is necessary so that the loaded practice cartridge will feed essentially the same as the service round. A bullet of the same weight will be driven at the same velocity and thus produce essentially the same recoil impulse as with the service load.

The bullet should be of a plain, flat-base, or slightly beveled-base design, and it needs no more than one substantial lubricating groove. If used for a revolver, it will require a properly located crimping groove that will permit the case mouth to be crimped in the groove. Overall cartridge length will be approximately the same as that of the service round. For autoloaders, the bullet needs no crimping groove and should not contain one. Bullets should be cast of a relatively hard alloy. The best general-purpose alloy that is readily available and has been proven quite suitable is Linotype metal. You can use a slightly softer alloy in revolvers, but the harder alloy will feed best in an autoloader. If Linotype is not available, Lyman Alloy #2 will usually work well. A fairly economical source of new metal is hard shot for shot shells, usually containing up to 3 percent antimony. This will require the addition of about 5 percent tin to make bullets of the proper hardness. Ordinary scrap lead is usually too soft, though automobile-wheel weights work well in revolvers and reasonably well in autoloaders.

Only perfect bullets should be loaded, even in practice ammunition. Cast bullets should be inspected and culled before sizing and lubrication. These operations often cover defects that will interfere with accuracy. Bullets should be sized to barrel-groove diameter or not more than 0.0015 inch (.038 millimeter) greater. Bullets more than 0.0015 inch (.038 millimeter) over groove diameter do not group as well.

It is especially important that the lubricator-sizer be closely fitted and that the top punch (which forces the bullet into the die) be accurately aligned (concentric) with the die.

The cavity in its lower end should fit the nose of the bullet closely. If these conditions are not met, a percentage of your bullets will not be sized concentrically and will not deliver their full measure of accuracy. Any of the modern Alox-type bullet lubricants will work well, and it is important that the lubricating groove(s) be completely filled. It is also important that there be no excess lubricant on the bullet base where it might contaminate the propellant. If this does occur, clean the bases by wiping them across a solvent-moist cloth on a firm surface. Careful adjustment of the lubricator-sizer die and punches will keep lubricant off the base. If necessary, take the bottom punch to a machinist and have a shallow cavity cut in its upper end. This will allow the outer edge to seat tightly against the bullet base and prevent the intrusion of lubricant.

Selecting the proper propellant charge is not difficult; however, there are several things to keep in mind. A charge that would give a certain velocity to a 9mm, 90-grain (5.83-gram), jacketed, expanding, service bullet will not give the same velocity to a similarly shaped 90-grain (5.83-gram), cast-lead bullet. Even if the two types of bullets are of exactly the same weight, shape, and dimensions, they will offer different resistance to ignition and combustion of the propellant; and they will produce differing values of bullet pull, engraving pressure, and bore friction. Generally, less of the same propellant is required to drive a lead bullet at the velocity of the jacketed bullet. If you used the same propellant charge in a service load and a practice load, the lead bullet of the practice load would be driven somewhat faster, perhaps as much as 5–7 percent faster. The result will be slightly greater recoil, but not necessarily a noticeable amount. If a chronograph is available, reduce the charge of the practice round in small increments until the desired velocity is produced. If your service load is in a factory product, check loading-data tables for an efficient propellant charge that will produce the same velocity with a lead bullet of the same weight. A minor amount of interpolation may be necessary to come up with the charge weight. Ideally, you should own (or have access to) a chronograph. With this instrument, it is a simple matter to measure the velocity of the service load in your particular gun and then adjust the propellant charge in your practice load until it produces the same velocity.

In typical law-enforcement calibers, which are principally the .38 Special, 9mm Parabellum, .357 Magnum, and .45 ACP, Hercules Unique propellant will serve especially well for full-charge, light-bullet, practice loads. Unique will also do quite well in the .38 Colt Super Auto, while the .380 ACP that is quite popular as a hideout or off-duty caliber may require a somewhat faster burning propellant, such as W-W 231. Once the question of propellant selection and charge weight has been settled, you must seat the bullet and crimp the case.

For convenience, you should obtain a fixed-charge powder measure. Several types are available, and those with inter-changeable charge bushings offer the greatest versatility. While most references insist that the powder measure be bolted securely to a bench or table and that the cases be passed under it to receive their charges, excellent results can be ob-tained more rapidly by holding the measure in one hand, set-ting it down over each case in a loading block, and operating it with the other hand to drop the proper charge in each case. Theoretically, this should not produce as high a degree of charge uniformity as a rigidly-mounted measure, but as a practical matter there is no noticeable difference.

Once the cases have been charged, they should be in-spected carefully under good light to ascertain that all the charges are approximately the same. None should appear sig-nificantly higher or lower in the case than the others. If there are charges not uniform, dump them and recharge the cases. Take care that the propellant does not spill over during han-dling; this happens very easily when the charge nearly fills the case, especially when ball propellants are used. Ball pro-pellants handle almost like water, while the extruded kind cause less trouble.

As soon as the cases have been charged and checked, bul-lets should be individually hand-started in each. Every effort should be made to align the bullet as accurately as possible in the case. Since light bullets are short bullets, and short bul-lets are more likely to tip during seating, alignment is important. Press the bullet firmly into the flared portion of the case mouth so that it will not fall out in transferring the round from the loading block to the press.

Seating and crimping are most often performed simultaneously in a single-combination die. Nevertheless, crimps tend to be more uniform, and the probability of shaved bullets is less, if seating is done as one operation, followed by crimping. A great deal of time will be saved if a four-die set is purchased for these operations. The typical, handgun-caliber, three-die set employs a single die for seating and crimping. It may be adjusted to do both simultaneously, or adjusted first to seat bullets and then readjusted to apply crimps. Frequent readjusting of the seat/crimp die is avoided with the four-die set, since it contains separate dies for each operation. Adjust the seating die so it forces the bullet into the case to the proper depth. For revolvers, the case mouth must just barely cover the crimping groove around the bullet. For autoloaders, the overall cartridge length should be equal to that of the service load. The cartridge rim should seat fully into the shell holder, and it is wise to guide the bullet into the die mouth with thumb and finger, slipping them out of the way after the full length of the bullet has entered and before the shell holder smashes them against the die. As the bullet nose contacts the seating punch—and it is necessary that the cavity in this punch fits the bullet nose closely—you should take note of the added resistance generated as the case is forced up over the bullet. If an unusual amount of force is required, either the case or bullet may be damaged, and that will affect accuracy and functioning. Even if no damage is done, that cartridge will place its bullet outside the target group. On the other hand, if unusually light pressure is all that is required to seat a particular bullet, that cartridge should also be discarded because it will produce less than normal velocity.

Once the bullets are seated to the proper depth, the die must be adjusted to apply the requisite amount of crimp. Revolver loads require a heavy roll crimp to secure the bullet against forward movement out of the case during recoil. The die should be adjusted so that it turns the case mouth in sufficiently so that it bottoms solidly in the crimping groove. Even a bit more crimp than this will not be amiss, providing it does not cause any visible bulging or wrinkling of the case. This heavy crimp is required to ensure maximum uniformity of ignition and combustion of the propellant charge. Too little crimp means less resistance, and the inevitable result is slightly less velocity, which will lead to a vertically enlarged target group. Automatics require a taper crimp rather than the roll type.

The headspace of an automatic handgun is generally measured from a shoulder inside the chamber of the barrel against which the mouth of the cartridge rests. If a heavy roll crimp is applied, the cartridge enters the chambers more deeply until the curved portion of the crimp strikes the chamber shoulder and the primer moves farther away from the firing pin. The result is less-uniform ignition and somewhat less accuracy. When target loads are assembled, a roll crimp is sometimes used; and the bullet is seated sufficiently far forward so that it wedges in the chamber throat and supports the cartridge. You cannot do this and still duplicate a service load, so the taper crimp is advised. It leaves the mouth of the case unaltered except in diameter and allows proper headspacing. A taper crimp requires squeezing the case mouth in upon the bullet at a slight taper. This is done by running the cartridge into a slightly tapered die cavity adjusted so that the case-mouth diameter is reduced by 0.01–0.015 inch (.25–.38 millimeter). This forces the case into the lead bullet, but the deformation produced is uniform and concentric so it does not interfere with accuracy.

The tightness of the case upon the bullet, the grip of the taper crimp, and the slight shoulder beneath the bullet base (produced by the expanding method described above) all combine to support the bullet solidly against feeding impacts. Were it not for these factors, the bullet might very well be driven into the case when it strikes the feed ramp. This would likely cause a feeding malfunction; or if there were no feeding malfunction, the receding bullet would cause increased chamber pressure, which would lead to a slightly higher velocity for that shot. It is absolutely essential that the bullet be held securely enough in the case so that it will not be dislodged during feeding. If the factors already mentioned do not hold the bullet tightly enough, a slightly greater degree of crimp may be applied. In addition, a smaller-diameter expander plug may be used; however, this may necessitate a smaller-diameter resizing die. As a last resort, a cannelure may be rolled into the case after resizing and expanding. This cannelure should be located with its upper edges about 0.03125 inch (.794 millimeter) above the position where the bullet base will come to rest. The depth of the cannelure should be regulated to the minimum that will positively prevent rearward bullet movement. If the cannelure is made too deep, it may deform the case so that chambering difficulties are encountered, and it may also weaken the case so that it will fail after very few reloadings. The canneluring tools on the market have positive mechanical stops so that once the required depth has been determined, the adjustment may be set and locked to ensure uniformity. If you discover that you have loaded a substantial quantity of ammunition and that the bullets are not held securely enough, the cartridges may be salvaged by rolling a shallow cannelure in the case centered over the lubricating groove in the bullet.

Once loading has been completed, the cartridges should be carefully inspected and cleaned. During the loading process, they pick up fingerprints, grease, and bullet lubricant. All this can be wiped off with a clean, dry cloth, or the cartridges can be tumbled clean in peanut hulls. This cleans and polishes the cartridges very nicely and removes the mold-parting lines on the bullets, giving them a factory-loaded appearance. Once all the loading operations have been performed, package and label the ammunition. Its identity should be preserved so it does not get confused with a different load that looks like it.

When a practice load is first being developed or when it is made for the first time, sufficient shooting should be done with it to make absolutely certain that it is compatible with the gun and that it produces 100 percent reliability before you load a large quantity. Once a given load has been tested and found acceptable, no further testing is necessary. However, if any component is changed or if you make any significant changes in loading methods or techniques, the live-fire test should be repeated. Sometimes some insignificant-appear-ing factor, such as switching to a slightly different shape or weight bullet, may affect the load's reliability.

For loading service ammunition, follow essentially the same steps. However, there is one particularly important difference. Service loads should be assembled in factory-new cases. This should not prove to be costly, since you probably will not consume more than two hundred new cases per year, including initial targeting of the gun, periodic test-firing, and regular disposal of the ammunition you carry. If you can afford to handload, you can afford this modest expenditure for new cases. There are two important reasons for using new cases. The first is that initial firing with a full-charge load might weaken the case so that it will perform less than perfectly when reloaded. Such a reloaded case presents no great hazard in practice load, but could be fatal in a combat situation. The second reason is with each firing and reloading a case loses some of its ability to hold the bullet tightly. Working the case mouth through firing, resizing, expansion, bullet seating, and crimping work-hardens the brass and changes its physical characteristics. Because of this, a case that has been fired and reloaded several times will produce less velocity than it did when new.

The making of the brass does not matter, but it should be checked for length. Length is important for use in revolvers only insofar as it affects the uniformity of the crimp. Usually this can be solved by gauging or measuring the cases, and if there is more than 0.01–0.015 inch (.25–.38 millimeter) variation in length, set aside the shorter ones so that the batch you load for service does not vary. If you want to be more meticulous, you can set up a good case trimmer and trim the entire lot to uniform length. In autoloaders, case length is important to ensure proper and uniform ignition; a case too short will be driven forward by the firing pin against the headspacing shoulder, which will cushion the firing-pin blow, sometimes resulting in weak ignition. Factory-new cases in autoloader calibers are often much shorter than many experts believe they should be, and a case that is too long may prevent the slide and barrel from going fully into battery and thus cause a failure. The possibility of an overly long case is remote, but check carefully. There really is nothing you can do to make cases that are too short useable. Check autoloader cases for length and set aside those that are the shortest for nonservice use, segregate those that fall in the middle of the length range for targeting and testing, and use those that are the longest for duty.

New cases are not flared, so you will have to perform this operation. In addition, the inside mouth diameter for many new cases is not quite small enough to grip the bullets as tightly as desired. This is due to the fact that loading plants do not depend as much upon tightness for bullet security as the handloader of combat ammunition should. Consequently, the case should be run into the full-length resizing die to reduce the mouth. The mouth is then expanded and flared as described for practice loads.

Once the new cases are fully prepared, you must select your defense load. The bullet is, of course, most important. It must produce the highest degree of lethality possible at a safe velocity. In an autoloader, this means a jacketed, hollow-point design, with the jacket covering the core completely up to the mouth of the nose cavity. There are some bullets currently available that demonstrate excellent feeding, even though a portion of the soft core is exposed ahead of the jacket; but from a practical stand, the bullet with the full-length jacket offers the best feeding reliability. As for shape, the truncated-cone or semi-round nose are essential to good feeding. Maximum lethality will be produced by the bullet with the thinnest jacket and softest core, which together permit maximum expansion. While the major ammunition makers do supply excellent bullets of this type to handloaders, they are generally not as available as the products of Sierra, Hornady, and Speer, which all produce excellent bullets of this type.

High-performance, jacketed, expanding bullets are often of less than barrel-groove diameter. (For practice loads, a lead-bullet diameter of at least groove diameter is recommended.) With some high-performance bullets running smaller, it may be necessary to use a smaller-diameter expander rod than was employed for practice loads. It is even more important for duty ammunition that the bullet and case assembly be quite

tight. Do not overdo this, however; with the bullet seated
there should be a barely perceptible ring around the case over
the bullet base. If there is a pronounced bulge there, the case
is too tight upon the bullet and has been either reduced too
much in the sizing die or not expanded enough. Seating the
bullet is the same as described for practice ammunition, but it
is even more essential that the head of the seating stem fits
the bullet nose precisely.

Choice of a bullet for revolver use is not quite as critical.
Shape is not important to revolver functioning. Therefore,
the use of a bullet with at least modest exposure of lead at the
nose is not only acceptable, it is desirable because it will allow
greater expansion in animal tissue. It is essential that the
jacket carry well forward over at least two-thirds of the ogive
to prevent leading. A jacket shorter than this may allow bare
lead to contact the bore when the exposed, unsupported, soft
core upsets under acceleration forces. Any significant contact
will produce leading, and that will affect accuracy.

If the revolver bullet has a fairly deep crimping cannelure,
it may not be necessary to resize the mouth of the new case.
If the bullet enters the unsized case with reasonable tightness, a heavy roll crimp will secure it solidly against recoil
forces. However, if the cannelure is shallow, it limits the
degree of crimp that can be applied, and a tighter case and
bullet assembly may be necessary to prevent the bullet from
shifting during recoil.

Once the service loads are completed, they must be carefully inspected. Every cartridge that you carry on duty should
be cycled through the action of your autoloader or checked in
the chambers of your revolver. While the possibility is remote, there is the chance that at some point in the loading
process a dent, bulge, or other defect has been produced that
might interfere with proper gun functioning. In addition,
samples (at least 5 percent, and perhaps as much as 10 percent) of each batch should be function-fired in the gun for
which they are intended.

There is one other operation you might wish to perform
on service loads. Factory ammunition is sold as oilproof and
waterproof. The loads you have assembled are probably just

as resistant to water and oil. However, you can further water-proof the primer by placing a small drop of thin, clear lacquer at the junction of case and primer. The lacquer will run along the entire joint and penetrate any minute gaps, sealing the assembly tightly when it hardens. If the idea of applying lacquer to each primer individually does not appeal to you, make a wood or cardboard holder with holes to support the cartridges with only the heads exposed. With a pressurized can of clear lacquer, spray the heads lightly. A thin coat is all that is needed, as this will flow into the joints, but the buildup on the case heads will not be sufficient to cause any functional problems in revolvers or automatics. Waterproofing the case and bullet joint is not quite as easy, but for the number of rounds that require it no great amount of time or effort is needed. With a small, pointed, artist brush, flow a narrow bead of thin lacquer directly into the joint as the cartridge is rotated. This will provide a waterproof seal when the lacquer hardens. Additionally you can flow thickened lacquer between the bullet and the flared mouth after seating but before crimping. While the lacquer is still tacky, apply the crimp and wipe away any lacquer squeezed out in the process. This should provide a better seal than the simple method, but many handloaders feel that it is not worth the extra effort.

Always keep in mind that nothing less than absolutely perfect components, faultless techniques, and continuous inspection and testing is acceptable when combat ammunition is being assembled. Ammunition choice is even more critical to survival in combat than gun choice. Even the very finest weapon cannot ensure your survival unless the ammunition is carefully chosen with a view towards maximum lethality, accuracy, and functional reliability—characteristics you can have with handloading.

10

Tuning for Target and High-Performance Ammunition

ANY NEW BROWNING, Colt, Smith & Wesson or other centerfire autoloader fresh out of the box will probably feed standard, round-nose, hard-ball ammunition with acceptable, if not perfect, reliability. Note the word "probably;" in recent years there have been new pistols that simply would not function reliably with even that most basic autoloader cartridge. Several mechanical problems have been identified as reasons for this type of failure. In two cases—Colt and Smith & Wesson—it has been traced to improper machining of the slide-breech face, burrs on the breech face and extractor and ejector openings, improperly cut chambers, bad magazines, and assorted ill-fitting and incorrectly finished parts.

Even a gun that meets the original specifications and performs properly with ball ammunition often will not perform acceptably (100 percent reliability) with either light target loads or high-performance combat ammunition. The same procedures that will adapt the average autoloader to proper reliability with light, low-velocity, lead-bullet target loads will also usually lead to the best functional reliability with high-pressure, high-velocity combat loads. To understand what is involved in adapting an automatic for use with high-performance ammunition, the user must understand how the typical, recoil-operated, autoloading pistol functions. The Colt Government Model of 1911 furnishes a good example.

First, the gun is cocked, the breech locked, the safety disengaged, and a cartridge is in the chamber. The rearward movement of the trigger rotates the sear out of engagement with the hammer, allowing the hammer to be driven forward by its mainspring, striking the firing pin, and then being halted by an abutment at the rear of the slide. At the instant the hammer is halted, the firing pin—being of the inertia-type and thereby shorter than the tunnel in which it rides—has not yet reached the primer. After the hammer halts, the firing pin continues forward under its own momentum, simultaneously compressing the firing-pin retracting spring to indent the primer and thus crush the priming compound against the anvil to ignite it. The jet of flame produced by the firing compound then passes through the flash hole to ignite the propelling charge in the cartridge.

At this point, the propelling charge burns and converts to a very large volume of heated gas, whose temperature may reach 3000 degrees F (1649 degrees C) or more. As this heated gas expands, it first expands the case radially into firm contact with the chamber walls, sealing the gases in and thus causing its tight grasp upon the bullet to be eliminated. Almost simultaneously, the gas begins to force the bullet forward out of the case and into the rifling of the bore.

According to universal laws of motion, for every action there is an equal and opposite reaction. Therefore, as the bullet begins to move forward, there is an equal force exerted rearward upon the slide breech. With the slide breech locked to the barrel and frame, the gun thereby begins to move rearward ever so slightly as the bullet moves forward; measured in a linear manner, of course, the much heavier gun travels far less distance than the bullet. The recoil of the gun begins while the bullet is still confined within the bore. However, the much greater mass of the gun prevents any significant rearward movement from taking place until the bullet has exited the muzzle. At that point, recoil becomes a significant factor, and all components of the gun begin to accelerate rearward.

Able to move independently of the frame, the barrel and slide—locked together—accelerate more rapidly than the frame and move rearward in relation to it. During the initial portion of this movement, barrel and slide remain locked solidly together. But as they pass a certain point, the barrel is cammed downward, disengaging its locking ribs from their corresponding abutments in the slide. Assuming the gun is properly timed, shortly after the locking ribs have cleared their abutments, the barrel is halted by appropriate surfaces in the frame, and the slide continues rearward by the momentum it has been given during that short initial movement. All factors being correct, the slide has developed sufficient momentum to move fully rearward, with the extractor withdrawing the fired case from the chamber and the slide compressing the recoil spring to store energy for counter-recoil movement. Simultaneously, the slide rides over the hammer, forcing it to the cocked position where the sear will engage and hold it. At the appropriate time when the empty case has been pulled completely clear of the chamber, it will be struck by the ejector, pivoted about the extractor claw, and hurled from the gun. As the slide moves rearward, the uppermost cartridge in the magazine is pressed tightly against its underside by the magazine-followers spring. And as the slide-breech face clears this cartridge, that spring forces the cartridge up into firm contact with the magazine-feed lips and into the path of the slide.

Shortly thereafter, the slide will be halted by appropriate abutments in the receiver, and after a very brief pause the compressed recoil spring will assert itself and begin to accelerate the slide forward in counter-recoil travel. As the slide moves forward, the lower edge of the breech face strikes the upper portion of the rim or base of the cartridge in the feed lips. The recoil spring possesses sufficient power so that the slide overcomes the friction of the cartridge against the feed lips and drives it forward in a nearly horizontal direction, parallel to the feed lips proper.

As the cartridge moves forward, it moves out from under the feed lips. At the instant the head, or rim, clears the forward edge of the feed lips, it is forced further upward by the follower spring, and thus moves vertically across the breech face with the rim moving between the extractor claw and the breech face. As the slide moves further forward, the nose (bullet) of the cartridge is driven against the feed ramp—at which point the nose of the cartridge is deflected upward at a rather acute angle, generally toward the mouth of the chamber. As the slide continues to push the cartridge forward, this angular movement usually causes the bullet nose to next strike the underside of the barrel tang or the underside of the top wall of the chamber near its mouth. This impact causes the cartridge nose to be deflected downward, into the mouth of the chamber as it continues to travel forward, perhaps striking the bottom wall of the chamber and rebounding again to become aligned longitudinally with the chamber axis. During chambering, the cartridge may oscillate fairly violently in a vertical plane, literally chattering against the chamber mouth.

From this point onward, the cartridge (now firmly seated in the breech face and gripped by the extractor) is thrust fully into the chamber, and the slide-breech face strikes the rear of the barrel. This impact carries the barrel forward with the slide, and the barrel is then cammed upward to engage its locking ribs with their corresponding abutments in the roof of the slide. At the instant this locking engagement is completed, appropriate surfaces in the frame—combined with others in the slide and barrel—halt the barrel, which in turn halts the slide. At this point, the hammer is at full cock, a fresh cartridge is chambered, and the breech is fully locked. The gun is now ready for the next shot to be fired.

With conventional, round-nose, jacketed-bullet ammunition and with guns made to standard specifications, these mechanical actions take place with regularity and reliability. However, there are several points during this movement where interference can develop. If it develops to a sufficient extent, it absorbs energy from the moving slide, leaving insufficient energy to properly close and lock the breech after chambering the cartridge. Further, if interference is such that the direction and magnitude of cartridge deflection exceeds allowable limits; then the cartridge will jam in some awkward position and not enter the chamber fully. Obviously, if it does not enter the chamber to its full depth, the breech cannot close and lock properly, and the gun cannot be fired.

If there is unusual roughness, irregularity in profile, or a ridge where two parts of the feed ramp or other deflecting surfaces meet, the bullet deflection will not be normal, and the cartridge may not chamber. This is particularly true in the case of two-part feed ramps, such as found in the Colt Government Model. If one portion of the ramp, particularly that part integral with the barrel, overhangs the other, a sharp ridge is formed. This ridge may well be sharp enough to actually dig into the surface of the bullet and halt the cartridge at that point, also preventing chambering.

Several other factors also affect the reliability of the manner in which the cartridge is driven out of the magazine and into the chamber by the slide. Of special importance is the condition of the magazine-feed lips. If the feed lips are as they should be, the cartridge is first pushed directly forward and then pops upward, striking the feeding surfaces at the proper angle. However, if the lips are dented or pinched too closely together, the cartridge will strike the feed ramp too low and not be deflected properly into the chamber. If the lips are excessively worn, spread, or bent outward, then the cartridge will either strike the feed ramp too high or may pop clear of the lips too early and thus be unguided at a critical point in feeding.

In most contemporary designs, as the cartridge head clears the magazine-feed lips, it slides up over the breech face and under the extractor claw. Thus, excessive roughness on the breech face or burrs upon the extractor interfere with this movement. Likewise, burrs on the firing-pin hole, a protruding firing pin, or dimensional inconsistencies in the breech face will prevent the head from rising smoothly into position. The result of this is simply that the case head is too low at the instant the cartridge nose is reflected by the feed ramp, so the cartridge enters the chamber only part way before it is jammed against the lower part of the chamber mouth by the slide breech. This condition is aggravated when there is a sharp edge where the upper portion of the feed ramp blends into the chamber wall. Such a sharp edge will dig into the soft, brass, cartridge case and prevent proper chambering. When all of these factors are recognized, it becomes quite evident that the feeding of a cartridge from magazine to chamber is far from the simple and uncomplicated operation it often seems to the casual observer. In fact, it is amazing that the operation can be performed with the degree of regularity achieved with modern guns and ammunition. But this does not end the list of pitfalls that await the cartridge as it is stripped from the magazine.

Rimless cartridges, which obtain their headspace dimensions at the mouth of the case present a sharp 90-degree shoulder at the front of the case. Many production guns present a corresponding shoulder at the mouth of the chamber. Considering that the chamber and case are almost cylindrical, there is little clearance for the squared-off case mouth to enter the squared-off chamber mouth. With just the slightest bit of lateral deviation as the cartridge heads for the chamber, the case mouth may hang up on the chamber mouth. Ideally, this problem is eliminated by rounding off the chamber mouth and putting a very slight crimp on the case mouth.

Occasionally in Browning-type automatics, which have the tang extending rearward over the chamber mouth, a cartridge is deflected so high that the bullet bangs into the lower edge of the tang. If the tang is sharp-edged at that point, it may dig into the bullet and halt the cartridge.

The casual shooter is often tempted to check the feeding of an autoloading pistol by slowly cycling the slide manually. Almost invariably this produces a failure to feed. Autoloading pistols are designed to feed reliably when the slide and other recoiling members are moving at the high velocities given them by the standard recoil impulse. This high velocity is essential in maintaining proper alignment of the cartridge during certain portions of its travel from magazine to chamber. The cartridge is thus stabilized in direction by the powerful thrust of the slide against its base. If the slide is moving only slowly, there is insufficient thrust to provide this stabilization. This is particularly true in any gun attitude other than normal upright. If the gun is turned upside down and cycled manually, it will jam hopelessly every time; yet, it can be fired upside down with complete functional reliability. Only when the cartridge and recoiling parts are moving at or above a certain minimum speed, or velocity, can feeding and chambering be correct. Speed is essential to functioning.

To improve the functional reliability of your automatic handgun with all ammunition, consider the following points.

1. **General:** Check all recoiling parts for free, but not sloppy, movement throughout their travel. Polish any rough-sliding areas, such as that part of the slide that rides over the hammer and disconnector. Make certain the inward lug of the slide stop protrudes far enough to be acted upon by the follower, but not far enough to contact cartridges rising in the magazine. Make certain all springs, especially the recoil spring, are the proper size and strength. Reduce friction and eliminate binding throughout recoiling parts by deburring and polishing.

2. **Magazine:** Depress the magazine follower fully with a dowel. If the follower binds at any point, remove the obstruction. If the spring cramps or kinks, replace it with a new one. Make certain the magazine seats fully into the gun butt and that the magazine catch engages properly. Inspect feed lips and edges of magazine mouth for sharp edges and burrs. Remove any by polishing or stoning. Fill the magazine with cartridges, noting how smoothly and easily they enter. Remove any interference that might be found. Then strip each cartridge forward out of the magazine, noting if there is undue friction on the feed lips or the follower. Polish the follower, especially if the last cartridge hesitates.

3. **Slide:** Inspect the breech face and extractor claw and stone off any burrs or heavy tool marks. Lightly bevel the underside of the extractor claw so it will not dig into the brass case as the cartridge slides up under it. Press a cartridge up into the breech face under the extractor and watch for binding. It should slide into position smoothly, and the extractor should grip it with just sufficient force to hold it there. If the

case rim binds in the breech face, the counterbore is too small and must be opened up slightly. This is a common failing of one lot of Smith & Wesson M39 pistols. Remove any burrs around the ejection port that might interfere with fired-case travel or with extracting a loaded round to clear the gun.

4. **Barrel:** Lightly round off the inner edge of the chamber mouth and polish smooth. Inspect the chamber walls under strong light, and if it is unusually rough, burnish heavily with steel wool on a spinning mandrel or polish with crocus cloth and oil similarly applied. Gently polish or stone the sharp edge where the feed ramp breaks into the chamber wall. Remove no more metal than necessary to produce a smoothly polished transition from ramp to chamber.

5. **Feed ramp:** This is one of the most common problem areas, and different types need different treatment. Examine the Colt Government Model's ramp with the barrel fully rearward in recoil. If any of the barrel portion overhangs the frame portion, carefully polish until the two form a single, unbroken surface. Then polish the entire ramp as smoothly as possible without changing its shape or angle and without removing any significant amount of metal.

Early Smith & Wesson ramps contain a hump in the middle that often causes trouble. It is best to remove this hump entirely, making the ramp straight from top to bottom. The tendency is to let the curved chute formed by the ramp become too narrow as this is done. When that occurs, bullet noses may bind at that point. Take care that the original radius is maintained along the full length. It is a good idea to have a late-model, straight-ramp, M39 barrel to use as a pattern and copy its ramp exactly.

Plain, straight ramps, such as on the Browning Hi-Power, Smith & Wesson M59, and late M39, require only careful polishing. The ground finish on most Smith & Wesson ramps is not smooth enough for trouble-free service, but the shape is excellent.

Generally speaking, all guns with two-part ramps and mobile barrels require the same treatment as the Colt Government Model. Fixed-barrel guns with two-part ramps (for example, the Walther PP series and the Astra) require careful checking and polishing to ensure that there is not a hairline sharp edge where the two parts meet. This edge may be so slight as to be invisible, but it will still dig into bullet noses and cause a serious feed failure. In general, all one-piece ramps need to be treated just as the Browning and Smith & Wesson. Some fixed-barrel guns may require that the lower end of the ramp be cut just a small amount deeper.

Keep in mind that every automatic should be broken in by firing at least 200 rounds before any serious use is made of it. More often than not, such initial firing will clear up most malfunctions through simple wearing and thus eliminate the need for much of what we have just described. Whether you fine-tune your gun as outlined or just shoot it until it works right, no automatic can be considered suitable for combat use (or potential combat use) until it will fire 100 consecutive rounds of the combat load without malfunctions of any sort.

11

Accessories

ONCE A COMBAT handgun has been chosen, there are dozens of additional items that can be purchased as accessories. Some, such as holsters and cleaning equipment, are more essential than others. Some are a good investment; others are a waste of money. A brief look at some contemporary accessories will give the user a better idea of what is available and what is useful.

Holsters. Since holsters are essential for the carrying of combat handguns, a few words about them will be helpful. There are two basic kinds of holsters—those to be worn exposed, and those to be worn concealed.

The exposed holster should be made of very heavy, saddle-skirting leather, preferably from the back of the hide, and assembled with high-quality thread and stitching. The main seam of the pouch should have an extra strip of leather to act as a spacer. At the top, additional spacers (welting thicknesses) should be employed as necessary to shape the opening to fit the contour of the gun. Extra welting is not as necessary with thin, flat autoloaders as it is with revolvers, whose protruding cylinders pose a design problem. Every point of unusual strain in a seam should be reinforced by either additional stitching or solid rivets. The most important places for this additional reinforcement are at the closing at the back of the mouth where the trigger guard and frame stress the seam heavily and at the bottom corners of the belt loop on the back of the holster. As initially formed, the belt loop lays flat, but the body to which the belt forces it to conform is curved, and this places excessive strain on those corners. If they are not reinforced, the stitching may pull out, break, or work loose.

The shank, the portion above the pouch opening to which the belt loop is attached, should be reinforced in some manner so that constant flexing of the holster on the belt will not eventually make the leather limp and allow the holstered gun to move back and forth on the belt. This reinforcement is sometimes made from additional layers of leather stitched in place, but a formed metal plate stitched between two layers of leather is a better method. Ideally, this metal plate should be malleable enough so that the user may bend it to fit his body, but stiff enough so that it will not distort during normal use. Although this metal reinforcement is most desirable in holsters with a drop loop, it is still an excellent feature to be included in high-rise or high-ride types, which sit well up on the belt.

Holster leather, of course, must have first-class tanning and be acid-free and salt-free. For many years, makers regularly supplied holsters made from oil-tanned leather. That leather is impregnated with some type of oil, which makes it more flexible and gives it some degree of water resistance. Oil-tanned leather, however, cannot be properly shaped and made to hold its shape to fit the gun properly. It has no place in a modern combat holster. The leather should instead be vegetable-tanned, a process that uses the tannin of many different kinds of trees and plants.

The fit of the handgun in the holster is important. If the holster is simply a loose pouch in which the gun is free to

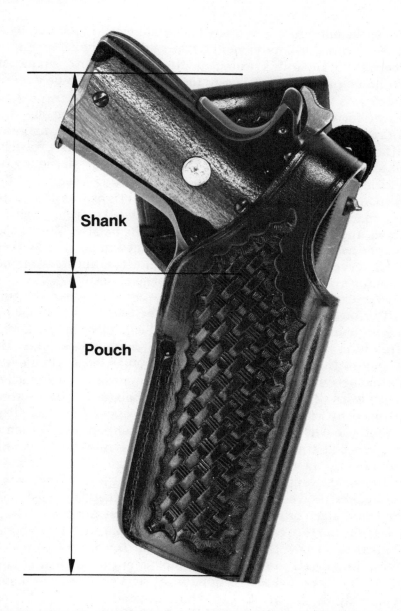

Shank

Pouch

Bianchi Deluxe Border Patrol holster is typical of the better molded holsters currently being manufactured in the U.S. The thumb break strap blocks the hammer on single-action automatic pistols. A steel-reinforced sight channel protects the front sight of the handgun. Although it rides low, it is designed to permit the wearer to sit comfortably in an automobile. (Courtesy Bianchi)

move, the handgun may easily be lost unless it is secured by a safety strap. Also, movement of the gun in the holster rapidly wears away the gun's protective finish. On the other hand, if the holster is too tight, heavy finish-wear will also be experienced; and in the case of autoloaders, the slide will be pushed out of battery, possibly causing a malfunction when the gun is drawn. Further, an excessively tight holster will make it difficult to draw the handgun. When a holster is properly fitted to the gun, the leather of the pouch follows all the major contours closely. This type of contour fit is best done by hand, a process called blocking. The initial tightness of a properly made holster can be overcome by twenty or so practice draws and by moving the gun about in the holster. Where the leather has been boned down into recessed areas, the leather itself serves to retain the gun in the holster, and there is no need for a separate safety strap or other security device.

An exposed holster is generally worn on a separate gun belt or on a very heavy waist belt. The belt leather must be the very highest quality, stiff and thick, in order to avoid stretching and sagging. The belt loop of the holster must fit closely to the belt. If the belt loop becomes loose, then even normal activity may cause the holster to move unnecessarily. When worn on an external gun belt, the holster can be secured in place by rubber bands or leather keepers fitted tightly around the belt on either side of the holster belt loop. When a trousers belt supports the holster, some extra security can be provided by the trouser belt loops if they are properly located and spaced. Simply thread the belt through the loops with the holster between two loops, which will keep the holster in the same place on the waist, even if the belt moves.

If the bottom of the holster is tied on one's leg by a thong or strap, as it is with some military and frontier tiedown holsters, it is forced to follow every movement of the leg. If you sit, the holster swings to horizontal. If you climb or move your body in any other way, the holstered gun must follow your leg. If a swivel-type holster is used, the holster is not damaged by such movements, but if the holster is of the fixed-belt-loop type it certainly can be. If the holster is tied to the leg, the position will differ according to the attitude of the

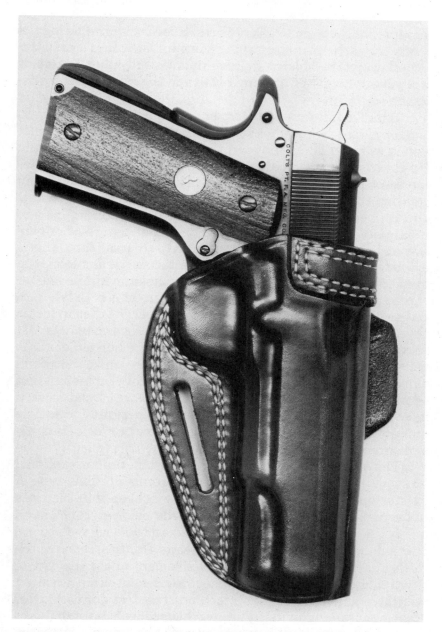

This Bianchi-made Askins Avenger holster is a good example of a molded or blocked holster. Shown here for the M1911A1 Government Model Colt, it is also made for a number of other automatic pistols. (Courtesy Bianchi)

leg, forcing the user to alter his reach for the gun. The leg tie-down is clearly an undesirable device for the combat shooter. By allowing the holster to be supported only by the belt, it will generally be upright and always in the same relationship to the torso.

Today's uniformed officers spend a great deal of time sitting or riding in automobiles. When a relatively short handgun is worn on a high holster, there is no particular problem. However, if a heavy-frame revolver with a 4-inch (101.6-millimeter) or longer barrel is carried in a holster, the act of sitting will jam the bottom of the holster against the seat, forcing it and the belt up uncomfortably into the wearer's ribs. The gun is jammed into a position where it cannot be easily drawn. Swivel holsters offer a partial solution to this problem. This is a holster in which the pouch is connected to the belt loop by a metal swivel or pivot. As one sits, the bottom of the holster can be swung forward to rest on the seat. This is only a partial solution, for while it eliminates the wearer's discomfort it still leaves the butt of the gun in a cramped position where it cannot be drawn quickly and freely. When a swivel holster is worn, the gun may swing fore and aft freely upon the swivel when the wearer is walking. A plain swivel is usually tight enough when new to prevent this movement, but as it is worn it will loosen. For this reason, some makers supply lock-type swivels, which may be freed for sitting down or locked to prevent movement when standing.

The cross-draw holster is far superior to the conventional or swivel hip holster for wear in an automobile. This type of holster differs from the standard hip model only in that it is not dropped below the belt, and the belt loop is attached at an angle so the butt of the gun is tipped well forward and toward one's abdomen, so as to be within relatively easy reach of the gun hand. It is worn on the weak side (left side if the user is right-handed) and is named cross-draw because the gun must be drawn across the user's stomach. The cross-draw holster makes the handgun fairly accessible to both the dominant and the weak hand. When drawing with the dominant hand, the individual reaches over and takes the gun out of the holster and swings on the target. When drawing with the weak

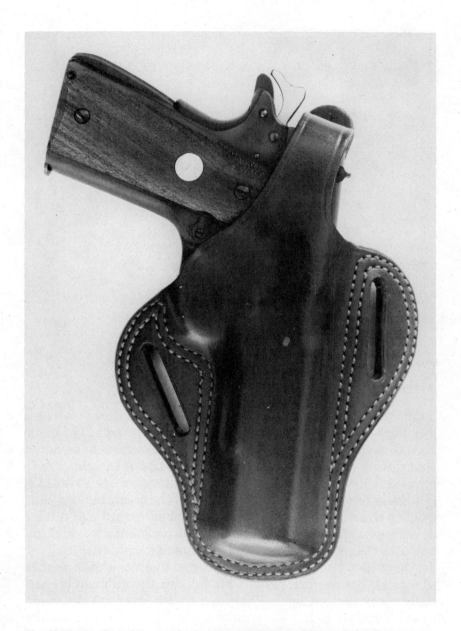

The Shadow is Bianchi's very high-riding concealment holster. It has been precontoured to the waistline curves of the average person. (Courtesy Bianchi)

The Judge, a swivel-type holster by Bianchi, is shown here with a Smith & Wesson Model 19 .357 Magnum revolver. This holster is the front-opening type for quick drawing in combat situations. (Courtesy Bianchi)

hand, the hand is rotated palm out and slid down between gun butt and body; the gun is drawn and rotated at the same time to bring it to bear on the target. Some critics have noted that during this weak-hand draw the muzzle of the gun points momentarily at the shooter's body and that an accidental firing could injure the shooter. Normally the weak hand will be used to draw the gun only when a very serious situation has developed. The very slight chance of accidentally shooting one's self is preferable to losing the target opportunity.

Shoulder holsters are widely used when the user wishes to conceal his weapon (with a hip holster the gun can be partially concealed if the user has on a coat or jacket). The traditional shoulder holster is simply a leather pouch to hold the gun hung from a shaped strap that passes over the weak side shoulder. The strap is held in place by an elastic band or nar-

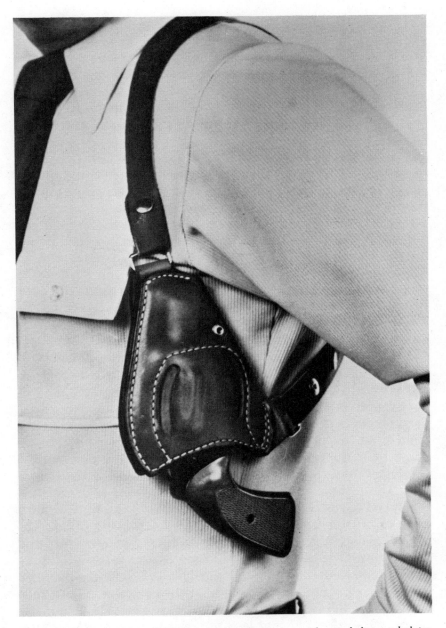

Bianchi's Special Agent shoulder holster can also be used as a belt-type holster. (Courtesy Bianchi)

row strap crossing the back and looping around the right shoulder and under the armpit. Fitted in this fashion, all the strapping is concealed by one's coat, with nothing visible to indicate that a holster is being drawn. The pouch hangs directly beneath the weak arm, where the gun is concealed and protected by the arm. However, there are drawbacks to this type of shoulder holster. Even with its bottom attached to the user's belt, drawing the gun can be quite awkward. First the wrist must be bent sharply to obtain a satisfactory grip on the butt. The gun must then be lifted nearly straight up to clear the holster before it can be swung on the target—not a very fast or convenient system. More recent and much more efficient are the spring-front or break-front shoulder holsters, which consist of the same harness carrying a modified pouch open down the front and containing a spring, elastic, or other tension or compression device to hold the gun securely in place. With this type of holster, the individual need only get a firm grip on the gun butt, then pull forward overcoming the restraint of the spring or elastic. Unless fitted with a very strong spring or an auxillary safety strap, this type of holster does hold the gun in a less secure manner than the pouch type, but this does not present any great problems when considering the added efficiency and speed it offers.

A more modern and even more desirable variety of shoulder holster is the kind that has a split, spring-loaded pouch similar to the break-front. It hangs upside down from the same type of harness. When properly worn, it hangs more to the front than the other types, fairly close to the left breast with the muzzle of the gun pointing upward and the butt down and to the right. Drawing the gun from this upside-down type of holster involves slapping the strong hand over the butt of the gun, grasping it firmly, pulling down and out, and swinging on the target. The process is much faster and more convenient than with the upright holster. This upside-down design was originated for short-barreled revolvers with relatively large-diameter cylinders and recoil shields. Thin, flat automatics are somewhat less secure in such holsters. This is overcome in some designs by stronger and more closely shaped springs and in others by mechanical retaining devices. A

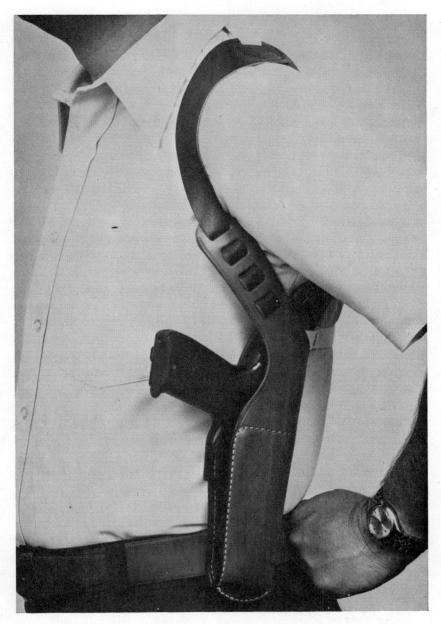

The Bianchi X-15 shoulder holster is shown here with the SIG-Sauer P220 in .45 ACP. (Courtesy Bianchi)

spring-loaded plunger or lever protruding through the trigger guard has been used on this type of holster; the retainer is depressed by the trigger finger to allow the gun to be pulled clear.

Inside-trousers holsters, sometimes called inside-waistband holsters, have some advantages over the holsterless waist carry. The principal advantages of this type of holster is that the holster prevents wear or stains on clothing and protects the gun when it and the holster are laid aside. Generally, an inside-trousers holster is made from very thin, soft leather and fits the gun rather loosely. It has a metal-spring clip that snaps down over the belt or waistband to secure it into position. Sometimes a patch of Velcro or a snap fastener is substituted for this clip. Without some means of securing the inside-trousers holster to the belt or the waistband, the possibility exists that the holster may come out with the gun when it is drawn. While this would not necessarily prevent firing, it probably would cause a malfunction. If an inside-trousers holster is required, the very thin, but sturdy, Bianchi sight-channel design occupies hardly any more space than the usual, soft-leather pouch and provides better protection for both the user and the gun. In addition, it eliminates the possibility of the front sight snagging on the holster or clothing. Inside-trousers holsters have become very popular in recent years with the advent of beltless slacks. Any kind of gun belt would seem superfluous on beltless trousers if the user wishes to partially conceal his gun.

Pocket holsters are somewhat unusual and are not extremely popular. They can be made to fit almost any pocket, but the standard models are generally shaped and dimensioned to fit most hip pockets. They usually consist of nothing more than two flat pieces of leather sewn together around its perimeter and around the outline of the gun, then blocked to fit the gun. This produces a pouch-style holster in the center of a large, stiff panel of doubled leather, which fits the pocket and thus holds the gun upright. Some models are made to position the butt of the gun in only one direction, usually outward toward the strong side. Others are more or less symmetrical, so that by simply flipping the holster in the pocket the butt

The Bianchi Waistband Holster Model #6 is typical of the soft, self-molding type used for the concealed carrying of handguns. (Courtesy Bianchi)

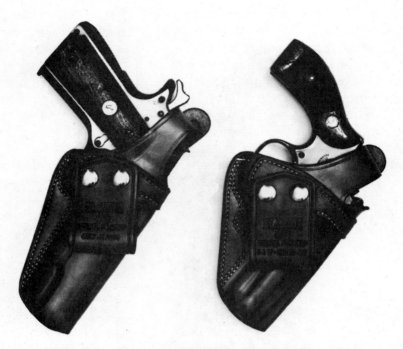

The Bianchi Pistol Pocket is designed to be carried inside the waistband just behind the right hip. In many cases, holsters of this type can be worn under loose shirts and short jackets without being noticed. In addition to being available for the 2-inch (50.8-millimeter) barrel Smith & Wesson, Colt, and Charter Arms revolvers, it is also made for the Smith & Wesson 9mm automatic pistols, Colt's automatic pistols, and the Walther PP and PPK. (Courtesy Bianchi)

can be pointed either way for right- or left-hand use. A closely fitted, hip-pocket holster may come out of the pocket with the gun if it is not secured with tabs that attach to the belt, or with Velcro tabs, or snap fasteners. If concealment is especially important, then most hip-pocket holsters are unsatisfactory because they leave the gun butt totally exposed. If the user stoops or bends, the outline of the pistol grip is also clearly visible through a light jacket.

There are a few carrying devices that serve the same function as holsters. Most common is the belt slide, which in its simplest form is a rectangular piece of leather slotted at both ends to slip over the trousers belt. With this slide slipped over the belt, the gun is simply pushed down between belt and slide where it rides quite comfortably and is secure. Another carrying device is the belt hook, which originated during the matchlock era to hang massive pistols onto the individual's sash. In its modern form, the belt hook consists of a thin piece of spring steel attached to the automatic pistol by screws or clamped under one of the grip plates. It is bent outward and then parallel to the slide, leaving just sufficient room between to accommodate the waistband and belt. The gun may then be slipped down inside the waistband with the clip or hooked over the belt. By means of its spring action, the clip clamps the gun securely to the trousers. This type of belt hook may easily be converted to outside wear by reversing it on the gun and slipping the hook inside the waistband while the gun remains on the outside. This way of carrying the automatic is not nearly as safe as carrying it inside the pants.

Holsters and belts are not the only type of carrying equipment to be considered. When an automatic pistol is used, at least one—and preferably two—loaded, spare magazines should also be carried. It is a poor policy to drop loaded magazines into your pocket where they will gather lint, dirt, and other foreign materials. Carrying a spare magazine in this fashion can result in a malfunction. It also enhances the chance of denting or otherwise damaging the magazines. Spare magazines can be carried in a leather pouch slipped over the belt. The pouch is shaped to hold the magazines mouth down. Such a case should incorporate a close-fitting but easily-opened cover. If the gun is carried on the right hip, it is most practical to carry spare magazines in the area of the left hip. When the gun is empty, the left hand goes for the spare, while the right hand ejects the empty. The spare magazine can be inserted with the left hand, and the automatic is ready to use again.

One other form of carrying equipment should receive some attention here—a suitable storage container for the gun. A rigid, plastic case with foam padding is very suitable for this purpose. Soft, fleece-lined, leather or plastic pistol rugs provide less protection for the gun, but are much more compact. They consist of a sheet of outer covering folded over in the middle and fitted with a slide fastener. Lined inside with fleece, they protect guns quite well except from heavy impacts.

Grips and sights. After holsters, the most commonly encountered accessories for handguns are replacement, or custom, stocks and target-type adjustable sights. Replacement grips are easier to install and are generally more worthwhile than finely adjustable sights.

Experts agree that typical target-type grips do not belong on a combat handgun. Nearly all of the handguns suitable for combat are sold with plain grips, which are quite good for combat use. While a Colt Government Model (M1911A1) pistol can be vastly improved for target shooting by special grips, very little improvement can be obtained for combat by changing grips. Grips must offer a secure hold when the gun is grabbed and hurriedly drawn, even though the hand may be wet or greasy. Grips must also be as unobtrusive as possible, but still offer a large enough handle for secure control of the gun. The shape, texture, and size of the grips must be such that the gun can be drawn properly, even if the hand does not contact the butt in the optimum position.

Except for persons with unusually large hands, the best conventional replacement grips are of checkered walnut or similar wood made to the same shape and size as the originals, but tapered thinner at the front and rear edges and made thinner overall than those with which the gun was originally equipped. Unfortunately, most of the replacement grips available for combat handguns are made in exactly the same pattern as the originals or are even thicker and more bulky. Considering the scarcity of proper combat grips, an alternative solution is to take the standard, factory, wood stock and file or sand it to one-half or one-third of its original thickness, then refit and shorten the grip screws accordingly, and blend the lines of the grips into the gun's butt (see chapter 7).

Frank Pachmayr of Pachmayr Gun Works has introduced an excellent combat-type grip called the Signature grip. This is a one-piece unit molded from a fairly soft, rubber-like material that wraps around the gun's front strap and folds back over into the normal grip position where the side panels are

Right side of a "Custom Colt" by Trapper, showing a Browne and Pharr belt clip. This pistol also has the Pachmayr Signature grips. (Courtesy Tom Wagster)

retained by the standard screws. The side plates are molded around steel reinforcements so they maintain their shape and fit the butt closely. Externally, the Signature grip carries nicely molded checkering and has a somewhat tacky feel, as well as a small amount of rubbery resilience. These characteristics make possible the most secure hold. Even when the hand is wet or greasy, the gun will not tend to slide around during the cumulative recoil effect experienced during rapid firing. The Pachmayr Signature grip is available for the Colt Government Model, the Browning Hi-Power, and the Smith & Wesson Model 39 and Model 59.

Sights are another area in which common sense should prevail in choosing replacements. There has been considerable argument in recent years about the desirability of target-type, fully-adjustable, rear sights on autoloaders for combat use. Many thousands of dollars have been spent by combat handgunners to modify the slides on automatics for installation of adjustable sights and to add massive, fully-adjustable, rear sights and matching front sights. In most cases, the guns were already equipped with perfectly satisfactory and much more durable fixed sights. While adjustable sights possess a distinct technical advantage and while they do allow changing sight settings for different ranges or loads, they are in most other ways actually inferior to the traditional patridge-type fixed sights with which most production automatic pistols are supplied.

A pistol carried for combat should always be used with the same high-performance cartridges and should, from the beginning, be properly targeted with that loading. Subsequent training and practice with that gun should be conducted with the same loading. In short, once an individual has begun serious sidearm training, he should not have occasion to change the ammunition loading or alter the rear-sight setting of his gun. Since handgun combat normally occurs at ranges of less than twenty feet (2.76 meters), there is unlikely to be any advantage in making sight changes. Adjustable sights, compact enough to be used with a combat weapon, must, of mechanical necessity, be relatively fragile when compared to the sturdy fixed sights found on most production guns. Even the Smith & Wesson-type revolver sight that is often installed on automatics can be misaligned by an accidental impact, which would have no affect on a Colt automatic fixed sight. A handgun carried in an exposed holster is frequently banged into door frames, automobile doors, and other obstructions, and a single impact can bend or break an adjustable sight. In addition, the typical adjustable sight has sharp corners that snag on holsters, clothing, and skin.

It is generally believed that adjustable target sights are more accurate than the fixed type. This is not true. Properly shaped and positioned, target and fixed sights can be aligned by the same eye with equal precision, but this does not make the two types equally accurate. Manufacturing and functional tolerances among the many movable parts in an adjustable target sight combine to produce a certain amount of play in the mechanism. The amount of movement may be small, but it will result in angular displacement of the line of sight from the bore of the gun; and this inherently makes the adjustable

CORRECT AND INCORRECT GUTTERSNIPE SIGHTING PICTURES

IMPACT LEFT   IMPACT RIGHT   RIGHT ON   IMPACT LOW   IMPACT HIGH

The Armament Systems and Procedures ASP has a single-unit sight called the guttersnipe, which eliminates the need for a front sight. (Courtesy Armament Systems and Procedures)

sight less accurate than fixed sights from a mechanical point of view.

The difference in mechanical accuracy between the two systems is at most a fraction of an inch at 50 yards (45.7 meters). Translating that into the much shorter typical combat range makes it clear that there can be no discernible affect on combat accuracy. There is a wide variety of both fixed and adjustable replacement sight systems that lend themselves to improving combat suitability of big autoloaders, however.

Of the fixed sight manufacturers, Micro Sight Company produces a sight for the Colt Government Model that may be adapted to any other tubular-slide gun. The set consists of a new rear sight and a front sight of compatible height. The dovetail base of the rear unit fits the sight dovetail of the Colt Government Model, while the front sight has a tenon that fits the front sight mounting point. This sight set differs from the standard only in that the two elements are higher, wider, and sturdier. The rear element contains a properly formed square notch matched to the 0.1- or 0.125-inch (2.54- or 3.18-millimeter) width of the front blade. Installation of the Micro Sight is quite simple. Drift out the old rear sight, drive the new one into the dovetail, and stake it in place after proper targeting. The front sight must be installed with silver soldering after the original sight has been heated and punched out of its seat in the slide.

Robert A. Sconce of the Miniature Machine Company (MMC) in Demming, New Mexico, is offering a High Visibility Sight System for the Colt Government Model-type automatic. This fixed-sight system was designed to provide a quick, clear picture in a variety of lighting conditions. The basic sight elements (front and rear) are sandblasted and then given a black-oxide finish. One series of sights has white inlaid markings for better sighting under poor lighting conditions. While the width of the rear-sight notch and the front-sight blade might offend some target shooters who would consider them too coarse, these sights are excellent for combat purposes. Sconce notes that the sighting plane has been raised 0.062 inch (1.57 millimeters) above that found on fixed sights mounted by the factory in an effort to obtain quick sight determination in a combat situation.

There is a wide variety of adjustable sights available from Micro Sight Company, MMC, Bo-Mar, and other small manufacturers. However, with the exception of the Low Micro from Micro Sight, these adjustable sights are too bulky, sharp, and angular, and they raise the line of sight too

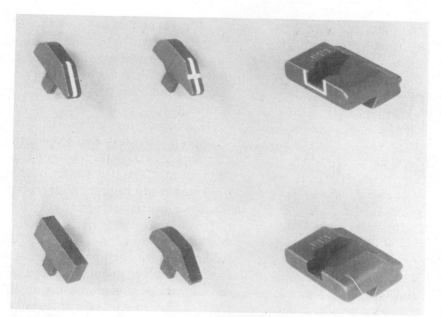

Sight elements for the MMC High Visibility Sight System for the M1911A1 Colt Automatic Pistol. The top row has the white inlaid markings, while the bottom row shows the plain black. (Courtesy MMC)

The MMC High Visibility Sight System as seen by the shooter. (Courtesy MMC)

Micro Sight Company's low-mounting Micro Sight on a commercial Colt M1911A1 automatic pistol. The mounting of this sight requires milling of the slide. (Courtesy Micro Sight Company)

much for combat use. The Low Micro is designed to be compatible with the original sight height of the Colt Government Model and is acceptable for holster use.

In addition to standard target-type sights, Bo-Mar offers these same sights permanently installed on a light-alloy rib that can be screwed to the top of the slide to provide a raised, nonglare sighting plane. These combinations are made for Colt, Smith & Wesson, and Browning big-bore autoloaders and require only the drilling and tapping of securing screw holes in the slide for proper installation. When installed, these combat ribs give the impression of a relatively low line of sight, but the line of sight is actually higher in respect to the bore than it is with standard Bo-Mar sights installed in the usual fashion. Fitting the rib simply fills the gap between front and rear sights, causing them to protrude only slightly above the surface of the rib, but still being far above the center of the bore. These units do make the gun feel and handle well, but they add 4–5 ounces (128–142 grams) of weight, and it is not possible to obtain a standard holster that will accept a gun so fitted.

Instructions for Low Mounting Micro Sights
Colt 45 ACP & 38 Super (3P and 4P)*
Browning 9mm Hi Power (27P)**

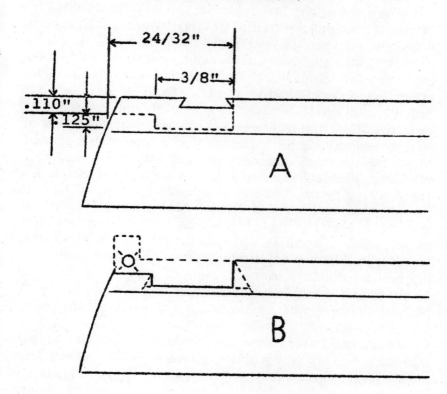

(Drawings not to scale)

A   *Mill flat on top of slide to length of 24/32 inches, depth of .110 inches, mill additional cut 3/8 inches to depth of .125 inches as in figure A.*

B   *Cut dovetail with 65-degree angle cutter, or hand file dovetail using three-cornered file.*

Micro sight installed from right to left maintaining a tight fit. To avoid damaging sight during installation, we recommend using a fiber block to drive the sight in.

  **Micro 3P set with front-blade height of .200 inches fits .45 ACP and .45 Commander. Micro 4P set with front-blade height of .175 inches fits Colt .38 Super and .38 Commander.*

  ***Micro 27P set with front-blade height of .250 inches fits Browning 9mm Hi Power.*
  (Courtesy Micro Sight Company)

(Note the amount of metal that must be removed from the slide in order to install these sights. This is no task for the amateur gunsmith.)

The MMC adjustable sight is an unusually compact, easily installed, adjustable rear sight intended purely for combat use. The sight is very low in profile, and when installed in the original rear sight dovetail of Colt or Browning autoloaders, it is no higher than the issue sight and is compatible with the original front sight. Most users can install the MMC combat sight in a few minutes. No alteration is required to the gun, other than a very light file cut at the front of the dovetail to provide additional clearance. To achieve its unusual compactness, the MMC unit utilizes a less-precise adjustment system than the bigger sights. Windage is obtained with a slotted-head screw of small dimensions, fitted with tactile and audible clicks, while elevation adjustment is obtained with a tiny screw with a pyramid-shaped point, which bears on the base and produces tactile clicks. In view of this, the MMC sight is less sturdy than the big target sights, but being so small it is far less likely to be damaged in normal activity. It is available for Colt and Browning autoloaders and can be modified to replace the original spring-leaf sight of the Smith & Wesson Model 39 and Model 59 series. Further, it may be bought with plain black leaf or with a white inlaid outline around the notch.

Magazines. Magazines are obviously essential to the autoloader. Every new gun is supplied with at least one, and most experts agree that combat shooters should have three magazines—one in the gun and two spares. For combat use, except where concealment requirements may preclude it, an individual should always carry two, fully loaded, extra magazines on his person.

As an after-purchase accessory, magazines can not vary a great deal from the original equipment. Oversize magazines of increased cartridge capacity are available from several sources, including the Triple-K Manufacturing Company. At first consideration, the idea of being able to carry ten rather than seven rounds in a Colt .45 Automatic or fifteen rather than nine in a Colt .38 Super has considerable appeal. Unfortunately, the only way in which this can be accomplished is by extending the magazine body below the butt of the gun. When a gun is being carried openly, perhaps as much as an

Exploded View - Base # 1

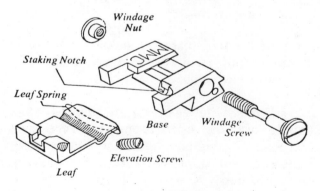

Windage Nut

Staking Notch

Leaf Spring

Base

Windage Screw

Elevation Screw

Leaf

Specifically for Colt M-1911 & variations.
Adaptable to other pistols.

Two illustrations of MMC's adjustable sight for the M1911A1-type pistol. (Courtesy MMC)

Swenson-type ambidextrous thumb safety on a Colt M1911A1, customized by James W. Hoag. (Courtesy James W. Hoag)

inch (25.4 millimeters) of extra magazine can be tolerated protruding from the butt, but if the gun is being carried concealed that is unacceptable.

Manual safeties. Safeties on automatic pistols have been a topic of debate for many years. As noted in chapter 2, several recent European designs have eliminated manual safeties in favor of internal safeties. Other contemporary handguns seem to have too many levers to manipulate. A compromise between these two extremes that would render a loaded handgun completely safe to carry and handle but allow it to be placed into action quickly is preferable. Of the currently available domestic and foreign, single-action, automatic pistols, none have a manual safety that meets all combat

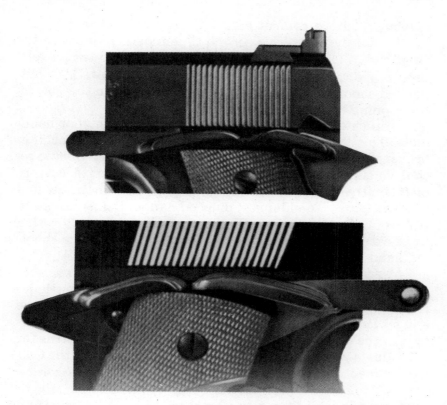

M-S Safari Arms has developed an ambidextrous thumb safety lever for the Colt M1911A1-type automatic. That safety is shown in these two photographs (top view, left side; bottom view, right side) along with an extended lever for the slide release. (Courtesy M-S Safari Arms)

criteria. For this reason, so-called combat safeties have been designed and are available as add-on accessories from Behlert Custom Guns, James W. Hoag, M-S Safari Arms, and Armand Swenson.

While methods differ, combat safeties are produced mainly by extending the Colt/Browning-type, thumb-piece safety forward and outward, sometimes curving it slightly downward so that as the gun is drawn there is greater area for the thumb to engage the safety. In addition, the forward extension provides greater mechanical advantage for overriding the detents (which hold the safety in engaged and disengaged positions) and allows easier and smoother operation. Often combined with a combat safety is an ambidextrous or left-handed safety, in which a second thumb piece or lever on the right end of the safety shaft has been added so that it falls naturally under the left thumb as the gun is drawn by a left-handed shooter. No internal changes are made in the gun, so functioning remains the same.

Grip safeties are of questionable value on combat hand-guns. This type of safety is often responsible for pinching, bruising, or cutting the web of the shooting hand during re-coil. To eliminate the unnecessary grip safety, most custom pistolsmiths will make the original part nonfunctional and pin it in place. To eliminate pinched hands, Behlert Custom Guns offers on an exchange basis a rebuilt grip safety with a large extension that extends back over the web of the shoot-ing hand to protect it.

Triggers. The shape and size of the trigger and the trigger reach (the distance from the back strap to the center of the trigger face measured parallel to the bore) can be quite impor-tant to the control of a combat gun. This is especially true for individuals with unusually large or small hands. For the Colt Government Model-type automatic pistols, triggers can be obtained in at least three different lengths. In addition, trigger shoes are available from several makers and may be fitted and reshaped to provide the correct feel. Trigger shoes are also available for most other makes and models when replacement triggers of nonstandard dimensions are not. For Browning, Smith & Wesson, and other guns, the only practical trigger accessory is a shoe.

More and more specialty accessories are being introduced for combat handguns every day. The serious combat-handgun user should follow the discussions of accessories in the arms journals, and when in doubt about the utility of a particular item look for a product review in a magazine. Two especially good sources of reliable information are the "Dope Bag" re-ports in the *American Rifleman* and the various columns of *American Handgunner.* Before you buy a new accessory, ask yourself bluntly: "Do I really need this?" "Will it improve my combat effectiveness?" Under no circumstances should you buy a gadget just because it is for sale. The manufacturer will appreciate your generosity, but a drawer full of useless accessories will be of little help to you. Your money would be more wisely spent on extra ammunition for practice with your combat handgun. It is the ability to shoot well and accurately that is most important, not the number of new accessories you have added to your weapon.

The "Handgun Trade Directory" at the end of this book lists names and addresses of accessory manufacturers.

12

Combat Handguns:
Care and Maintenance

MAINTENANCE OF YOUR autoloader has but one goal—
to ensure that any time it is called upon, no matter what the
conditions, it will fire the first round and as many subsequent
rounds as you require with absolute reliability and standard
accuracy. Since a sidearm that does not perform reliably can
mean death to the professional gun handler, firearms care
and maintenance are important considerations.

Unfortunately, gun maintenance to many users means
patches and oil. They believe that a clean, well-oiled gun with
a gleaming exterior will function every time. To maintain
your automatic handloader, you must expect to do more than
wipe it down occasionally. Consider the following guidelines.

Do not leave the gun in a wet holster or other carrier.

Do not pitch the gun on a dresser or table when you come
off duty.

Do not tighten grip or sight screws excessively.

Do not fiddle idly with sight-adjustment screws.

Do not flood the inner workings of the gun with oil or pre-servative.

Do not let oil soak into wood grips.

Do not attempt to disassemble the gun without the assistance of a trained armorer unless you have detailed, illustrated instructions and proper tools available.

Do not put the gun where it will pick up grit or dirt.

Do not apply synthetic, aerosol-spray preservatives and lubricants to a loaded gun or allow them to come in contact with cartridges.

Do not disassemble the gun any more often than absolutely necessary for proper cleaning.

Do not use replacement parts, particularly magazines, that are not intended for the particular gun in question or are known to be of questionable quality.

Do not attempt to do gunsmithing for which you are not qualified or equipped.

Do not let anyone other than a fully qualified armorer or gunsmith work on your gun.

Do keep the gun clean and dry, both inside and out, utilizing the minimum of lubricants and preservatives necessary to ensure reliable functioning and prevent rust.

Do inspect the gun thoroughly at the beginning and end of a duty period, making certain that every component functions as it should.

Do place the gun in a covered box or plastic bag or in some other dirt-free place when it is not being carried.

Do keep the dirt and grit cleaned out of your holster so it will not harm the finish and sights of the gun.

Do make certain chamber and bore and interior of magazines (and any other parts in contact with cartridges) are kept free of oil or preservative, especially the aerosol type, which can dissolve the waterproofing seal around primers and bullets and cause misfires.

Do wipe off perspiration or other moisture whenever it is on the gun.

Do keep a full set of cleaning equipment and tools available alongside the gun so you will not put off cleaning, care, or maintenance.

Do fire all the cartridges in your several magazines periodically (every three months), then exercise the magazine springs at least twenty cycles with a dowel, then recharge with fresh ammunition.

Do check tightness of grip screws and other screws at least weekly and inspect to ensure that all pins and interlocking parts are fully and properly seated.

Do exercise the gun at least once weekly, preferably by firing at least one magazine full of service cartridges, after which you rotate one of your spare, filled magazines into the gun; recharge the empty one and carry it as a spare.

Do clean the gun thoroughly as described below after each episode of firing.

Cleaning is the most essential part of care and maintenance. Presented here is a guide for cleaning a typical big-bore autoloader, such as the Smith & Wesson Model 39 or the Colt Government Model. First, clear the chamber and lock the slide back and remove the magazine. Do not just glance at the ejection port and assume the chamber is empty; examine the chamber closely to be absolutely certain that it is empty. Shuck all the cartridges out of the magazine manually and make certain that none of them has been nicked, dented, or otherwise damaged. If any have, set them aside for practice or plinking. Also note if the cartridges, particularly around the primers, are oily or greasy. Any that are cannot be considered safe for duty use.

Disassemble the magazine. Take particular care if you are disassembling a Colt Government Model magazine that the follower is not bent in the process. Wipe off follower and spring and check for any damage. With a tight-fitting wad of cloth on a cleaning rod or special rod made for the purpose, thoroughly scrub clean the inside of the magazine with solvent. If you discover patches of rust or other stubborn material, use steel wool or a bore brush to remove them completely. Lightly oil the inside of the magazine with a tight patch and reassemble. Fill the magazine with cartridges; be sure that they enter as freely and smoothly as they should.

Field strip the gun according to directions and remove the grips. If the gun has not been fired since the last cleaning, pick up the barrel and run a tight-fitting patch or mop several times through the bore and chamber. Just push and pull the patch through the bore; on the chamber use it from the rear with a vigorous rotating motion. Wipe off the outside of the barrel and inspect it for nicks, burrs, or any excessive wear or damage. Wipe the barrel inside and out very lightly with a water-displacing oil and set aside.

If the gun has been fired, first use a tight-fitting, brass, bore brush twisted and rotated through several full revolutions in the chamber. Wipe the chamber clean and dry, inspect carefully under good light, and if there is any doubt whatsoever that it is not thoroughly clean, repeat the process. This is especially important, inasmuch as powder fouling from some cartridges can accumulate rather quickly, clinging tightly to the chamber walls and forming a rough layer that makes extraction more difficult.

If the gun has not been fired, use a stiff brush to scrub out all recesses and grooves in the slide. Follow by wiping those surfaces clean. Inspect the guide grooves and the breech face for nicks or dents. Check the extractor by pressing it sideward with a punch or screwdriver to make certain it functions smoothly and is not obstructed by foreign material. Depress the firing pin its full travel with a punch applied to the rear, making certain it moves smoothly. While the pin is fully forward, wipe it clean. Check any other moving parts mounted on the slide (except an adjustable rear sight) for free movement. If you encounter any undue hesitation, remove those parts and clean. Wipe all of the slide surfaces inside and out very lightly with a water-displacing oil.

If the gun has been fired, powder residue, and occasionally primer residue, will have penetrated every recess and opening. For this reason, the slide must be completely disassembled (except an adjustable sight), and the recesses and the parts therein wiped free of residue. This is particularly important to the firing pin and becomes absolutely vital if corrosive-primed, military-surplus ammunition has been fired. The residue of the corrosive primer is not corrosive itself, but it is composed largely of a salt that resembles common table salt. Salts absorb moisture from the atmosphere, and that moisture will cause rust to develop on metal surfaces in a few hours, depending upon humidity. This salty primer residue cannot be adequately removed merely by wiping. The surfaces require washing in hot, soapy water to completely dissolve and flush away the salts, after which the parts must be dried and then immediately oiled lightly. Do not let freshly scrubbed parts air-dry overnight; you will find them rusty in the morning. Once powder residue has been properly removed, proceed as above.

Pick up the frame and look down in the recesses where the barrel seats and in all other recesses (particularly the magazine well and feed ramp) to the rear of the chamber. If the gun has not been fired, simply wipe those areas clean. If it has been fired, carefully scrub away all sooty powder residue with a cut-down toothbrush. Firing will have driven it into almost every place conceivable. Look carefully inside all frame recesses for foreign material—such as lint, thread, grass—that might interfere later with functioning. If you use household cloths for cleaning, make certain fragments or threads of them are not left in crucial places. While you have the field-stripped frame in hand, check the functioning of every movable part. Wipe everything down.

Direct your attention to the loose small parts—barrel bushing, recoil spring, grips, grip screws. Wipe or scrub all metal parts clean and oil lightly. Inspect for nicks and burrs. Check the recoil spring for kinks or bending. You should also have a new replacement spring on hand; compare the existing spring with the new one for free length. If the new spring is at least 10 percent shorter, discard the old one and replace it with the spare. As feeding is highly dependent on adequate recoil-spring energy, a partially collapsed spring will not guarantee 100 percent reliability needed in combat use. With a clean toothbrush, scrub dirt, grit, and other debris off the stock or grips. Wipe off any excess oil and check for splits, cracks, chipping, or looseness on the gun. If the grips appear to be getting dry, moisten the toothbrush with linseed oil and scrub it in.

Reassemble the gun and check it. Manually run one magazine full of cartridges through the gun by jerking the slide back hard and releasing it and letting it slam forward under the full force of the recoil spring. If it is not cycled sharply and allowed to run forward hard, you may well get an indication of feeding failures when none exists. If the gun does not chamber, extract, and eject every cartridge in the magazine, it is imperative that you determine why, even if live firing on the range is necessary. As a last step, put a drop or two of oil in the slide grooves, a drop around the barrel where it passes through the bushing, and a drop in the locking lug-area. Put a slight smear of molybdenum disulphide grease on the underside of the slide where it rides over the hammer.

About every six months, a more detailed cleaning should be undertaken. This involves all of the above, plus cleaning and relubricating all the small internal parts. All movable parts should be removed in accordance with the manufacturer's instructions. Each of these parts must be carefully cleaned to remove any rust that may have developed and inspected closely for any damage or excessive wear. These parts, too, should be wiped lightly with oil before reassembly, but this is intended primarily as a preservative and is not adequate lubrication for long-term use. Every pivot point, every sliding or bearing surface should be very lightly coated with molybdenum disulphide grease. The simplest way to do this is to rub the grease into a cleaning patch and wipe all of the affected areas with the patch. This serves well on all sliding surfaces and pins, but it leaves pivot holes unattended. For them, take a toothpick or cotton swab and apply a very minute quantity of grease inside the hole. When all parts are assembled, they will be protected from corrosion and will move with hardly any friction. Incidentally, molybdenum disulphide grease is very black and difficult to remove, so be careful of your clothing and the cleaning surface.

Maintenance does involve more than cleaning. You may carry an automatic for thirty years and never require a replacement part, or you could have parts break almost any time you are on the range. Generally speaking, when a gun (any gun, not just an autoloader) gets through its break-in period without any parts breakage, it is not likely to experience any for at least 2000 rounds.

Nevertheless, a small kit of replacement parts should be kept on hand. This is particularly important for the individual who is not supported regularly by a trained armorer with a stock of parts or for the user who cannot afford the time that might be required before a replacement part can be sent from the manufacturer. A parts kit need not be expensive. It should include those parts with the highest incidence of breakage and those parts that are easily lost during cleaning (small springs, pins, plungers, screws). Purchase new parts, not surplus. Three parts that will break most frequently in the automatic are the extractor, hammer notches, and sear nose. A spare hammer, sear, and extractor (complete with spring and pin, if applicable) will probably last you many years. In addition, a spare firing pin is a good idea, and a spare recoil spring should always be included because of its propensity to slowly collapse over time. In addition, one spare magazine spring may be useful. Magazine springs are surprisingly sturdy and generally will last for many years as long as the magazine is occasionally emptied and the spring exercised. If you discover, however, that one of your magazine springs will no longer lift that last cartridge tightly against the feed lips, nothing less than a new spring will affect a permanent repair.

Actual repairs that can be classified as maintenance are quite limited. If a sear pin wears loose, replace it. If the sear itself becomes chipped or defective, replace it; but do not attempt to recut the sear nose. Likewise, if the extractor fails, you may replace it; but do not attempt to repair the defective part. This holds true throughout the gun, at least until you have developed sufficient experience and skills with the tasks of an armorer. The rule is simple—replace rather than repair.

Daily care of your automatic handgun should take no more than a few minutes; inspect the gun and wipe it down if needed. Weekly cleaning of an unfired gun should not take more than five minutes. If you have fired the weapon using corrosive ammunition, you should spend approximately fifteen minutes in a thorough cleaning. Very little effort or time is routinely involved in conducting all of the maintenance necessary to keep your gun in first-class condition, but a very great deal depends upon your doing so.

Handgun Trade Directory

FOLLOWING IS A basic listing of manufacturers, distributors, and specialists involved with combat handguns and accessories.

A. R. Sales Co.
92624 Alpaca Street
South El Monte, CA 91733

M1911A1-type pistol frames

Lindsey Alexiou
Trapper
28019 Harper
Saint Clair Shores, MI 48081
(313) 779-8750

Custom pistolsmith

Arcadia Machine & Tool
11666 McBean Drive
El Monte, CA 91732
(213) 442-2504

AMT automatic pistols and parts

Armanent Systems and
Procedures, Inc.
P.O. Box 356
Appleton, WI 54911

ASP conversions of Smith &
Wesson Model 39 automatic pistol

Bar-Sto Precision Machine
633 South Victory Boulevard
Burbank, CA 91502

Automatic-pistol barrels and parts

Austin F. Behlert
The Custom Gunshop
725 Lehigh Avenue
Union, NJ 07083
(201) 687-3350

Smith & Wesson and Browning
conversions and accessories

Bo-Mar Tool &
Manufacturing Co.
P.O. Box 168
Carthage, TX 75633

Pistol sights

Browning Arms Company
Rte. 1
Morgan, UT 84050
(801) 399-3481

FN Browning Hi-Power automatic
pistols

Charter Arms Corporation
430 Sniffens Lane
Stratford, CT 06497
(203) 377-8080

Charter Arms revolvers

Colt Firearms
150 Huyshope Avenue
Hartford, CT 06102
(203) 278-8550

Colt automatic pistols and
revolvers

Crown City Arms
P.O. Box 1126
Cortland, NY 13045
(607) 753-0194

M1911A1-type automatic pistols

Detonics .45 Accessories
2500 Seattle Tower
Seattle, WA 98101

Detonics .45 automatic pistol

Devel Corporation
28749 Chagrin Boulevard
Cleveland, OH 44122
(216) 292-7723

Combat conversions of Smith &
Wesson Model 39

Essex Arms   M1911A1-type pistol frames
P.O. Box 345
Phaerring Street
Island Pond, VT 05846

Heckler & Koch Inc.   Heckler & Koch automatic pistols
Suite 218
933 North Kenmore Street
Arlington, VA 22201
(703) 525-3182

James W. Hoag   Custom handguns
H & D Products
Suite C
8523 Canoga Avenue
Canoga Park, CA 91304
(213) 998-1510

Interarms, Ltd.   Star, Walther, and Mauser
10 Prince Street   automatic pistols
Alexandria, VA 22313
(703) 548-1400

Micro Sight Company   Pistol sights
242 Harbor Boulevard
Belmont, CA 94002
(415) 591-0769

Miniature Machine Company   Pistol sights
Robert A. Sconce
210 East Poplar
Deming, NM 88030
(505) 546-2151

M-S Safari Arms   Enforcer automatic pistol
P.O. Box 28355
Temp, AZ 85282
(602) 966-0445

Navy Arms Company   Mamba automatic pistol
689 Bergen Boulevard
Ridgefield, NJ 07657
(201) 945-2500

Pachmayr Gun Works
1220 South Grand Avenue
Los Angeles, CA 90015
(213) 748-7271

Custom gunsmithing and
pistol grips

Pacific International
Merchandizing Corporation
2215 J Street
Sacramento, CA 95818
(916) 446-2737

Vega .45 automatic pistol and parts

L. W. Seecamp Co., Inc.
P.O. Box 255
New Haven, CT 06502
(203) 877-3429

M1911A1-type pistol, double-action
conversions, and other custom work

Sile Distributing
7 Centre Market Place
New York, NY 10013
(212) 925-4111

Benelli automatic pistols

Smith & Wesson
2100 Roosevelt Avenue
Springfield, MA 01101
(413) 781-8300

Smith & Wesson automatic pistols
and revolvers

Sterling Arms Corporation
211 Grand Street
Lockport, NY 14094
(716) 434-6631

Sterling automatic pistols

Sturm, Ruger & Co.
Southport, CT 06490
(203) 259-7843

Ruger revolvers

Armand D. Swenson's .45 Shop
3839 Ladera Vista
P.O. Box 606
Fallbrook, CA 92028
(714) 728-5319

M1911A1 Colt Custom Pistols

Triple-K Manufacturing
Company
568 6th Avenue
San Diego, CA 92101

Pistol magazines

Wildey Firearms Company Inc.   Wildey Automatic Pistols
P.O. Box 284
Cold Spring, NY 10516
(914) 561-5200

Appendix **B**

Police Handgun Usage

THIS CHART REPRESENTS a summary of findings from a nationwide survey of state police agencies concerning their handgun usage. It was taken from New York (State), Division of Criminal Justice Services, *A Special Report to the Governor of the State of New York, Hon. Hugh L. Carey, Police Handguns and Deadly Force* (February, 1976): 92-97.

STATE POLICE AGENCY	OFFICIAL SIDEARM	AUTHORIZED AMMUNITION FOR FIELD USE	AUTHORIZED AMMUNITION FOR FIREARMS TRAINING	SIDEARM FORMERLY IN USE	COMMENTS
ALASKA	.357 Magnum	.357 semi-jacketed hollow point	.38 calibre wadcutter	changed from .38 calibre in 1967	Satisfied that present weap. has more "stopping power" and longer range.
ARIZONA	.38 Special Smith & Wesson Model 15	.38 Special 110 gr hollow point	target wadcutter and service loads	personally owned .38s or .357's changed 1969.	The change was made to standardize and control both weapons and ammunition within the department.
CALIFORNIA	.38 calibre Colt or Smith & Wesson with 6" barrel	.38 calibre 150 gr lubaloy high speed Winchester (considering change to .38 cal 90 gr SJSP)	.38 148 gr wadcutter	No change anticipated.	Prohibit the use of Hollow point, wadcutter, armor piercing, military ball for official use.
CONNECTICUT	.357 Magnum model 66 with 4" barrel	.357 calibre jacketed hollow point 125 gr	.38 calibre 148 gr semi wadcutter. (Will change to .357 calibre ammo when they obtain .357 reloading equipment)	Transition from .38 calibre Colt is currently taking place.	Found the .38 calibre weapon ineffective in neutralizing opponent.
COLORADO	.357 Magnum Colt Python	.357 calibre 125 gr jacketed soft point	.38 calibre 158 gr semi wadcutter	Transition from .38 calibre Colt and the 38/44 Smith & Wesson currently taking place	
DELAWARE	.38 calibre Smith & Wesson Model 10	.38 calibre, 125 gr jacketed hollow point	.38 calibre, 148 gr wadcutter and 125 gr jacketed hollow point	Changed from .38 calibre Colt to present weapon several years ago.	Feel that by their choice of ammo. they maintain a performance capability compatible with the .357 Magnum.

State	Weapon	Ammunition	Ammunition	History	Comments
DISTRICT OF COLUMBIA	.38 calibre Smith & Wesson Model 10 or Colt in 2" & 4" barrels	.38 calibre 158 gr lead round nose	.38 calibre 148 gr wadcutter	Always been the official sidearm.	Satisfied that it meets department needs.
FLORIDA	.357 Magnum	.357 calibre 158 gr jacketed hollow point	.38 calibre 148 gr wadcutter reloads	Changed from .38 cal. Colt in 1958.	Dept. felt it wanted weapon with more velocity and penetration.
GEORGIA	.357 Magnum	.357 calibre 158 gr lead ball	.357 138 gr wadcutter reloads	Changed from .38 cal. Colt in 1956.	Desired more firepower for disabling vehicles and in barricade situations.
IDAHO	.357 Magnum 4" bbl. model 28 Smith & Wesson	.357 calibre 158 gr ¾ jacketed flat-nose (also issue armor piercing bullets on limited basis)	.38 calibre wadcutter reloads	Changed in 1954 from 38/44 Smith & Wesson with 4" bbl	Desired increased penetration or "car stopping ability". Satisfied with change.
ILLINOIS	9mm Semi-Automatic Smith & Wesson Model 39	Special Police Service Load with minimum foot-pounds of energy approximately 400 F.P.E.		.38 calibre .357 calibre	Transition was due to desire to issue a state-owned firearm which by design and weight and overall competency would serve as both on-duty and off-duty weapon and maintain a training program for that one gun.
IOWA	.38 calibre Smith & Wesson for uniform .357 Investigative Force	.38 calibre, 125 gr	.38 calibre, wadcutter	.38 calibre .357 calibre	The investigative division currently using the .357. The Patrol Division will make switch shortly to the .357 Magnum.

STATE POLICE AGENCY	OFFICIAL SIDEARM	AUTHORIZED AMMUNTION FOR FIELD USE	AUTHORIZED AMMUNTION FOR FIREARMS TRAINING	SIDEARM FORMERLY IN USE	COMMENTS
KANSAS	.38 Special Smith & Wesson	.38 special 158 gr lead round nose	.38 calibre 148 gr semi wadcutter	Changed from a .357 Magnum in early 1950's	Satisfied with current weapon but are aware of limitations with present cartridge.
KENTUCKY	.357 Magnum	.357 calibre 158 gr jacketed soft point	.38 calibre 148 gr wadcutter	Changed from the .38 calibre Smith & Wesson with 4" bbl in 1966.	Found that penetrating and "knock down power" was not sufficient in .38 cal. weapon.
LOUISIANA	.357 Magnum	.357 jacketed hollow point weight is matter of officer's choice	.38 calibre 148 gr wadcutter reloads		Satisfied that .357 provides superior fire power for Dept. needs.
MAINE	.357 Magnum	.38 calibre 158 gr (changeover is currently taking place and men have not yet qualified with .357 ammunition)	.38 calibre 158 gr	Transition from .38 Spec. is currently taking place.	Found the .38 Spec lacked sufficient velocity and shocking power.
MARYLAND	.38 Colt Official Police 6" barrel .38 Smith & Wesson Model 10, 4" barrel .357 Smith & Wesson Model 13, 4" barrel commissioned officers -2" barrel Colt or Smith & Wesson	.38 calibre 158 gr ball	wadcutters for bulls-eye, 158 gr ball for combat training	.38's listed at left. 75 .357's issued this year.	Some officers like 6" barrel, but the 4" makes it possible to carry service weapon off duty, thereby eliminating added expense to the Trooper.

State	Weapon	Ammunition	Ammunition		Comments
MASSACHUSETTS	.38 Special Smith & Wesson Model 10 6", 4" heavy barrel; plainclothes .38 Special Smith & Wesson Model 49, 2" barrel	.38 Special 158 gr semi-wadcutter	.38 Special 148 gr mid-range Wadcutter	.38 Special Smith & Wesson Model 10, 6" standard barrel changed in 1967	Found the 4" barrel easier to handle in combat situations. Not contemplating change at present but recently tested S&W Model 59 9mm semi-automatic for possible future use.
MICHIGAN	.38 calibre Special	.38 cal. 125 gr Special +B jacketed soft point	.38 calibre 148 gr wadcutter		Satisfied with present weapon, contemplate no change.
MINNESOTA	.38 calibre Smith & Wesson with 4" bbl	.38 calibre 158 gr lead high velocity blunt nose	.38 ca. 148 gr		Smith & Wesson is currently making a stainless steel .357 Magnum which will replace the present weapon.
MISSISSIPPI	.357 Magnum	.357 calibre 158 gr lead nose & 158 gr steel jacketed	Star reload wadcutters	FIRST STATE TO USE THE .357 MAGNUM	"Would not recommend for city use."
MISSOURI	.38 Special Combat Masterpiece S&W	.38 calibre 158 gr lead alloy hollow-point Winchester	.38 calibre 148 gr wadcutter	Always .38 calibre.	Satisfied with present weapon not contemplating change.
MONTANA	.357 Magnum	.38 calibre semi-jacketed softpoint, high speed or super vel. load	.38 calibre wadcutter	Have discontinued the use of .357 ammunition due to the heavy recoil which has affected shooter accuracy.	
NEBRASKA	.357 Magnum	.357 calibre 158 gr jacketed softpoint	.38 calibre wadcutters	.38 calibre Colts & Smith & Wesson 4" bbl.	Found .38 bullet ineffective in gunfight.
NEW JERSEY	.38 calibre Colt or S&W with 6" bbl	.38 calibre 125 gr semi-jacketed hollow point, Remington	.38 calibre 148 gr wadcutters and 125 hollow point		Satisfied with current weapon since transition to ammo. currently used.

STATE POLICE AGENCY	OFFICIAL SIDEARM	AUTHORIZED AMMUNITION FOR FIELD USE	AUTHORIZED AMMUNITION FOR FIREARMS TRAINING	SIDEARM FORMERLY IN USE	COMMENTS
NEW HAMPSHIRE	.357 Magnum	.357 calibre 158 gr hollow point S&W	148 gr wadcutters and .357 158 HP	Changed from .38 Model to S&W 1973	All members of Division are very much satisfied.
NEW MEXICO	.357 Magnum	.357 calibre 158 gr semi wadcutter	.38 calibre 158 gr wadcutters	Changed from .38 in 1964.	
NEW YORK	.357 Magnum Smith & Wesson Model 10	.357 calibre 158 gr lead soft point Winchester Western	.38 calibre 158 gr lead roundnose	.38 calibre Colt or Smith & Wesson 4" barrel	
NEVADA	.357 Magnum	.357 calibre 110-125 gr semi-jacketed HP .357 calibre 158 gr lead	.357 Wadcutter	Changed from the .41 calibre Magnum in 1969	.41 Magnum caused a lack of shooting proficiency because of its considerable recoil and loud report. Men became "gun shy".
NORTH CAROLINA	.357 Magnum	.357 calibre, 125 gr semi-jacketed hollow-point	.38 calibre, 148 gr wadcutters .357 calibre, 158 gr semi-jacketed soft pt.	Changed from .38 calibre M&P in 1971.	The greatest disadvantage to present weapon is adjusting to the noise and recoil. The physiological affect of the large weapon outweighs any disadvantage to date.
NORTH DAKOTA	.38 calibre Smith & Wesson	.38 calibre Armor Piercing	.38 calibre wadcutter	Prior to 1958 used .38 calibre Colt.	Satisfied with present weapon no change contemplated.
OHIO	.38 calibre Smith & Wesson Model 10	.38 calibre, 125 gr semi-jacketed	.38 calibre, 148 gr mid-range wadcutter	Prior to 1967 used 38/44	Satisfied with present weapon no plans to change.

State	Weapon	Officer's Choice	Ammunition	History	Comments
OKLAHOMA	.357 Magnum .41 Magnum .44 Magnum	Officer's Choice	Target wadcutter, mid-range	Prior to 1971 used .38 calibre S&W Model 15	85% of Troopers carry .357 but after recent shootings more are turning to the .41 & .44 Magnum.
OREGON	.357 Magnum Smith & Wesson or Colt 4" barrel	.357 calibre, 158 gr semi wadcutter	.357 calibre 158 gr semi-wadcutter and .38 calibre 148 gr wadcutter	.38 calibre Revolver 6" barrel changeover initiated in 1967 completed in 1972	Find the .357 Magnum has proven to be an entirely satisfactory police weapon.
PENNSYLVANIA	.38 calibre Colt Police Special 6" barrel	.38 calibre, 125 gr semi-jacketed hollow point	.38 calibre, 158 gr roundnose, lead		Feel that the .125 grain, semi-jacketed hollow point ammo. negates the need for a Magnum weapon.
RHODE ISLAND	Uniform: .38 calibre S&W Detective: 9mm S&W Model 39	158 gr hollow point 115 gr hollow point	.38 calibre 158 gr Reloads	Prior to 1958 .45 calibre Colt	Find the .38 calibre more accurate, cheaper and lighter to carry.
SOUTH CAROLINA	.38 calibre Smith & Wesson Model 10 4" bbl.	.38 Special (MS) 158 gr hollow point Lead, Winchester	.38 calibre, 148 gr lead wadcutter		Feel that increased recoil and noise level make the .357 difficult to keep on target.
SOUTH DAKOTA	.357 Magnum Model 19 Smith & Wesson Chrome Finish	.357 calibre, 125 gr jacketed hollow point	.38 calibre wadcutters .357 replacement ammo. to maintain proficiency	Prior to 1972 .38 calibre.	Transition took place because of age of .38's and general consensus of uniform members
TENNESSEE	.38 calibre Model 15 4" barrel	.38 calibre, 158 gr lead, round nose	.38 calibre, 148 gr wadcutters	Always been the official sidearm.	

STATE POLICE AGENCY	OFFICIAL SIDEARM	AUTHORIZED AMMUNITION FOR FIELD USE	AUTHORIZED AMMUNITION FOR FIREARMS TRAINING	SIDEARM FORMERLY IN USE	COMMENTS
TEXAS	.357 Magnum	.357 calibre, 158 gr metal jacketed soft point - Remington	.38 calibre wadcutters	38/44 Revolver	Officers are satisfied because of the confidence they have in the weapon. Have monthly firearms training to improve officer performance.
UTAH	.357 Magnum	No restrictions on type of .357 ammo. to be used.	.38 calibre semi or full wadcutters. Some Magnum reloads to familiarize men with heavier recoil.	.357 for 30 yrs.	Feel that it is top all-round weapon for law enforcement. Also .38 calibre ammo. can be used for training which is an economic factor to the department.
VERMONT	.357 Magnum	.357 calibre, 158 gr jacketed soft point Remington	.38 special wadcutters	Prior to 1968 .38 Special	Changed because of the general inability of the .38 cartridge as commercially loaded to meet the needs of a rural police agency in terms of penetration and stopping power.
VIRGINIA	.38 calibre M&P Special 4" barrel	.38 calibre, 158 gr lead round nose	.38 calibre 148 gr lead wadcutters	Prior to 1967 used .38 calibre with 6" bbl.	Satisfied with current weapon; not contemplating change in either weapon or ammunition.

State	Weapon	Ammunition	History	Comments
WASHINGTON	.357 Magnum 6" barrel Model 28-2	.357 calibre, hi-speed 158 gr soft point Remington	.38 calibre 158 gr semi-wadcutter	Prior to 1961 used .38 calibre revolver with 6" bbl.	Dept. experience indicates the weapon has been accurate, dependable and adequate for most State Police applications. Changeover due to fact previous weapons in use over 15 yrs. Replacement cost was only slightly greater than repair.
WEST VIRGINIA	.357 Model .19 Smith & Wesson	.357, 158 gr Soft Point Remington	.38 calibre wadcutters some .357 158 gr	Until 1966: .38 Special Official Police 1966-69; Colt Trooper	Originally issued two types of ammo. for field use. .357 semi-wadcutter normally. .357 full metal jacket for maximum penetration through autos, houses, etc. Found to be unworkable, men used full jacketed ammo. exclusively and found it went right through assailant without knocking him down. Now testing 110 grain and 125 grain jacketed soft point ammo. for future use.

Index